A FOND FAREWELL FOR THE TOBACCO GIRLS

LIZZIE LANE

Boldwood

First published in Great Britain in 2023 by Boldwood Books Ltd. This paperback edition published in 2024.

I

Copyright © Lizzie Lane, 2023

Cover Design by Colin Thomas

Cover Photography: Colin Thomas and Alamy

A CIP catalogue record for this book is available from the British Library.

Paperback ISBN 978-1-83617-898-9

Large Print ISBN 978-1-80048-534-1

Hardback ISBN 978-1-78513-693-1

Ebook ISBN 978-1-80048-537-2

Kindle ISBN 978-1-80048-535-8

Audio CD ISBN 978-1-80048-529-7

MP3 CD ISBN 978-1-80048-530-3

Digital audio download ISBN 978-1-80048-533-4

Boldwood Books Ltd
23 Bowerdean Street
London SW6 3TN
www.boldwoodbooks.com

MIX
Paper | Supporting
responsible forestry
FSC® C171272

1

MAY 1945 – VE NIGHT

Carole Thomas laughed and laughed, danced and twirled as she was passed from one outstretched male hand to another. Feeling happier than she'd ever felt in her life, she kept on dancing her way around the joyful circle until she'd danced her way back into Joe Shaw's welcoming arms.

'You've come back to me,' he laughed, and looking up into his warm brown eyes, she laughed with him. All was gaiety. All was relief. The war in Europe was finally over and everyone who could was out celebrating.

The streets, squares and thoroughfares around Bristol city centre were packed with people. The night was warm and dry, though it wouldn't have mattered if it had been pouring down with rain. The city, and the country at large, had been waiting for this moment for five years. Nothing was going to stop them from dancing till dawn if that was what they wanted.

Dancing in the streets was like playing sardines, though the crush in this case was taking place outdoors, the air alive with noise, laughter and a lot of drunken singing.

A woman enveloped in the arms of a sailor bumped into Carole, breath smelling of drink, her hat tilted at a jaunty angle. 'Isn't it bloody marvellous,' she shrieked. 'It's over. It's over at bloody last.'

Joy was infectious. Laugher was infectious. Carole danced on, caught up in the excitement of the crowd who bustled and sang, shouted and swigged from upturned bottles of brown ale.

Midnight. It was the beginning of summer and always a reason to celebrate, but this year the end of the war made it doubly so.

Carole was as happy as anyone, more so because she was looking up into the velvet brown eyes of Joe Shaw. She'd only known him for a few months, though long enough to be going steady. They saw each other when he was home on leave, which wouldn't be appreciated as much in peacetime, but in war, sweet moments between serving one's country and seeing your girl were snatched and savoured.

'All over,' he whispered as he ruffled her hair and smiled down at her from his greater height. He was broad in comparison to her slight frame and dark in contrast to her near white blonde hair that owed nothing to a bottle of peroxide dye but was, rather, Carole's natural colour.

'All over,' she whispered in breathless response, her eyes fixed on his and feeling as though she could drown in his smile.

His battledress strained across his chest when he heaved a big sigh. He licked his lips as though in preparation to say something very profound, or at least something very important.

After readying himself, hugging her closer and kissing her until she was breathless, he spoke. 'Now we can make plans.'

Small words that said a lot.

'Plans? Ah yes.'

'For you and me. For our future together.'

For a second, her smile faltered, was recovered and her aspect of surprise laughed off. Once she had regained control of her expression, she gazed at him with undisguised affection. 'Our future? You and me?'

'Well, we have been going steady. Might as well make it permanent and put a ring on yer finger.'

Her breath caught in her throat. Her eyes sparkled. 'Are you sure?'

'Of course I am.'

He pretended to be offended, but his smile and the warmth in his eyes told her the truth.

Her cheeks couldn't have coloured up any more than they were already and her feelings confused her. She felt surprised and embarrassed, but excited too.

'That's lovely. Really lovely.'

Drinking in his good looks was accompanied with a nervous tightness in her chest. He was the one, the man of her dreams, and he seemed as much in love with her as she was with him. But he didn't know that she had a child. Paula was not born of love, but Carole loved her.

'You all right, darling?' he asked.

Carole pushed away the sombre thoughts and laughed. 'Course I am. Tonight of all nights! Old Adolf is gone and good riddance too.'

There had been several times when she'd almost told him about Paula, who was now a robust toddler of two and a half. Once she did, he might change his mind about getting married.

On reflection, she decided the nervousness had been there from the moment they'd met. It had been love at first sight. He was the one for her and it seemed also that she was the one for him. Such a brief time together, but such a wonderful one. She couldn't believe it when it so happened that he was as in love with her as she was with him. He'd exclaimed with unfettered exuberance that she was the girl he'd been seeking all his life and that he knew her better than he knew himself.

The trouble was that he didn't know as much about her as he thought, there was much more to know. He knew the address where she lived, but she'd never invited him inside. He also knew nothing of the circumstances that had brought her to living in Totterdown. She'd mentioned Maisie as being her aunt and she was living with her because her mother had remarried and lived up north. She'd lied to him that her father was dead. So far, they had not bumped into Eddie Bridgeman who insisted the role was his. Not only would he declare her his daughter but he'd likely take Joe to one side and, in as fatherly a manner as he knew how, warn him not to mess with her. He'd probably also mention her daughter, Paula, a bonny toddler with her looks and the same head of off-white hair.

She'd told herself that if he did ask her to marry him, she would instantly tell him the truth. That moment had come but still she couldn't bring herself to tell him. Like most men of his generation, he wasn't likely to countenance taking on another man's child. It wouldn't matter that the father had got her drunk and raped her. Society, not just men, always seemed to take the view that it was the girl who'd been flaunting herself and invited what happened. It hadn't been that way at all, but for now at least she was keeping the truth to herself.

And it didn't stop there. He'd asked her where she worked.

'I keep house for my aunt. She works at the tobacco factory. I used to work there meself but...' She'd shaken her head. 'I'm keeping house for now until I get something better.' She'd made it seem as though Maisie was incapable of running both a house and holding down a job. It couldn't be further from the truth and Carole hated herself for taking that line. But until she could bring herself to tell the absolute truth, she let it be.

He hadn't quizzed her further, hadn't asked why she'd never joined one of the armed forces.

'I love you, Joe.' She said it softly and with feeling, an appeal to stab at his heart. It was hard to keep her secret. Harder still to hope and pray that he wouldn't cast her aside once he knew of her past and Paula. People had histories they preferred not to mention and she was certainly no exception. If she'd been a widow, it might not have mattered. But she wasn't. Paula was the result of an older man taking advantage of her, a night she'd prefer to forget but couldn't. Paula reminded her of it every day.

Life was cruel and the truth would likely destroy this sudden semblance of happiness and Carole so craved that happiness.

'Do you really mean it?' she asked him.

He was about to answer when a band of merrymakers crashed into them, forcing them together.

His voice whispered into her ear, 'I'll get down on bended knees here and now if you want me to. Do you know what I'm saying?'

Yes, of course she did.

A space cleared, although the crowd continued to whirl around them, jostling until they were pushed together again. The crush was greater now, more people pouring into the city, thronging the streets. She smelt his masculinity and that of his battledress – heavy wool alongside the tang of Brylcreem and shaving soap.

His arms wound around her protectively, his lips whispered into her ear: 'I'm going to marry you, Carole Thomas.' His voice was heavy with emotion and his breath warm in her ear.

Declining to answer, she buried her face against his shoulder so he wouldn't see the fear in her eyes and her unsmiling lips.

One hand clutched at his sleeve and the other thoughtfully fingered the epaulettes on his shoulders and the insignia that proudly declared he was a member of His Majesty's forces – a tank commander who had served at El Alamein in North Africa.

'Are you sure?' she asked pensively.

'That's a daft question. Of course I'm sure.'

'But we haven't known each other very long.'

He leaned his shoulders away from her. She raised her head and looked up at him.

'I've known you long enough to know that you're the girl for me.'

She shook her head, and despite the joy reverberating the very air, she couldn't get that shared joviality to return. 'You know nothing about me. Not really.'

His furrowed brow was accompanied with a disbelieving smile. ' I know everything about you. I did from the very first time I saw you. In fact, I said to myself, that's the girl, the sweetest woman in the world, so Carole Thomas has got to be the one for me.' His frown deepened. 'There's nobody else is there?'

She shook her head. 'No. No, there isn't.'

'So you'll marry me?'

Her heart filled with joy. 'If you'll have me, I'll marry you. But give me a little time to adjust. There's a load of things I need to sort out first and more things you need to know about me. Please be patient. That's all I ask.' She eyed him plaintively, lips still smiling.

Joe beamed. 'You take as much time as you like, sweetheart. I'll wait forever if I have to.'

She hugged him as tightly as she could and determined that she would never let him go. She was in love. She'd never known love before, the odd crush, but that was it. But Joe. He was the one, the love of her life, the man she wanted to be with forever.

The crush of dancing people encompassed them, hands and arms, feet and legs an unstoppable force of movement that made their feet begin to move too.

'Might as well join them,' Joe shouted over the din as the crowd took them along.

'I should be going home. It's getting late.'

'The night is young.'

'It's gone midnight.'

'Come on. It's not time for breakfast just yet.'

'Breakfast! Joe Shaw, you're crazy.'

'Yes,' he said. 'Crazy about you!'

'What about...' She almost said, *What about Paula. I need to get home for my daughter.*

'What about what?'

'Nothing. I just don't want to be like Cinderella and find that my coach and horses have turned back into a pumpkin and four mice. I hate mice.'

He laughed. 'It's a pound to a penny that they're more afraid of you.'

Carole abandoned all thoughts of going home, after all Maisie had told her to go out and enjoy the making of history.

'It's something you'll remember for the rest of your life. In twenty years' time, people will ask where you were on Victory in Europe night. Don't worry about Paula. She'll be fine with me.'

Carole knew beyond doubt that her daughter couldn't be with anyone better than Maisie, who had loved Paula from the moment she was born – perhaps even before she was born when Carole had been so distraught and wanted the situation to go away.

It seemed unthinkable now that she'd considered giving Paula up for adoption. Maisie had been appalled and put many obstacles in her path. In the end, Carole had relented and realised she just couldn't go through with such a terrible thing and now she couldn't imagine life without Paula.

They danced some more, caught up in the exuberance of the crowd, the astonishing outpouring of joy now that the war – in Europe at least – was finally over.

At around four o'clock in the morning, one of Carole's heels wedged in a gap in the pavement and snapped off.

'Now I have to go home,' she insisted.

'I don't think there's any buses. I'll get us a taxi.'

'That's expensive.'

'Nothing's too good for my girl. It's either that or I carry you.'

'Don't be daft.'

'Darling, it's too late for you to go home by yourself. I'm coming with you, like it or lump it.'

Joe proceeded to jump out in front of one of the few taxis running at that time of night.

'Come on,' he shouted, opening the door.

When she lingered, he grabbed her arm and dragged her onto the back seat.

'Just remind me of that address again.'

Still she hesitated.

'Come on. We won't get there until you give us the address. Now what is it?'

'OK.' She gave him the address but insisted he dropped her at the end of the street.

The taxi pulled away into the dawn of a peacetime morning. Peacetime. It was funny to think that. No more bombing. No more fire watching up on the roof and in time there would be no more rationing, though as yet nothing had changed.

'Driver, can you please get a move on?'

'She's trying to get rid of me,' Joe quipped to the driver.

'No such thing, Joe Shaw. You could find yourself in the Glass 'Ouse if you're late back.' The Glass House was a prison barracks in Catterick. No soldier worth his salt wanted to go there.

'I'd put up with it for your sake.'

'Don't be daft.'

'Are you ashamed to introduce me to your family?'

'No. Of course not.' She shook her head at the same time as forcing a smile back to her face.

'Then why have you never let me take you to your front door? It's always the end of the street. When do I get to meet yer Aunt Maisie?'

'Won't be long now,' she laughed. 'Now that we're almost engaged.'

'Almost? Hang on. Let's make it official.'

After fumbling around in his pocket, he brought out what looked like a washer.

'Wait a minute.' He cleaned off what looked like oil in his handkerchief. 'There you are. Give me yer finger.'

It was hard not to laugh as he pushed it on her finger.

'I now announce in front of a witness that me and you are engaged to be married. Ain't that right, cabbie?'

The cab driver agreed that it was and that if Joe wanted to kiss the bride, that was all right with him.

Joe's kiss was sweet and she really did feel that something in her life had suddenly changed.

'From this day forward, Carole Thomas. Ain't that what they say?'

'Yes,' she murmured.

She couldn't tell him the truth just yet and certainly not in front of a witness. Neither could she tell him that she did have a brass curtain ring at home that she wore as a wedding ring when the occasion required it. If there was the slightest suspicion that a young woman was unmarried, a quick look at a gold band on the wedding finger was evidence enough that all was proper.

'You've got to get some sleep before going home.'

He agreed that he did. Ahead of him was a long train journey to Liverpool, where his family, including his beloved mother, would be waiting for him.

'That's true. It could be my mother's last chance to see me in a uniform. After that, I'll be standing in the demob queue, and the sooner I'm demobbed, the better.'

'Can't imagine you not being in uniform.'

'Can't wait to get out of it.'

'Hope I'll still recognise you.'

'Course you will, and once I'm demobbed, the sooner we arrange a date for you to meet my mother.'

'Do you think she'll like me?' Carole asked nervously.

'If I like you, she'll like you. That's all there is to it. Then you can introduce me to your Auntie Maisie and the rest of your family. Should be quite a party.'

She laughed with him, joyful because he was joyful – at least that was what she showed on the surface. Inside, she imagined both his and his mother's opinion changing when they heard the truth: that she was an unmarried mother with a daughter named Paula and a mother who had once sold her favours for money.

A sudden surge of courage took hold of her. Now or never. In the back of a cab. 'Joe. There's something I have to tell you.'

'That you're going to say yes. There's no other answer you can give me.'

She looked up into the strong face she loved so much – the crinkles at the corners of his eyes, the chipped tooth that only showed when he smiled, and he smiled a lot.

'Perhaps we should talk it over...'

'Come on, baby. This is no time for talking. We're young, we've been through a war and now we're going to build a future together. Nothing else matters. Just you and me and all the kids we're going to have.'

At the mention of children, it felt as though her heart had stopped beating and the very air in the back seat of the cab seemed to heave with apprehension.

2

Maisie's neighbours had shouted and sang most of the night and made music on an ad hoc collection of instruments. Those who didn't have a mouth organ, an accordion or even a tambourine used boiler sticks to bash a noisy drumming out of an ashbin lid.

Amazingly, Paula slept through it all.

Maisie indulged for a short while, standing at her front door and accepting a drink and a Spam sandwich from one of her neighbours. More than one neighbour was running up and down with a tray of sandwiches, cups of tea and glasses of questionable alcohol.

The sandwiches and even slices of cake kept coming until she declared herself full and used Paula as her excuse for going back indoors.

Once the door was closed on the rowdy celebrations, she checked on Paula before sitting in a chair in the quiet coolness of the front room.

She didn't quite know what triggered it, but suddenly there were tears trickling down her face. So much had happened in the last five years. People she knew had died and others had been born. She'd grown up in York Street, where some days the small, terraced houses had been shrouded in the stink from the bone yards and the soap factory. That was where her mother had died and where she'd found out that her father was not her natural father. Finding out who he was had brought her to this house in Totterdown.

At this time of night, it was easy to imagine her grandmother, Grace Wells, doing her accounts at the old bureau upstairs. Grace had been both a moneylender and an abortionist. The money accumulated, plus this house, had passed to Maisie on her death. She didn't need to go to work at the tobacco factory, but she loved the camaraderie, the cheeky jokes, the bubbling conversation. There would have to be a very good reason indeed why she would stop working there.

Carole too had worked at the tobacco factory. Then Paula had come along. She adored that little girl to the depths of her soul. Earlier that evening, before she'd gone out, Carole had confided in her that she'd fallen in love with a man called Joe Shaw.

'I've never felt like this before.'

There'd been an expression of wide-eyed disbelief, as though she'd been hit by a thunderbolt and had very much enjoyed it.

Maisie's feelings had been divided. She was happy for her but also concerned. If the affair was serious and she married him, she would move out and take Paula with her. 'I take it you're meeting him tonight.'

'We've agreed to meet, yes, only... if you could look after Paula.'

She'd told Carole to go out and enjoy herself with the young man she'd met.

Carole had given her a bear hug and cried out over and over again, 'Thank you, Aunt Maisie. Thank you, thank you, thank you!'

It had only been for the last few months that Carole had called her aunt and Maisie quite liked it. They weren't related, but it made her feel as though they were.

'Why don't you bring him here for tea?' she'd suggested.

Carole's natural exuberance had evaporated when asked the question. Her countenance had fallen. 'I haven't told him about Paula.'

'Oh.'

'The thing is that I've held off telling him. I thought I would wait and see if it was just a flash in the pan.'

'And is it – a flash in the pan?'

Carole had hung her head so that her hair fell forward, almost hiding her pink-lipped secretive smile. 'No. I think he's going to ask me to marry him.' Her lips had twitched as though she was tasting something bitter and wanted to spit it out. Eventually she did spit it out. 'I held off telling him about Paula up until now, but if he does ask me to marry him, I'm going to have to tell him. But I'm so scared, Aunt Maisie. What if he doesn't listen? What if he thinks me just a cheap floozie and doesn't want to have anything more to do with me?'

Maisie had reassured her that if he loved her enough it wouldn't matter. The war had altered many lives. What was unacceptable before the war might not be so important once it was all over.

Though what would I know, she'd thought to herself and was suddenly overcome with a great tide of nostalgia.

In 1939, just before the outbreak of war, she'd joined the workforce at the tobacco factory. It seemed a long time ago now, the heady days when she'd become one of the three Ms – Phyllis Mason, Bridget Milligan and her, Maisie Miles. They'd become firm friends. The three of them had laughed, cried and got through more than a few dramatic moments together. Then the war had come and it was just her left at the factory – unmarried and alone – until Carole had come along. Carole Thomas had, like Maisie, not long left school. She had arrived mid-war at the factory and Maisie had taken her under her wing.

A moment of melancholy descended as she thought of the past

five years. With hindsight perhaps, she should have stayed outside, danced and partied, instead of sitting here in front of an empty grate. The room didn't usually seem so gloomy, but it did tonight. The feeble light from the overhead bulb inside its pigskin shade helped hide the shabbiness of the old furniture. Not that Maisie was worried about that. It was the future that concerned her, especially the fact that she would never regain the comradeship of Bridget and Phyllis. Bridget was married to an American and Phyllis to an Australian. Both would be settling with their new husbands very far away, whereas she...

Even Carole's beau was from Liverpool, so she too was likely to move away from dear old Bristol. The worst thing about it was that Carole would take Paula with her – although that depended on whether Joe was willing to take on another man's child. For her own selfish reasons, Maisie hoped he would not. But that was selfish. Carole loved him. She also loved Paula. Whatever happened, they had to make their own life.

As for you, Maisie Miles... you'll be alone. An old maid, unless...

An unending and empty future stretched out ahead of her. She let the tears fall.

'The war's over,' someone shouted, not far from the front of the house. Loud and drunk, the same voice broke into a rendition of 'Land of Hope and Glory' and was joined by more voices rising in song, slightly drunk and out of tune.

Maisie mopped at her wet eyes with a clean cotton handkerchief. Like a lot of other things, it was cut down from something else, something that had been worn out. In this case, one old pillowcase had become a quartet of handkerchiefs.

'It's over. It's over.'

The same words kept recurring, echoing between the rows of terraced houses high on the hill in Totterdown.

She turned her head in the direction of the living-room window, and although her shout was not likely to be heard outside, she shouted it anyway. 'The war's ended in Europe, but not in Japan.'

There was one old friend who was currently far away and had been since the fall of Singapore. Sid was still a prisoner of war and Japan had not surrendered.

3

CHANGI – SINGAPORE. TWO MONTHS LATER

'Changi is hell.'

Sid heard the same comment every day.

'Could be worse. Could be over in the old jail.'

There followed grumbles of acceptance and argument. The original civilian jail had been built to house six hundred. It now housed three thousand. Military prisoners were kept in what had been the British Selarang Barracks. They too were stuffed to capacity, the conditions basic, the men's mental health as badly affected as their bodies.

Three years of captivity, heat, humidity and hunger took their toll on even the strongest of men. When the rains came, Sid could almost believe he was at home, though not quite. England was wet. Everyone knew and accepted that. Singapore could be wet too, but the rain was different. It was never cool and once it had stopped, there was no rainbow. He'd looked but never found one in that mud-coloured sky. Not here. It must be something to do with the humidity that clung like a second skin, sapping energy from body, soul and the clothes he stood up in. Once upon a time, the rags he wore had been a uniform. Not now.

Cloth rotted. He still had the jacket, but the shorts and under-wear were gone, replaced with a native sarong – healthier in this fetid climate.

He yearned for an English downpour, raindrops hanging like crystals in the air. Pierced by light, they made the bridge that was a rainbow. He recalled the old legend of there being a crock of gold at the rainbow's end. His own personal rainbow was England and if gold was a person, it was Maisie Miles. That was the gold he longed for when, and if, he survived and got back home to Bristol. It was writing to her and her writing back that had kept him going. They'd even joked about being engaged. He'd held on to that hope with both hands. If she was still single, he would ask her to marry him. He didn't want to believe that she was married. She hadn't said as such in her letters, so he presumed not. Hopefully, she was still waiting for him.

In the darker moments, the times when he couldn't even find the strength to swat at the mosquitoes that made a fizzing sound as they flew, she was there in his mind with someone new. That was his nightmare. He knew he was becoming paranoid, perhaps being driven mad. That was how bad it was to be incarcerated in this terrible place. Starvation, brutality and hopelessness had become the norm.

When his spirits were lowest, his jealousy fed anger, and almost hatred, and not just against the Japanese. That went without saying. But he also nurtured anger against those that had sent him here, those who'd been in charge, those who had not had to endure the isolation, the living in an alien world of beatings and hard labour. There were moments when he saw his own death in the contorted features of a camp guard, or the bleary world of sickness, the dizzying pain of starvation.

In those dark dreams when he seemed to be drowning in despair, he forced himself to resurrect her face from memory. For the most part, he remembered how she looked, but feared he might not recognise her once he returned to England, once he was free.

In the mornings, he would get out the faded photograph he'd carried with him all this time. A factory outing to Weston-super-Mare, a fresh breeze blowing off the sea. The smell of fish and chips, of donkey dung on the beach, and the taste of sand on his tongue.

Through all this, the heat, the cruelty, the starvation and the unending hopelessness, Maisie Miles was his life raft, the vision he recalled and clung to when it felt as though he was going under, never to come back up again.

In those many moments of fever, tossing and turning, out of his head with pain and sickness, he vowed that if he died, then the fates would decree that she would too. In his fevered mind, he told himself that for her sake, not for his own, he had to keep going.

Stripes of dawn light glowed a bluish silver. Daybreak. He welcomed daybreak, the advent of surviving another day, for which he was seriously thankful. Get through the day, then get through the following night. Mark it off on the rudimentary calendar scratched onto the baked ground behind the hut he shared with many others.

He sighed. Might as well get up and face the day.

First stop, see how his mate Claude was doing.

He called to the emaciated, yellow-skinned man lying on what passed for a bunk next to him. 'It's light, Claude.'

Claude had been with him on the ship out from England. They'd checked into Singapore barracks together. Checked into the Japanese prisoner of war camp too.

Claude made no comment.

Sid thought he heard a sigh, but it might just as well have been a slight breeze disturbing the palm-leaf roof.

He needed to know that someone else was still alive, so carried on: 'Don't blame you for sleeping on. When I'm asleep, I'm always somewhere else. Wish I could sleep until this bloody war is over. I could cope better then. Wouldn't notice it was still going on. How about you Claude?'

Unable to turn onto his side – without much flesh to pad them, his bones ached too much – Sid turned his head.

'Claude? Did you hear what I said?'

A dark shadow filled the hut door. Raffia sandals scuffed across the hard-packed earth floor.

Glover, the army medic – not a doctor; he'd died some time ago – leaned over Claude and shook his shoulder. On getting no response, he took hold of his wrist to take his pulse.

Sid felt an upsurge of anxiety as he watched every move, not wanting to believe, yet knowing deep down that the inevitable had finally happened.

There was a respectful slowness to the way the medic placed Claude's hand back to where it had been. Sid felt a tightening in his chest. He knew what came next.

'Gone,' said Glover.

Sid said nothing and turned away. It was easy to get upset but damned dangerous to give up. He would give up for a while, pretend that he wanted to die. But then he would remember Maisie and carry on. In the meantime, Claude's loss would be a raw wound, forever imprinted on his memory.

Glover came around the edge of the bed – a makeshift thing of splintered wood and straw mattress. 'You all right?'

Glover was one of the few medical orderlies they had left.

Sid closed his eyes. 'I'm tired.'

Glover said nothing. There were few medicines and little hope.

The only way Sid could connect with hope was behind his closed eyelids. Hope or death, the stuff of dreams and nightmares, the road to oblivion.

4

A shopping bag hanging from the handlebar of the pushchair brought a smile of satisfaction to her face. Every so often, Maisie peered down into it, hardly daring to believe her eyes. Rationing wasn't entirely over, but there was more in her bag today than there had been a few months back.

Butter, bacon, a tin of corned beef, a loaf of bread, milk and sugar, plus vegetables, offal and pork bones. A feast! She'd even managed to buy a bar of Fry's Five Boys – dark chocolate with a sweet creamy middle. She'd make it last a week – had to, in fact, seeing as sweets were still rationed.

'Well, you're looking pleased with yerself,' said one of the neighbours as she manoeuvred the pushchair into the front door.

'I didn't have to queue for too long and Edwards' had onions.'

'Ooow. If that's the case, I might go shopping today instead of tomorrow.'

'They won't be there forever,' Maisie called back.

Happy feelings were still there when she unstrapped Paula from the pushchair and ripped a portion of crust from the loaf, which Paula grabbed with both hands.

Having done all the shopping and housework all week, it was Carole's afternoon to go clothes shopping with friends of her own age. They'd heard of a clothes swap taking place at the Central Hall and Maisie had been glad to have Paula to herself.

'Stay there and eat that whilst Auntie Maisie puts the kettle on. She's gasping for a cuppa.'

Auntie Maisie. She loved being Paula's auntie. It made her feel as though she really mattered in the little girl's life.

Dinner tonight would be liver and onions. The old-fashioned meal was a wartime staple for the simple reason that offal had not been rationed – well, not at first anyway.

Once the shopping was put away and the kettle had boiled, Paula came out asking for more bread. Maisie gave her another crust.

'We had a very good shop, Paula, and now we need to sit and catch our breath.'

Paula laughed.

Maisie blew on her tea and poured some into a saucer. 'Here you are, Paula. Wash that bread down with some of this.'

Paula waved it away and carried on with the bread.

Maisie sat drinking her tea, all the while smiling and thinking what a great change the little girl had made to her life. A wave of happiness swept over her. Things hadn't always been easy these last few years, but she did feel things were returning to normal.

'What is normal, Paula? Can you tell Auntie Maisie what normal means?'

Paula laughed and threw back her head, showing cool white milk teeth. 'Choc.'

'Chocolate. Well, that's a nice thought, although I don't quite remember things being that way.'

Normal was before the war, which seemed such a long time ago now. A sudden yearning to go back to those years at the tobacco factory took hold. Back then, the height of happiness had been making friends with Bridget Milligan and Phyllis Mason. It seemed a world away. All the girls had talked of in those days was getting married, having children and keeping house. They'd fully expected to spend the rest of their lives in the city they'd been born in with a fella they expected to be married to for the rest of their lives.

'Who would have thought. I wonder what next?'

Paula stopped chewing and looked at her. 'Bubby,' she said and handed her a sliver of soggy bread.

'No, you eat it up, darling.'

'Yeah, yeah, yeah.'

'Yes. It's yes, not yeah.' Though she'd always spoken with a strong Bristol accent, she corrected Paula. She would do whatever she could to have the little girl better herself.

'Yessss,' returned Paula, bright-eyed and determined to please.

'No matter what, I'm going to teach you what we went through.'

The little girl stared. Too young to understand, but she did like to be spoken to. She liked stories, she liked to hear someone singing.

'I think the more you're spoken to, the cleverer you will be,' Maisie said.

Perhaps Paula was impressed. She made noises, blew raspberries and pointed to things that she wanted to know the name of. 'That!'

'The wireless. You already know that, Paula.'

'Arless.'

'Well, that's near enough.'

She pointed to Maisie's shoe.

Maisie said shoe.

'Shoe. Shoe. Shoe.'

Maisie clapped. 'Well done. Now what about this?' She raised her teacup. 'Can you say cup?'

Paula pointed a sticky finger. 'Cup.'

'And what's in my cup?'

'Tea.'

'Well done! You are a very clever little girl.'

She gave Paula a big hug but regretted it when a piece of doughy bread stuck in her hair.

'Soup?' Maisie asked. 'Soup. Spoon.' The words came tumbling out. It was time for lunch and Paula was making no bones about it.

Early afternoon was time for Paula's nap and Maisie's chance to get on with some housework. This afternoon, there was ironing to be done. Many women she knew admitted to hating ironing. She wasn't one of them. Ironing was one of those times when she thought on all that had happened. Cities had been bombed and young people, barely twenty some of them, had been called up and sent into battle. Phyllis had served in Malta. Bridget had served in several hospitals throughout the country. Such a long time since they'd been at the factory and gone on that charabanc to Weston-super-Mare.

Sid. It seemed like another world, long ago, but also like yesterday. Thinking back made her well up with emotion.

Maisie set the iron onto a brass trivet, caught her thoughts and her feelings and relived them. Laughing, kissing and making fun of each other. He'd been so intense and she'd been... What had she been? A little frosty at times? That was the way it might have seemed, but in all honesty it hadn't been the way she'd felt. Sid had made her feel shy. No one who knew her would have believed that Maisie Miles, frightened of no one and as outspoken as you like, could be shy.

She smiled at the memory of seeing him off at Temple Meads Station. Dear Sid. He'd neglected to leave her a photo when he went away.

'I'm not going to be away for that long. You just see. I'll be 'ome in time for another factory trip to Weston. You just see if I ain't.'

He hadn't come home before the summer. Instead, he'd been sent out to Singapore. So very far away.

When the news came that Singapore had fallen to the Japanese, she'd been as shocked as anyone. In time, a card arrived from a prisoner of war camp. That was when she began writing in earnest. He'd sent coded messages, very simple affairs, but enough to fool the Japanese who had censored everything. Of late, she'd heard nothing and wondered, with unvoiced sadness, how he was getting on, whether in fact he was still alive.

The smell of singed cotton made her grab the iron, which unnoticed by her had fallen onto the ironing cloth.

'Damn!' She swore and rubbed at the brown scorch mark, though knew beyond doubt that it was a permanent fixture.

How long, she wondered, until Sid and the men who'd served in the Far East would be freed and finally return home?

She looked at the mantel clock. Its sonorous tick was constant, though its hands seemed a little slow. The news was broadcast on the hour. There was news of British troops in Berlin and what was happening in Europe before switching to the American advance on Japan. Overtures had been made to the Japanese government, but so far there had been no response.

So much of the reporting on the wireless was still of war and she was tired of it, tired of hearing about it.

Frustrated, she thudded her way upstairs, carrying the pile of laundry. The bedding went into the airing cupboard. Some of her clothes she carried into the bedroom, where she lay them on the bed. The colours of her favourite blouse sprang out at her. When she'd first worn it, she'd loved the vivid pink and green. Countless laundering had made the colours fade and the stitching was coming undone. *A bit like this country*, she thought. *A bit like all of us.*

'Perhaps I'm not being entirely fair,' she said out loud. 'Clothes aren't the be-all and end-all. Brave lot, us Brits.'

Though shabbily dressed and living amongst ruins, people were beginning to look forward to better times – 'the sunny uplands', as Churchill had termed it. An election was in the offing and, as yet, the outcome was unclear, though the Labour Party message, Let Us Face the Future, was ringing true with a war weary population who wanted to see some reward for their many sacrifices.

'Yes,' she hissed through clenched teeth. 'Let's see what tomorrow brings.'

* * *

The following day before leaving for work, a letter arrived that lifted Maisie's spirits. At heart, she dearly wished to hear from Sid to know he was alive, but this letter was from Bridget.

To her great surprise, she was still in London.

'I can't believe it. I thought she'd be in America by now,' Maisie remarked to Carole.

'She's still in London. What about her husband? Where's he?'

'I don't know.'

Carole was trying to disentangle herself from Paula's sticky grasp on her leg. Paula was walking but made use of her new skill to plaster herself to her mother at any opportunity. 'So what's she up to? Is everything all right?'

Eyes still fixed on the letter; Maisie's expression glowed with joy. 'Very much so. She writes such a wonderful letter. Wish I could write one as interesting as hers. Mind you, she always was a clever clogs – read books all the time and knew lots of history, especially about Bristol.'

Her comment was proved true as she read on.

Dear Maisie,

Lyndon is in America. He did arrange tickets for me to travel very soon, though I'm not quite sure if I'm ready. I feel guilty about letting him down but can't help it.

I'm planning to visit the family as soon as I'm able. I've arranged to stay at the Royal Hotel on College Green for three nights – who would have thought it back in the days at the factory, Bridget Milligan staying at a posh hotel? There's precious little room for me and Lyndon Junior at Marksbury Road. But I desperately want to see Dad as many times as I can before finally saying goodbye. Just the thought of leaving brings tears to my eyes.

Most war brides won't be travelling to the United States until next year, their husbands travelling ahead of them. Lyndon insisted that Lyndon Junior and I travel on one of the transatlantic liners that hasn't been requisitioned for war. He has both planta-tion business and an interview in Washington. He's hoping for some kind of political position. Goodness knows where he's going to find the time.

I'm excited at the prospect of beginning life in a new country, though sad to leave my family and friends. It seems such a long time since that day you arrived at the factory. It also seems a long time since I gave Lyndon a guided tour of St Mary Redcliffe and had him gawping with surprise at the tomb of William Penn's father. You may recall me telling you that William Penn was one of the founding fathers of the United States of America and gave his name to Pennsylvania.

It would be nice to meet up if you can get time off work. I have written to Phyllis, but as yet have received no reply. To be honest, I'm not sure where she is. I wrote to the last posting she had. Perhaps Mick's been posted overseas, and she's gone with him. It takes time for the mail to catch up.

Talking of mail, I'm not sure Dad has received my letter. I did think about phoning the telephone box at the end of the street. I recall the number from when I lived there – phoning the odd boyfriend my parents didn't know I had. I can still hear the drop of those coppers falling into the box and the pips going when my time was up. Goodness, but that old phone scared me! All so new at the time.

Anyway, even if I did ring and somebody picked it up, Dad wouldn't use it. Modern gadgets scare him. Clocks are mechanical and an entirely different matter.

Would it be possible for you to call in on him and make sure he knows I'm coming? Of course you will. You're one of my oldest and best friends. Who knows, you might also be able to find out what's happening with Phyllis too.

I must go. Junior is beginning to grumble for a feed. He's four months old now and well grown. You'll no doubt agree when you see him.

All my love, Bridget.

Laying the letter aside, Maisie sighed with pleasure, her face wreathed in smiles. 'She's coming to stay in Bristol in two weeks' time.'

Carole lifted Paula into her arms. 'Is she coming to stay here?'

'No. She's booked into the Royal Hotel on College Green. It's open again as a hotel. The troops have left – or most of them have.'

'The Royal Hotel! Wish I could afford to stay there.'

It occurred to Maisie that if Carole asked Eddie Bridgeman he'd probably arrange it for her. If Carole's mother was to be believed, she was his daughter and he certainly had the money. Before the war, and during it, Eddie had carried on with his criminal activities, including bumping off Carole's attacker and Paula's father. Nowadays, he was making money as a scrap merchant – there was certainly plenty of that about! The military no longer needed troop carriers, vans and cars. Eddie had put in his bid to buy many of these vehicles, at the same time becoming cheek by jowl with local politicians. It was even rumoured he would be running for city councillor.

Maisie kept well clear of him. He'd made overtures to her in the past and although he'd been good to Carole, she avoided him. Although he'd declared he was going straight now, becoming a councillor no less, she still couldn't forget his criminal background. If he ever did go straight it would be something short of a miracle.

'It makes sense for her to stay there what with the baby. He's four months old now. Doesn't time fly,' she added with a regretful sigh.

Carole agreed that it did. 'They grow up quickly.'

Maisie experienced a wave of contentment wash over her. Happily, it seemed Carole was content with her lot in life. She seemed to enjoy keeping house whilst Maisie went to work. Living with Maisie also meant she could go out on an evening to enjoy herself as any young girl wanted to do.

'I'll put the kettle on. You've got time,' Carole insisted.

Leaving Maisie with Paula, Carole thought about Joe. He had no idea she had a child, but the truth had to be disclosed sooner or later. There was also another truth. If Joe was still intent on marrying her regardless of Paula, then Maisie had to be told about the prospect of moving to Liverpool. Carole knew it would hit Maisie hard, but Joe was the love of her life and she truly believed that it was her last chance at happiness.

Whilst drinking tea, Maisie's thoughts were still on Bridget. 'I think her plan is to spend as much time as possible with her father before she leaves for America. It's going to hit him hard,' she said sadly and sighed. 'It seems a lifetime since we first met at the tobacco factory. I wonder what our lives would have been like if the war hadn't happened?'

Carole laughed. 'You'd probably be married to Sid by now with kids of your own.'

Maisie's attention immediately turned to Paula. 'Hmm. There's a thought.'

Inside, she felt a deep sadness she preferred not to show. She hadn't heard anything from Sid for a long while and neither had his mother, who'd been queuing outside the fresh fish shop in Bedminster, hoping against hope that there was a fish on the slab that she recognised.

'Fresh from Iceland,' the fishmonger had shouted.

'As long as it ain't that stuff from Africa,' somebody had grumbled. Other voices were raised in agreement.

The demand had been made to know what kind of fish had come in from Iceland. Any fish had been acceptable in the past five years, but people were beginning to request some of what they'd eaten before the war, like cod, herring and mackerel. Recognisable fish was beginning to trickle through, but there were still mines floating in the sea; one touch from their metal prongs and no more fishing boat – or fishermen.

Maisie and Sid's mother had hardly noticed when the queue began to move forward.

'I was hoping he might have written to you of late, if not to me,' she'd said, her face creased with worry. 'It's been a while now.'

Maisie had shaken her head. 'No.'

The fear of him never coming home showed in her eyes.

Maisie harboured the same concern but certainly wouldn't say so. His poor mother looked to be suffering enough, so for the rest of the time they'd spent queuing she'd talked about anything and everything. No news was good news. That's what they eventually stated, though it was of little comfort.

* * *

For the rest of that day whilst tearing leaves and overseeing the new input of workers, Maisie thought about the forthcoming visit from Bridget, which she was very much looking forward to. As for Phyllis, she convinced herself that everything was fine. She and Mick had got through the terrible bombing in Malta. To Maisie's mind, if they'd got through that, they could get through anything.

Life was going on in the sweet old-fashioned way at the tobacco factory. Working here helped Maisie cope with everything the war had thrown at her. She'd found friendship here and respect. Her steadfast nature and willingness to learn had also gained her promotion. She had responsibility for training new employees and there were certainly going to be a large number of them in future.

A batch of school leavers had recently been taken on, most of them fifteen years of age, in line with the new law coming in. The school-leaving age had been scheduled to increase from fourteen to fifteen a while back, but the outbreak of war had intervened. Things that were promised were now catching up. Thanks to the ending of the war in Europe, raw materials were trickling in from all corners of the world and tobacco was no exception.

Maisie didn't need to ask for an increase in wages but was told she was getting one anyway. It seemed she was valued because production would be increasing now that servicemen were expected home. They'd want their cigarettes, pipe tobacco and, those who could afford it, their cigars. Production would be increased and to that end they would be taking on more labour and needed experienced people to oversee their training and development.

The contingent of school leavers stood in front of her. Some glowed with confidence – sassy types – like Carole, she thought and couldn't help smiling. Others looked scared as rabbits, likely to bolt for cover.

As per usual, they were introduced to the stripping room, told the correct way to strip leaves and how it was best to wind sticking plasters around their fingertips to stop them bleeding.

Maisie imparted the same advice given to her when she'd first begun work at W. D. & H. O. Wills a few years ago now. She told them the times of the tea and lunch breaks, where the lavatories were, what time they clocked on and what time they clocked off. She also warned them of the cheeky boys pushing the trollies who weighed and collected the leaves.

Maude Potter, a senior in the department, leant into Maisie and assured her she'd soon knock the edges of the sassier girls. 'Right cheeky little mares some of them.'

'Go easy, Maude. We were all young once.'

She said it whilst recalling how she'd felt on first arriving in the factory. Working here at number one factory, East Street, Bedminster, had not been her choice but that of her stepfather – and then only for his own selfish ends. He'd wanted her to play a part in stealing cigarettes. Getting through that grim time still sent shivers down her spine. She'd entered the factory determined she would hate it but instead had made friendships she knew would last forever.

Over a welcome cup of tea in the canteen and despite the din of conversation going on around her, she thought of that long-ago summer and the coach to Weston-super-Mare. The firm's outing, the coach babbling with noise and all of them squashed in together in their summer frocks. She thought of eating chips and sandwiches with Sid that day on the seafront as an aircraft buzzed overhead pulling a banner about resisting the impending war. But the war had come regardless. Like many others Sid had gone to war. So far, he hadn't come back. She hoped he would. Sid deserved to live, but having not heard from him for a few months now, she was beginning to worry.

Looking on the bright side, she consoled herself with the memories of times past and the possibilities for the future. She smiled dreamily as she imagined his old chirpy self, strolling along the street, banging on her door and asking her if she'd like to go to the pictures. That's what they'd done on their first date – though it hadn't really been a date. They'd just been standing in the same queue and he'd barged in.

She wondered what he would think of Carole and Paula. Her letters had been brief, the paper precious, so news kept to a minimum. Carole was mentioned but not Paula. Her reasons for not mentioning them were varied.

'What you doin' this weekend then, Maisie?'

Ted Evans, one of the foremen, sat himself down at the canteen table without being invited.

She knew he was sweet on her and she quite liked him. She nonchalantly dipped a biscuit into her tea, then took a sip.

'Nothing much, though I promised my old friend Bridget I'd pop over to see her dad. She's coming down for a few days in two weeks and isn't sure he knows that she is. He's by 'imself since her mum died – well, not exactly alone. The kids are still there, except for the eldest. He was working as an apprentice gardener, but the moment he turned seventeen joined the army cadets. Can't be easy though.'

'That's good of you.'

'I don't mind. She's a dear friend.'

She winced as he lit a cigarette. Although she worked in the factory, she'd never taken up the habit and she couldn't help believing that her mother had died from smoking.

Noticing her reaction, Ted apologised and put it out.

'I suppose you'll 'ave a lot to talk about.'

'Nineteen to the dozen,' said Maisie with a laugh. 'Nobody will be able to get a word in edgeways once we start gossiping.'

Ted laughed with her. 'Sounds like a party.'

'Might be, though we're all grown up now. We've got responsibilities, though we do let our 'air down now and again – when the mood takes us.'

There was both fondness and bemusement in the look he gave her. 'That's what I like about you. You're not flighty. You've got responsible ways.'

She felt a rush of embarrassment, due only partly to what he was saying but mostly to the intense way he was looking at her. 'I don't know about that.'

He played with the cigarette he'd placed in the ashtray. 'I was thinking you might want to go to the pictures with me tomorrow night. *Fire Over England*. Vivien Leigh and Laurence Olivier are in it, down at the Town Hall. Fancy it?'

She couldn't help returning Ted's smile. He had an optimistic attitude to the world and a face to suit; kindly and cheery. His expression and disposition tended to rub off. Nobody could be miserable in Ted's company.

This was not the first time he'd invited her out. So far, she'd declined, but she hadn't celebrated VE Day. Carole had, coming home after four in the morning, eyes bright and full of herself. Panic had seized Maisie. The moment she'd dreaded had come. Soon she would be all alone. Up until now Carole, and more specifically Paula, had been the centre of her universe. Soon, very soon, everything could change. She'd put her own life and enjoyment on hold. It was time to make a new life for herself – whether or not Sid came home.

'OK. I fancy a night out – but only if you promise me fish and chips for supper.'

He responded instantly to her smile with a broader one of his own. 'Hamblins for fish and chips wrapped in newspaper after-wards – with loads of salt and vinegar and a few scrumps added.'

'Even better,' she laughed.

'Then that's settled. See you outside the town hall for a night at the pictures. See you at seven?'

'Yes. Seven.'

He wandered off whistling merrily.

Back in the stripping room, Maisie sat there, staring down at the piled-up leaves and asking herself if she really did want to go out with him.

'You goin' on a date with 'im?'

Gladys Edwards was one of the new intake straight from school and had been sitting close by in the canteen. She'd obviously heard everything.

Maisie's fingers began to fly, tearing and sorting, then piling to one side.

'Don't you think that I should?' she asked with as much confidence as she could muster.

Gladys sniffed. 'Couldn't 'elp overhearing. The fish and chips sounded nice. And the pictures. Unless you've got something you want to do more, you might as well go. Anyways, 'e ain't a bad-looking bloke and nice too – for a foreman.'

Suddenly, she had cold feet about going out with Ted. The other dates she'd been on hadn't come to anything. If she was honest, her days with Sid hadn't been the stuff of romance. They'd been friends. Perhaps that was their strength and the reason they'd continued to correspond. Ted was a different matter. He was nice, had twinkly eyes and a ready smile.

'I'd better 'ave a word with 'im,' she said, swinging one leg, then the other from beneath the table.

The small booth labelled 'Production Foreman' was at the far end of the ground floor. Particles of tobacco dust hung fog thick, tickling the nose and settling on hair, clothes and face. In the outside world, her breathing was fine. Just half an hour after arriving at the factory particles of grit lined her throat.

She knocked on the obscured glass dividing the office shared by three production foremen with the factory floor. Someone shouted, 'Enter.'

'Is Ted around?'

Two foremen, one with a red, round face, the other with a monkish style border of white hair around his scalp, shook their heads.

'Gone to the cricket ground with the factory team to inspect the grounds.'

'I didn't know Ted liked cricket that much.'

'He's married to it, sweet'eart. No doubt about it.'

She knew better than to ask if he'd be coming back that day. It was a Friday. They played matches on a Saturday, sometimes even on a Sunday, but a fragrant Friday evening was set aside for practice and inspecting the pitch.

'I don't suppose I could get a message to him?'

A shaking of heads again.

'Sorry, love.'

A snigger passed between them, followed by a wink.

Not being one afraid of coming forward, Maisie challenged them to explain. 'Is something funny?'

Still chortling at their shared joke, they shook their heads.

'Oh for goodness' sake!'

Once she was outside their office, the obvious truth hit her. Out here all she could smell was tobacco dust. There had been another smell in the office that had smothered that of tobacco. Beer.

Angered by their rudeness, she went back in to give them a piece of her mind. The inebriated pair hadn't expected her back and didn't have time to hide the opened bottles of stout they'd brought out from beneath their desks.

'Drunk on duty? Drunk in charge of machinery? I think this should be reported to the management, don't you?'

Their jaws dropped. The bottles were slowly slid back beneath their desks.

It was all they had chance to do before she slammed the door behind her.

'Drunks,' she snorted under her breath. Just like her stepfather. He'd spent every penny he could on beer and cigarettes.

She found herself wondering about Ted. Was he a drinker? She hadn't heard any rumours. Nevertheless, she was having second thoughts about keeping the date they'd agreed on. She didn't need a man in her life. Her world was wrapped around Paula and her mother. Hopefully it always would be. There again she couldn't let him down quite so harshly. She would put him off – perhaps suggest they leave it for another time – just until she didn't feel so threatened – so unfaithful to Sid.

To that end, she searched out anyone else who was heading in the direction of the cricket ground.

'Can you tell Ted Baker that I can't make it to the pictures. Something's come up.'

* * *

At Maisie's urging, Carole took full advantage and went out herself. Maisie stayed at home with Paula, a pile of ironing and feeling just a twinge of regret for letting Ted down.

'Never mind,' she said as she spit on the base of the iron and watched it sizzle. 'There'll be another time.'

5

As she'd promised Bridget, Maisie made her way to the Milligan household in Marksbury Road. The road had that Sunday slumbering about it. Bees buzzed, vying with the sound of children lately released from Sunday school, dressed in their Sunday best and bursting to change before climbing trees, playing hopscotch or rolling marbles along the gutter.

The house in Marksbury Road didn't feel as crowded as it used to be when Bridget was still at home and her mother was alive.

'They're all out,' said Bridget's father as he invited Maisie into the living room. 'The younger ones are at the park, the older ones out walking with boyfriends. I keep thinking they're too young, but when I look back to my own younger days I realise, they're not at all. And, of course, our Sean is in the sea cadets.'

'Do you hear much from him?'

'He writes when he thinks about it. Never wrote as much as my Bridie.' A wistful look flickered in his eyes. He'd always been closest to Bridget, even though she wasn't his natural daughter.

'That's true. She asked me to come over and let you know she was coming down next week. She wasn't sure you'd get the letter in time.'

'I did,' he said. A knowing smile curved his lips, accompanied by a mischievous twinkle in his eyes. 'That's just her, I think, wanting to keep an eye on me and sending you to do the job.'

Maisie was inclined to think he was right. Bridget worried about her father. The house hadn't changed much, but she sensed Patrick had. Even though he'd received an injury to his leg during the Great War, necessitating having to wear a false leg, he'd always struck Maisie as an energetic and well-adjusted man.

She couldn't quite put her finger on why he'd changed. He was older, of course, his hair had thinned and deeper lines scoured his face, but that was only to be expected. His clothes looked clean and ironed and he looked well fed. Bridget would be relieved.

Tea was offered. Maisie said she would love one.

'I missed the bus to the centre and had to walk. It's made me thirsty. Luckily it's a lovely day.' She fluttered a hand in front of her face. 'Quite warm too.'

She followed Patrick out into the kitchen and watched whilst he held the kettle beneath the tap and filled it.

'Sorry I took a while to answer the door. I was out in the garden, planting carrots – and other things.'

'Are you serious?' she asked laughingly. Patrick had never been a keen gardener but had kept busy mending watches and clocks.

She sensed an uncharacteristic furtiveness about his manner, as though there was something he wasn't divulging.

He threw a half-smile over his shoulder. 'Let's get this kettle on.'

The gas jet ignited at the touch of a match.

'Come and see.' He led her out of the back door whilst the kettle sang on the gas.

The garden was not as she remembered it. Six months ago, it had looked a muddy mess. Now, burgundy, yellow and purple dahlias grew in regimented rows, butterflies landing delicately on the nectar-laden flowers. Bees buzzed as they hopped from flower to flower. Birds dived in and out the tallest of the privet hedges and sparrows peeped out from the eaves of the roof.

Maisie voiced her admiration. 'They're beautiful. I'm amazed you never grew them before.'

He grinned sidelong at her. 'Our Sean showed me how and made me promise to keep growing them.' He nodded at the flowers, which in turn seemed to nod back in the warm breeze. 'They were Mary's favourite flowers. She used to try to encourage me to grow them but didn't press too hard. She knew I was far from a keen gardener.' He shook his head. 'I don't know where my boys get their interest in gardening from.' He chuckled. 'From their mother obviously. Certainly not from me.'

Naturally their conversation turned to Bridget. He expressed himself happy for her but regretted that she would be going to America to live.

'I'll miss her. But don't you go telling her I said so. I wants me girl to be happy.'

'You do have other children. That's some consolation.'

'Won't be long before they've all flown the nest.'

A sad look came to his eyes, though only fleetingly. Once back inside, he began to fidget, tapping his knees with the palms of his hands, glancing at the clock, the window and the door.

Was he expecting someone?

Three chimes rang out from the walnut mantel clock.

Again a hint of furtiveness in the way he glanced up at the clock.

Maisie read the signs and couldn't help commenting, 'I'm sorry. Am I interrupting something?'

He looked away and cleared his throat. 'There's something I should tell you...'

The sound of a key turning in the front door stopped him from saying more.

'Cooeee! It's me!'

The voice was that of an adult. The plump homely features of a middle-aged woman appeared around the door. Her eyes, which seemed almost the colour of ripe plums, swept from Patrick to Maisie.

'Oh. Company.' She blushed and placed a finger coquettishly on her chin, eyes flashing between Maisie and Patrick, settling on the latter in what Maisie could only describe as a girlish manner. 'I didn't know you had company, Pat. I ain't interrupting anything, am I?'

Patrick got to his feet, rubbing his hands down his thighs. He looked bashful, like a younger man introducing his sweetheart for the first time. 'Maisie, this is Ethel Ellard, a friend of mine.' He then explained who Maisie was. 'She's a friend of my daughter's. She came round to check on me because Bridget asked her to. She's coming down from London shortly but wasn't sure I'd received her letter.'

Ethel, who had a pleasant face, smiled and gave a curt nod. 'Well, that's nice. Pleased to meet you, Maisie.'

'You too, Ethel.'

'Any more tea in that pot for me?'

'Help yourself,' said Patrick.

Ethel shook the pot, then turned up her nose. 'It needs fresh.'

'Well, you know where everything is.'

Without a backward glance, Ethel took the pot to the kitchen.

Maisie wondered whether Bridget suspected and that was the real reason for having her check on him.

They sat awkwardly across from each other. From the kitchen came the sound of Ethel singing.

Maisie broke the silence. 'I shouldn't have come.'

'No, no, no,' he said, shaking his head. 'It's good to see you. Reminds me of when you, Bridget and Phyllis used to go out on the town.'

'Hardly the town,' Maisie laughed. 'The pub or the pictures.'

'I remember you getting caught in that raid in November 1940. What a night that was. Me and Mary were worried sick. There was the city centre on fire and you three walked through it. Mary said more than one prayer that night and so did I, for that matter.'

Ethel came back with a fresh pot of tea. 'And I've got biscuits. Welsh cakes – well, after a fashion. I can't always get the right ingredients. I get what I can and improvise.'

'You made them yourself?'

Ethel beamed. 'Oh yes.'

'They look delicious.'

'Ethel's quite a cook.'

Maisie chose to believe that the look that flashed between them was one of mutual respect – though it could just as easily have been love.

The Welsh cake, the consistency of which was more like a biscuit, melted in her mouth.

'Have another,' said Ethel, pushing the plate towards her.

'I can't resist. You're a good cook.'

'I try to be, though it's hard with rations. Still, I manage. It's only me now since Sam died and my children 'ave...' Her voice trailed away.

It was obvious that Ethel was consumed by a great sadness at mention of her children. Heaven forbid, but perhaps they'd been killed during a bombing raid. Or perhaps a childhood disease had taken them.

Whatever it was, Patrick patted Ethel's hand. 'There, there, me darling. It's a hard cross you bear.'

'Obviously you've suffered some kind of loss?'

Ethel's cheery expression drooped with sadness. She nodded and the way she sipped her tea made Maisie think it was a subject that was difficult to talk about.

'Look. You don't have to tell me. It's your business.' *And your tragedy*, she thought, desperately not wanting to intrude.

'I was ill. Albert was away fighting and was injured. He was in a hospital in Palestine for a long while. I did ask my mother to look after the kids, but she was already a bit past it by then. My sister took the youngest, but the older ones...' The corners of her mouth were downturned and her eyes turned watery. 'They took my older boys. The youngest was eleven. The other twelve.' She turned her cheek into her hand, cupping one side of her face and shaking her head. 'I was devastated when I came out of hospital.'

'Do they write?'

'I had one letter from each of them. That was a while ago now. Nothing since.'

Maisie felt a great urge to enfold the poor woman in her arms, but as they'd only just met didn't think it appropriate. She settled for telling her how sorry she was, then added, 'I hope they do write again, but you know how youngsters are. They get so caught up in their own world.'

It came as something of a relief when Ethel glanced pointedly at Maisie's left hand. 'You're not married?'

She shook her head. 'No.'

'No young man then?'

'Possibly. He's still a prisoner of the Japanese.'

'Oh. Let's 'ope he gets home soon then. Let us all get on with our lives.'

There was sincerity in Ethel's tone and kindness sparkling in her eyes.

'Any more tea? Another biscuit?'

'No thank you.' Maisie glanced at the clock. 'I think I should be going. I might be able to get a bus back if I hurry. Thank you, Patrick. Thank you, Ethel. Nice to meet you.'

Patrick, showing an obvious stiffness in his gammy leg, also got to his feet. 'I'll see you to the door.'

At the front step, he suddenly caught hold of her arm. Rarely had she seen him look so intense.

'You don't condemn me, Maisie? You see, I was lonely. What with Mary dead and Bridget and our Sean left home. Our Michael will be off soon and then the girls. Time flies so fast.'

She shook her head. 'You're old enough to think for yourself.'

'You won't tell our Bridget, will you? I would prefer to tell her myself.'

Her heart went out to him. 'We all get lonely, Mr Milligan. It's a good thing to have someone in our lives. Best of luck to you.'

He nodded. 'Yes. Yes. 'Tis true. Ethel was in need of a friend herself since her kids were sent to Australia. Her husband died just after he came back from the fighting.' He shook his head. 'This war, this terrible war...'

There was nothing at all she could say to him that would help. All she did say was that knowing Bridget she had no doubt that she would understand.

'Bridget loves you. She'd want you to be happy.'

At the garden gate, she turned and waved at both him and his lady friend.

Up until this weekend she'd not felt in the least bit lonely. She had Carole, she had Paula, but seeing Bridget's father with his new girlfriend had affected her. Sid came to mind. So did Ted. She was divided between the two: the man who was to hand and the one who might yet come home. Either way, life was too short to remain lonely. Seeing Patrick and Ethel had brought home that she had nobody with whom to share the highs and lows of her life. It hadn't really mattered much up until now, but there was a new urge within her to seize the day and hope for happiness.

6

The summer sun glared outside. Inside, the hospital was cool and echoed with the footsteps of doctors and nurses.

Phyllis stared at the posters on the waiting-room wall without really seeing them. The smell of antiseptic and carbolic made her nose tingle. Everything she saw and smelt aggrieved her, but she had to be here. Her husband, Mick Fairbrother, was here, that fact alone was making her feel sick inside.

Clive Ansell, a colleague of Mick's, had found her at her new posting in Cambridgeshire and given her the grim news direct. It would have been better if she'd been nearer, but they'd both been in the last throes of active duty, both loving what they were doing, until she'd received this news.

'It's something to do with an injury to his head he received when he was in Malta. I thought it was better than phoning you. You might get worried,' Clive had insisted.

Get worried! Of course she was worried.

Clive had accompanied her into the adjutant's office and once he, a decorated RAF officer, had explained the situation, Phyllis was granted compassionate leave.

The adjutant was a white-haired man with a pink face. An old-fashioned handlebar moustache hung heavily on his upper lip. Those owning such had the habit of twirling the ends upwards with their fingers. This is what he had done as he thought about it and finally pronounced, 'Under the circumstances, I think it best to bring forward your demobilisation. Your husband needs you more than we do. The time has come for women to go back to their homes and have children. Their war is over.'

If she hadn't been worried about Mick, she would have taken him to task, asked him if it hadn't crossed his mind that it wouldn't necessarily be so. Women had spent the war years away from the kitchen sink. It was very likely they might no longer be content with their lot. Their experiences had changed them, but there wasn't time for arguments.

Packing only the necessities, Phyllis had numbly agreed for Clive to drive her to the military hospital at Stowmarket. Travelling by car took far less time than by train. They ran out of petrol at one point and Clive had to resort to using the petrol from the can in the boot. Her mind was occupied with how Mick would be, how ill he was and, worst of all, would he survive?

The head injury had been sustained on their wedding day in Malta following an explosion. Their wedding had not gone ahead, not in Malta anyway. After a recovery period, they'd married on the boat going back to Blighty, very romantic but not at all planned.

Why now? Phyllis asked herself. Now when the war in Europe had ended and they'd so much to look forward to? It seemed so unfair.

All is fair in love and war. Well, whoever had said that wasn't thinking straight. Life was unfair.

The antiseptic smell of the hospital had hit her the moment she'd walked through the door. On arrival, she was advised that Mick was in a specialist unit that dealt with head injuries.

Stark was the only word she could think of for her surroundings. Stark and pristine, from the cold, unadorned walls to the crisp veils of the nursing staff, the white coats of the doctors.

Phyllis felt numb. Trivialities broke into her mind. *Did I thank Clive?* She couldn't recall whether she had or not, in which case he must have thought her very rude. She couldn't even remember speaking to him very much at all. Two of them in the car, but she might as well have been alone. Never had she felt so isolated and in need of someone to reach out to, so in need of someone to weep with.

A nurse brought her a cup of tea. 'If you need anything at all,' said the nurse, eyes and voice full of compassion, 'I'll be in the ward office at the end of the corridor.'

The nurse left. A doctor arrived, introduced himself as Doctor Gilbert and asked if she was bearing up. She mumbled that she was.

His voice was soft. His hands looked soft too. She couldn't help staring at them, noticing the long fingers, the neatly trimmed fingernails. He wore a wedding ring. She wondered if he had children.

His words competed with her dizzying thoughts. 'I understand from his medical records that he was in the vicinity of an explosion when stationed in Malta.'

She nodded dumbly as the memory flooded back. 'It was supposed to be our wedding day. A UXB was being wheeled through the streets to be detonated away from the houses. He happened to be close by. We had to postpone the wedding. He ended up in hospital instead.'

'I'm sorry to hear that, Mrs Fairbrother.' He took a seat next to her. 'I know it's difficult, but I have to ask you a few questions. Can you cope?'

She nodded.

'Firstly, has he been getting headaches?'

She bit her bottom lip, aware she was twisting the strap of her shoulder bag, tying it in knots. She too was tied up in knots. 'Yes.'

He began shuffling papers in a brown manila folder. 'There's no record of this either in his service file or medical records.'

'He didn't think it important.'

'It *was* important. Very important. He should never have been allowed to fly again.'

'We didn't know that, and anyway he lived for flying.'

The doctor took a deep breath. 'I'm afraid there's been some internal bleeding and damage, which might not have happened if he'd not done so.'

Her mouth felt dry. Her blood ran cold. She didn't need to see her reflection to know that her face had turned ghostly white.

'Will he get better?' Her voice sounded far away yet echoed inside her head.

There was sadness in his eyes, sympathy in his kindness.

Fearing to see anything else, she looked down at the floor.

'We can't say for sure. The injury caused a kind of balloon of blood and suddenly it burst; that's what we think.'

She stopped staring downwards and turned worried eyes onto his face. 'Will he get better?' she asked it more stridently this time, seeing as he hadn't said anything reassuring.

'The greatest course of action is rest and relaxation. In time, it could heal itself, though we don't know for sure.'

One question quivered on her trembling lips. Will he...?

'Will he live?'

Not would he die. She couldn't bring herself to ask that. All she wanted to know was whether he would live.

'With care and not too much disturbance, the injury might right itself, but for now it's very fifty-fifty. He needs to live in a stable environment.'

'Once we get to Australia...'

'Australia! I'm sorry.' He shook his head. 'Let me make it quite clear. Travelling that distance is not an option. It would be best if you find somewhere to live in this country, not too far from here. Just an ambulance drive.'

She stared at him dumbstruck, her thoughts reeling, darting around like the needle on a compass. 'My home city is Bristol.'

'A good choice. Not too far and with good medical facilities. In fact, I'm thinking of applying for a post there myself. I could keep an eye on him. Fingers crossed that I get the post.'

'Mick loved flying. He'll hate being grounded.'

Doctor Gilbert tucked Mick's medical file beneath his arm and shook his head. 'It might have been different if he hadn't gone back to active service being jolted up and down in a military aircraft, but at least he's alive. That's what we must concentrate on – keeping him alive.'

'I want to see him.'

His bearded chin nodded. 'Yes. Of course you can. I thought it best to run through things first to prepare you. You might want to think about what you say – though it's up to you, of course.'

The sound of her footsteps echoed in her ears as she followed a nurse to the ward. There were other patients, but she didn't see them – not in detail. It was as if they were made of wax, placed there to relieve the lack of colour. The room was white. The pillows were white. The bedding was white.

It pleased her to see that Mick's tanned face made him look healthier than the wax effigies in the other beds. Living a life in the hot sun was responsible for that.

Nonetheless, tears welled in her eyes as she looked down at him. Only his face was showing. His head was bandaged. His neck was bandaged.

Like a mummy, she thought. He looked like an Egyptian mummy.

She heard the nurse say that she would leave her for a moment. 'Call me if you need anything.'

Phyllis nodded without once taking her gaze from his face.

Gently, afraid to cause injury or to have him jerk in surprise, she lightly stroked his hand. Peace and quiet. No sudden movements. He had to lie still. And never go home to Australia – at least not in the immediate future. What would his family think? What would they do? Would they come over to visit him? It was such a long way. At the heart of everything was the fact that their dream of setting up a vineyard in South Australia would come to nothing. He'd been totally absorbed with the idea, telling her of how good the soil was there. 'Can't understand why nobody ain't thought of it before.'

Well he had thought of it, had been enthused but now...

She bent over him, her lips only inches from his ear. 'Hello, Mick darling. It's me, Phyllis. Your wife. Can you hear me?'

She closed her eyes tightly and willed him to respond. Even the most fragile movement would be welcome. She looked for a flickering of his eyelashes, the hint of a smile, but there was nothing.

A sob caught in her throat.

She squeezed his hand. 'Mick, get better. Get better for me. We're having kids, remember? Can't recall how many we said. Might have been four. Might have been six, but whatever, kids take up a lot of a woman's time. A mother's time...'

She went on about everything she could think of regarding their future, though didn't mention it would have to be here, confined in a city, and for him in a country, far from home. Having children was all she could think of to make up for their dreams of a vineyard being put on hold for the foreseeable future – or perhaps forever. She couldn't tell him that. She had to give him hope as fragile as it might be. So she talked about work, about the countryside around here and that the famous painter Constable used to live somewhere nearby. She didn't quite know where.

Talking, talking, talking. How long did she go on? It was hard to know. Her eyelids felt heavy, but she gave them no account. Sleep could wait for now.

A nurse, a different one, came with yet another cup of tea. Phyllis didn't take it from her. Her eyes remained fixed on him, Mick Fairbrother, her husband, the man she loved.

She still had hold of his hand when the night had dispersed and daylight fell through the open window. She hadn't noticed anyone opening it but its freshness helped erase the fatigue and grasp where she was and what she was doing there.

She blinked, saw him and for no discernible reason except that he seemed so peaceful, so very still, panic set in. 'Mick?'

An iron fist squeezed her heart.

'Mick?'

She got up, stood over him and gave him a gentle shake.

'Mick. Wake up.' Her voice grew louder, so loud that it carried out into the corridor.

A nurse came running in and inspected the patient lying so still on the starched white sheets.

Phyllis stood back, her breath catching in her throat, her mind empty of any thoughts except fear of him dying. That terrible fear slid like a sharp knife into the depths of her brain. Fearing the worse, she covered her face with her hands.

Starched apron and headdress rustled as the nurse lay her hand on Mick's forehead, listened to his breathing and took his pulse.

Rigid with worry, Phyllis prayed as she had never prayed before. Suddenly, she felt a kindly touch on her arm.

'Don't worry, Mrs Fairbrother. Your husband's all right. In fact, I would say he's sleeping far less fitfully than he has for ages.'

Phyllis came out from behind her hands, her cheeks wet with tears. 'He's alive?'

The nurse smiled. 'He's alive. But tired. We did give him something to help him sleep.' She hesitated before saying, 'And I think you too are tired, Mrs Fairbrother. How about you get a billet close by, get some sleep and see him sometime tomorrow? There's a guest house just outside the hospital entrance run by a Mrs Crane. She'll look after you.'

Phyllis shook her head. 'I can't leave him like this.'

The nurse gently took hold of her arm and guided her away from the bed. 'I'm afraid I'm going to have to insist. The doctor wants him to rest. Sleep is a great healer, you know. Go along to Mrs Crane's. Out through the gate and turn left. It's the second house along. Rest, Mrs Fairbrother.' A sad look crossed her face. 'We all need rest. A great deal of rest after all we've been through during the last five years. Once refreshed, we can all get on with the rest of our lives.'

Phyllis allowed herself to be guided out of the ward and along to the hospital entrance. She sighed deeply. For a moment at his bedside, she'd thought she was losing him. 'At least he seems better now and knowing Mick he'll tell me off when he hears I got myself into a state. He'll pull through. He'll be his old self again,' she said with a sniffle and a smile. 'I know he will. Goodbye. And thank you. I'll see you tomorrow.'

'Goodbye. And make sure you get a good night's sleep.'

Phyllis lifted her hand in a wave before heading for the gate and the place where she would sleep. *Yes*, she told herself. *Mick is strong. He'll be back to his old self in no time.*

The nurse stood for a while watching as yet another war bride attempted to put a brave face on things, living in hope that everything would be as it was before, for her and for everyone. She'd seen enough of the carnage first hand to know that it wasn't necessarily so. Many people had sustained both physical and mental scars that would change their future from the one they'd envisaged. Unfortunately, Mick Fairbrother was likely to be one of them.

7

Maisie smiled to herself as she travelled back from work on the bus to her home in Totterdown, a place she was always glad to get back to and for a few good reasons. For a start, it was a vast improvement on the house she'd grown up in York Street. Secondly, Paula was there.

The sight of a sailor coming out of a pub turned her thoughts to her brother, Alf. It had been a long while since she'd heard from Alf, a scrawled message on a scrap of paper posted from Zanzibar, a routine stop-off for merchant ships making their way up to the Suez Canal. *I might come knocking on your door once this war is over.* That had been six months ago. She'd heard nothing since and had held on to the piece of paper, the pencilled words lifting her spirits when she was feeling low. The war was over but still no sign of him.

The bus passed bombsites and ruined buildings where stairs hung on to a single surviving wall. An ornate marble fireplace was, like the staircase, clinging on to what was left of the building it had once graced. It must have been a lovely house if that fire surround was anything to go by, she thought. Senseless. In a way, it would have been fairer if the bombs had fallen on York Street. As far as she knew, only the third bedroom on one house had ever been blown off and not the one she'd lived in with her family.

Her brother Alf, who was her half-brother, had been the only person in that house she'd truly loved and she missed him. *I wonder when he'll be home from the sea?* she thought. He'd been her lifeline and they'd been close despite the difference in their ages and finding out they were actually half-brother and -sister. Her father had turned out to be her stepfather and her downtrodden mother had dared not show her any affection purely to escape another beating. Cruelty, want and disease in smoke-filled lungs had sent her mother to an early death, leaving Maisie alone and vulnerable. The only thing that helped her get through it were the friends she made at the tobacco factory.

Sometime later she met up with her maternal grandmother who took her in and then left her money and property. Not that she could rest on her laurels. She'd kept her job at the cigarette factory and gained promotion. Unlike the others who had joined up, the tobacco factory was still the centre of her life, but she still looked forward to going home on an evening where Carole would have dinner waiting and Paula would be gurgling and tottering to meet her on strong little legs.

Maisie had seen something of herself in Carole Thomas. She too had come from an impoverished background where she'd been in danger of leading a far different life than she had now. Eddie Bridgeman, a local criminal and friend of her stepfather, had suggested a far from honest living. Carole too had been vulnerable to exploitation, though things changed when she found out that Eddie was her father. Since then, he'd doted on her and the little girl born of an assault by an older man.

'Just think. Me, a grandfather,' he'd declared the last time Maisie had seen him.

She chased the memories from her head to recall what Ted had said earlier. He was disappointed that she hadn't gone to the pictures with him but was still keen.

'We'll just go for a walk tonight,' he'd said to her. 'Up Perrett's Park if you like, while these fine evenings last.'

She'd agreed, though with one important proviso. 'I'll bring Paula if you don't mind being seen out with a woman with a kid in a pushchair.'

To her surprise, he'd gushed an enthusiastic response. 'Would love to. Makes me feel like a part of your family, not just a friend.'

'Well, that's a new one for a girl on a date.' She'd laughed. Laughter helped her cope with the look that came to his eyes. But he wouldn't push it. She knew he would give her time and who knows perhaps in the not-too-distant future they would indeed become more than friends. It all depended. There was still Sid to consider.

So tonight they'd go for a walk in the park, she thought as she alighted from the bus. Perhaps if Paula wasn't too sleepy, she might let her run on the grass. She was too little yet to go on a swing.

The smell of cheese pie greeted Maisie as she entered the house and although it made her taste buds water, she detected the strong smell of onions. Carole was always a bit heavy handed with the onions.

'I'm dishing up,' Carole called from the kitchen.

'Good.'

Paula was on the floor clambering up the fireside chair with plump little hands, her knees buckling a bit as she fought to get onto her feet. Her podgy fingers grabbed at Maisie's overall before she had chance to take it off.

'Let me take this off, poppet, and I'll pick you up.'

Paula gurgled appreciatively and made sounds that were words but not quite properly formed.

'Guess what? Tonight I'm taking you for a walk in the park. Would you like that?'

Sensing from Maisie's tone that this was something she would enjoy, Paula clapped her hands.

'Not tonight.' Carole was standing in the doorway. Her expression was worrying.

'Not tonight?' Maisie was taken by surprise. 'Ted's coming round. I thought you'd appreciate a night out with your friends and that new boyfriend of yours.'

A frown creased Carole's brow and she seemed nervous. 'That's just it. Joe's coming round here tonight.'

'Here?' Maisie couldn't help the disappointment in her voice.

'Yes.' A series of worry lines appeared on her brow. Her lips, so pink and perfectly formed, turned down at the corners. 'I wanted to introduce him to Paula. He must know the truth about me. We're serious about each other, but before it goes any further, I need to be honest with him.'

By now, Paula's head had fallen onto Maisie's shoulder, which meant the little girl had fallen asleep. Gently and lovingly, she put her down on the settee, her head resting on a red velvet cushion, one that had belonged to her grandmother.

Whilst Maisie covered her with a blanket, Carole placed their meal on the table. Cheese and potato pie – with onions, plus bread and butter.

'There was a bit of jam left so I made a roly-poly pudding,' said Carole as she pulled out a chair. Eyes downcast, she sat at the table.

Maisie sensed she was nervous about Joe's visit. 'I know you're worried he might drop you once he knows about Paula. But it's about time you told him after all.'

'What if he changes his mind?' Carole's pale complexion turned ashen.

Maisie did her best to reassure her. 'Then he'd be a fool. You're worth it, and anyway it wasn't your fault that you got pregnant.'

Carole hung her head, desolation twisting her fidgeting hands. 'I should have had her adopted when I wanted to,' she shouted, her eyes blazing.

Maisie was taken aback. 'You don't mean that.' She shook her head. 'No. You don't mean that.'

Carole stabbed at her food, moving it around the plate without actually eating anything.

Hungry after a full day at work, Maisie ate as she thought. She too was worried about Joe visiting. To her, it was a double-edged sword. If he rejected Paula, then Carole would be devastated. If he accepted the child, then he would marry Carole and they would set up home together. But where?

She raised another forkful from her plate. 'You've never told him anything about Paula? Not even hinted?'

As Carole shook her head, Maisie forked more cheese and onion pie into her mouth.

'Shouldn't you have done that first before asking him to visit?'

'I didn't have the courage,' Carole blurted.

Maisie put down her fork and sighed. 'I think you should have. It's going to be one hell of a surprise you're springing on him with no warning.'

Carole lifted her head. Her blue eyes had a liquid look about them, as if she was about to burst into tears. 'Maisie, I love him and don't want to lose him.' She looked down at her untouched meal and ran her hand over her anguished forehead – a soothing action, but not necessarily of much help. 'You don't mind me inviting him, do you?'

'Of course not, though he might have to put up with Ted talking endlessly about the factory cricket team. Anyway, you need to talk to him alone. As I said to you I think the best plan is for us to go out and leave the two of you alone. Do you want me to do that?'

Carole looked down at her plate as she thought about it. 'I don't think I want to be here by myself. I think I want to present a family picture. You and Ted could help.'

'I'm not sure how.'

Maisie held back on the other possibilities that Carole didn't seem to be facing.

What if he was furious that he'd been kept in the dark? It was likely he'd leave the house there and then. Was it likely that he'd easily accept another man's child without a second thought? That, she decided, was indeed a long shot.

There was another option, a possibility that she dare not voice, not yet anyway. What if he still wanted Carole, could accept what had happened, that Paula's father had foisted himself on her, but could not accept the offspring of that monster? What then?

Thoughts raced through her, head each one more bizarre than the next. Then reason itself took over. What she wanted was for Paula to stay with her, but who would that really benefit?

She sucked in her bottom lip. *You*, she told herself. *You don't want to lose Paula and if she goes away...*

Guilt and sympathy fought for precedence. Eventually, her meal mostly finished, she reached across and patted Carole's hand. 'Whatever happens will be for the best, and there is more than one solution – if you really love him, that is.'

Carole smiled haltingly. Her eyes were still big and luminous. She was doing a grand job of keeping the tears at bay. She was worried and had rights to be, but the predicament had to be faced.

Maisie pushed her chair away from the table. 'I'll take the plates out. Why don't you go outside for a smoke?'

'Thanks.'

Maisie balanced Carole's plate of untouched food on top of her empty one. Carole had barely eaten a thing.

'Not surprising,' she murmured as she emptied the leftover food into a bowl and placed it on the cold shelf. Sometime this week they'd eat bubble and squeak, the leftover vegetables fried in the pan and garnished with an egg. Making use of everything and wasting nothing had been ingrained into everyone during the war. The habit was going to be hard to break, though that was not a bad thing. Wasting food was criminal.

Carole's feet clumping up the stairs sounded like a retreating drumbeat. Maisie looked up at the ceiling, listening to softer footsteps now. She imagined her reaching for the stub of lipstick and remnants of face powder. There was little of each left, both still being in short supply. Carole was making herself look glamorous for her beau.

Seeing as Ted is coming, I should do the same, she said to herself. But like Carole, she was worried, though not quite for the same reason. Her big hope was that once married, Carole and Joe would set up home in Bristol. It was like Liverpool, where Joe was from, wasn't it? A sea port, though the northern city was bigger and had more heavy industry.

Although Maisie did her best to concentrate on the washing up, it was nigh on impossible. She found herself washing the same things repeatedly, some after she'd dried them. Deep down, she knew that wishing Carole and Paula wouldn't leave Bristol was grasping at straws, but she couldn't imagine a life without the little girl.

Giving up on the dishes, she flung the tea towel to one side whilst reminding herself that nothing was yet decided.

A movement through the kitchen window drew her attention. A pair of blackbirds had nested in the apple tree. They took turns flying in and out carrying food to their young. Good little parents.

As all parents should be. And two of them. Despite the neglect of her past, she still believed that children should have two parents.

Thinking of parents brought a bitter taste to her throat. When she swiped at a tear, a mixture of soap and soda from the washing-up water transferred to her eye.

This wasn't the first time Maisie feared Carole leaving and taking Paula with her. A while back, not long after Paula was born, Carole had almost had her child adopted. The experience had been horrible. The woman who'd claimed to represent a legitimate adoption agency had come from London specifically to collect Paula from her mother's arms – at a price. A baby farmer! Someone who brokered babies from unwed mothers and sold them on to childless couples.

Maisie had breathed a sigh of relief when Carole had had second thoughts. She'd thought the danger of losing the little girl was over, but here it was again, like a monster lurking in the darkness.

She pulled the plug from the sink with fierce finality and watched as the water ran away. What if I married? Would that be enough leverage to sway Carole into letting me adopt Paula?

The tea towel was already soaking wet and a clean one was needed. She spread the wet one over the plate rack above the stove and took another from the unit drawer. Cutlery clinked into the drawer and crockery clattered onto shelves. A butter plate fell to the floor and smashed.

'Nothing to worry about,' she said to herself as she picked up the pieces. 'Now concentrate on what you're doing. Whatever will be, will be.'

* * *

When Carole came downstairs, she informed Maisie that she was going to wait for Joe at the end of the street.

'I'd like a bit of time alone with him. Just a little talk before I spring Paula on him.'

Trying hard not to look aggrieved, Maisie agreed it was a promising idea. 'Take your time.'

The front door slammed.

Maisie dabbed the tea towel against her eyes.

'Peepo!'

Maisie lowered the tea towel.

'Peepo!'

Face sticky with custard, Paula laughed.

'Better get your face washed before your mum comes back.'

'No.'

'Yes. You've got jam and custard all over your face. Once your face is washed you can change into your pink party dress. Would you like that?'

Paula was easily swayed by the chance to wear her party dress, cut down from an adult dress to suit.

'Tonight we're having a party,' Maisie said once Paula's face was clean and she was buttoning up the dress.

'Cake?' Paula asked hopefully.

'No, but there might be some roly-poly pudding and custard left.'

The sound of the doorknocker reverberated through the house. It could only be Ted. Carole had a key.

Maisie went and opened the door.

'Maisie! Hope I ain't too early.'

Ted smelt of coal tar soap and had the look of a man who owned the horse that had won the Derby.

Smoothing back his tousled hair, he grinned at Maisie, then at Paula.

'You didn't tell me a fairy lived yer, Maisie.' He pointed at Paula.

The little girl giggled.

Maisie's cheeks dimpled as she joined in the fun. 'What makes you think there's a fairy living here?'

Ted drew in his chin and grinned. 'There's the fairy,' he said, nodding at Paula as they moved inside. 'She's wearing a pink dress. All fairies wear pink dresses. Don't they?'

Paula placed both hands over her mouth to hide her chuckles. They came out anyway. Her blue eyes peered above her hands and her blonde curls bounced as she laughed.

'Fairies go for walks in parks a lot – so I've heard.' His grin was for Maisie. 'But I don't think they allow ladies wearing slippers into the park. Unless they're glass, that is. Like Cinderella. Do you know about Cinderella?' he asked Paula.

The little pink mouth remained behind her hands, her cheeks round and laughter merry in her eyes.

'You're quite right. It's not allowed,' added Maisie. 'Oh well. That's it then. I can't go.'

Paula danced up and down. She only half understood what was said, but as with many small children, she caught the sense of fun.

Realising something else was going on here, Ted cocked his head sideways and mouthed, 'What is it?'

'Carole's gone out to meet Joe, her sweetheart. She expects me to be waiting for her. There's things to discuss. Look, I'm sorry, Ted. I'm letting you down again, but when I tell you what it's all about, I'm sure you'll understand.'

Ted looked puzzled. 'Do you want me to go?'

She sighed and rubbed her forehead. 'I'm not sure what's for the best. You can if you like, but on the other hand I could do with some support. I don't know how things are going to be after tonight.' She glanced worriedly at Paula, who was now doing a fairy dance.

'How about a cup of tea and you explain?'

She shook her head disconsolately. 'Not yet. We'll wait until Carole comes back with Joe. Can't afford enough tea leaves to make two pots.'

'You're worried about something.'

Maisie nodded, then bent down to pick up Paula. 'Joe's asked Carole to marry him, but there's a problem. She didn't have the courage to tell him about this little darling, so she's bringing him home so he can see what he's letting himself in for.'

'Ah! She's staking everything on him accepting the kid. Will she tell him that it wasn't her fault? That...'

'No.' She shook her head adamantly. 'She's told him nothing about how she got pregnant.' Anger and sadness blazed in her eyes. 'Nothing must be said.'

Ted nodded. He was one of very few who knew the circumstances surrounding Paula's birth, only because he drank in the same pub as Eddie Bridgeman.

Paula's dance came to an abrupt halt immediately in front of him. Getting down on his knees, he tickled beneath the toddler's chin. When she squirmed and giggled, he shook his head and there was sadness in his eyes.

'Who could fail to love the little mite?'

The fun look she'd had fell from Maisie's face.

Ted took in the concern wrinkling her brow. 'There's something else worrying you. What is it?'

Her dark eyes met his. 'He comes from Liverpool. He wants her to go with him and meet his mother.'

'Ah!'

'To my mind, that means he is serious about marrying her, which in turn means... Ted, I can't bear the thought of being parted from Paula. I really can't!'

Her dark curls floated about her face as she tossed her head from side to side.

Ted opened his mouth to say something more, but at the sound of a key being inserted into the front door, he exchanged a look of concern with Maisie and whispered, 'Once they're in here, you stay put. I'll put the kettle on.'

Before heading for the kitchen, he introduced himself and shook Carole's and Joe's hands.

'I know you've got things to discuss, so I'll just make meself busy in the kitchen.'

He closed the door behind him when he went, leaving Maisie feeling strangely alone. He was a big presence, the kind that made her feel protected.

It was Maisie now who shook Joe's hand. The moment she saw him, she understood why Carole was in love with him. He wasn't just good-looking but had a warm and friendly manner, a twinkle in his eyes that hinted at fun and laughter.

The only drawback was that he seemed a bit intimidated by the pretty little girl in pink. She was eyeing him coyly and, strangely enough, he was eyeing her in much the same way.

If the occasion hadn't had such serious overtones, Maisie might have laughed out loud. As it was, she only smiled.

Carole placed an arm around her daughter's shoulders. 'Say hello to Joe, Paula.'

Paula shyly obliged before disappearing behind the settee.

Maisie fetched her out again. 'Come along, Paula. No need to be shy.'

Carole looked expectantly at Joe, who got the message that he was supposed to say something.

Joe offered the little girl his hand. 'Pleased to meet you, Paula. You look just like yer mother.'

'She's got her party dress on. She's a fairy when she's wearing her party dress.'

Joe smiled nervously. 'I can see that.'

Maisie guessed that on their way here Carole had pretty much explained everything – at least that she had an illegitimate child.

Ted came in from the kitchen with a tea tray and a smile on his face. 'I found some biscuits. And one of them's got sugar sprinkled all over it.'

The last comment was directed at Paula, who looked up at him in wonder as he gave it to her.

'And a cup of milk for you, sweetheart?'

Paula squealed when he tickled her arm.

Carole took Paula onto her lap. She looked at Joe. 'So this is Paula.'

'Well...' said Joe, a sound that was almost relief but veined with surprise. 'Well.' He paused as though searching for what to say next. 'Paula. Lovely name.'

'I think so.' There was petulance and a sudden haughtiness and Maisie fancied Carole had pulled Paula more tightly to her chest, defensively almost.

Joe's broad shoulders remained tense. He shoved his hands into his pockets as though he didn't really know what to do with them in circumstances like this – which was no doubt true.

'I found some cake,' said Ted, who had gone back to the kitchen to replenish the pot.

Engrossed in her own thoughts, Maisie left him to refill teacups and pass around slices of cake.

Joe said little, his eyes flitting from Carole to the baby.

There was no doubt in Maisie's mind that he was in love with Carole, and who wouldn't be. She'd bloomed since having Paula. Gone was the flighty girl of the past. Near white, blonde curls still bounced around her face, but she was now a much more subdued version of the blonde bombshell she'd once been.

Two of Joe's fingers rummaged in the breast pocket of his jacket. He was still wearing uniform, but it wouldn't be long before he exchanged khaki for a demob suit. All those leaving the forces were getting them, a leg-up for when they applied for a job back in Civvy Street. A packet of Senior Service emerged. His fingers hurried to open it before passing it around.

Maisie had wanted a moment to have a word for him. The appearance of a packet of cigarettes gave her the chance. 'We don't allow smoking indoors, not with the baby.'

She saw the surprised look on Carole's face.

Maisie invited Joe to follow her out back. 'I'll share one with you out there.' She said it pleasantly enough, but although she worked in the tobacco factory, she'd never smoked, hated the smell of it in fact. In this instance, she would make an exception.

The setting sun stained the sky orange. Here and there, streaks of purple cloud formed a grid, somehow intensifying the golden glow.

Maisie led Joe along the garden path to where her grandmother's old shed leaned drunkenly against the back wall. The smell of cooking came from the houses to each side and over the back wall.

She needed to think what she was going to say to him. Would he accept Paula or would he pass? If the marriage went ahead despite the ready-made family, where would they live? Her nerves were on edge. It was a time for small talk to act like a gate opening slowly.

'That's a lovely sky,' she said as she blew the acrid smoke into the air.

Joe nodded and chanced leaning against the shed. It creaked in response. A panel of wood let go, swinging downwards, rusty nails poking out from the rotten timber.

Maisie remarked that it was getting on a bit and for him to be careful.

He agreed. 'On its last legs, by the look of it.'

She grimaced. The old shed was where her grandmother had stored the tools of her trade – back in the days when she 'helped out' young girls who'd got themselves in trouble. Sight of it still sent a shiver down her spine, after all Carole might have gone that way.

Joe fell to silence just as she'd expected him to. She guessed he was masticating his thoughts as he might chew a tough piece of meat.

'Carole's news about Paula must have come as a shock.'

She let the cigarette simmer without drawing on it.

He flicked ash onto the ground but kept his head on the glowing sunset.

'It did a bit.'

Was he getting used to the idea? Panic set in at the thought of it. She felt an urgent need to state her case.

'There is a solution if you want to marry Carole but don't want to take the baby on.'

'Really?' He continued to stare at the sky for a moment, then looked at her with a deep frown on his forehead.

She would have preferred him not to look at her, not to see the turmoil etched on her face.

Here goes, she thought and licked her lips. This wasn't going to be easy.

'I'm willing to adopt Paula. I can give her a loving home. I can be a mother to her.'

He hesitated. She could see he was unsure how to respond.

'I can understand how you must be feeling now you've found out.'

He jettisoned the half-finished cigarette into the row of leeks she'd been trying to grow – not too successfully. For a moment, he didn't speak but looked thoughtful.

'I must admit that it was a shock at first, though there were hints. I don't think she knew she was trying to tell me and I didn't know what it was she was trying to say.'

The disclosure surprised her. 'What kind of things?'

He shrugged. 'Not exactly telling me what had happened but stressing how she hated men who talked about women as though they were like old shoes, discarding them once they'd had the best from them. I must admit she opened my eyes to the way some of my mates behaved. At times, it made me ashamed to be a man, and tonight, when she told me what had happened...'

'She told you?'

Maisie was surprised. Carole had never said much about it.

'Yes. She told me what happened. If I could get hold of that bloke... But she told me he died not long after the incident. Is that so?'

Suddenly, Maisie found herself craving another cigarette, her who didn't smoke. 'Yes,' she said, swallowing the faint memory of fear she'd always felt about Eddie Bridgeman, who she suspected was responsible for the death of Reg Harris. 'So, what next?'

Joe's chest expanded with a heartfelt sigh. He turned from the fiery sky and looked at her. The moment she saw his expression she feared the worst, not the worst for Carole and Paula, but the worst for her.

'I'm going to ask Carole to come home with me to Liverpool to meet my old lady – my mum,' he added with a boyish smile. 'I reckon they'll get on like a house on fire. Besides, me mum's been going on at me forever about getting married and giving 'er grand-kids. She'll be dead pleased on getting a ready-made one.'

It was as if the ground had split wide open beneath Maisie's feet. 'Does she know that yet? Has she said that she'll go?'

'No to the first, so also no to the second.'

'I would urge you to think about it carefully. You may be accepting now, but after a few years of marriage, when the first flush of romance is over, you might think differently.'

He looked at her in a probing manner, wanting to understand what she was thinking and unsure of what she was saying. 'How would you know, seeing as you ain't married?'

Maisie felt as though she might explode. Her arms folded across her chest and her gritted teeth felt as though her jaw was near breaking point. 'I don't need to be married to know what happens.'

Some might say she was clutching at straws, but her heart would break without Paula in her life.

There was kindness in his expression when he looked at her, but also pity.

'You could be right, but it don't mean I shouldn't take the chance. I think we'd be good together.'

'And the baby?'

'She's part of Carole and if I want Carole, I have to have her kid too. I think we'll be fine. We'll be a family.'

'In Liverpool?' The question hurt her throat but not nearly so much as it hurt her heart.

'It's my home city and it's where I've sworn to go back to. I've done my bit in this war and now all I want is peace. I know you're a kind woman, Maisie, and if we did leave Carole's baby with you, you'd give her a loving home, bring 'er up right and all that. But...' He shook his head dolefully, his eyes sliding sideways. 'I just know me and Carole wouldn't work out right at all if she didn't 'ave her baby with 'er. She'd miss 'er something chronic.'

'But...'

She didn't like his scowl and what he said next hurt her deeply.

'P'raps you should think about getting married and 'avin' kids of your own. Beats being a spinster all yer life – if you don't mind me saying.'

She shook her head determinedly. The truth was that she did mind; she minded very much indeed. His reference to the possibility of her being a spinster all her life made her turn cold inside and a shiver crossed from one shoulder to the other before trickling down her back. The old saying about someone walking over her grave came to mind. She shook it off.

'Time to go in.'

Maisie led Joe back down the garden path to the house. Her feelings were mixed. Carole and Joe deserved each other. She'd decided that Joe would make a good father for the little girl.

The warmth of the kitchen came out to greet them as she pushed open the door. Ted was there to greet them.

'I've made another brew.' Ted held up the teapot. 'Hope you don't mind, only Paula kicked out a leg and sent Carole's cup flying. Little tinker!' He laughed as he shook his head.

Their eyes met and she wondered how long he'd been in the kitchen. Had he heard anything? It wasn't that far from the back door to the end of the garden.

On returning to the living room, Joe walked straight over to Carole, sat down beside her and wrapped his strong arms around both mother and daughter. It was a touching gesture and coupled with the words that followed, Maisie should have found it comforting. But she didn't. In fact, she wanted to tell him he had no business doing that. That both Paula and Carole belonged to her.

'Your responsibilities are my responsibilities. I'm willing to take them on if you're willing to take me on.'

'Yes. Oh yes!'

'Then that's settled. I think it's time you met my mother.'

A phantom dagger stabbed into Maisie's heart. Paula would be lost to her, perhaps forever.

'Will you come?'

Dry mouthed and wide-eyed, Carole nodded, then swallowed as a thought came to her. 'I'll go with you, but only if Maisie will look after Paula whilst I'm gone?'

'Of course I'll look after her.' The words were bitter on her tongue but she said them anyway.

Whether it was a result of their conversation out in the back-yard or an entirely fresh decision, her offer was turned down. 'No need,' said Joe. He kissed Carole on the cheek and threw a sidelong look at Maisie. 'We'll take Paula with us. My mum will love her.'

Maisie no longer felt as though a dagger had pierced her heart. It was more as though it had stopped beating. She pasted a smile onto her face, forcing herself to show she felt happy for the pair of them. For herself, she felt only despair at the thought of never seeing Paula again.

8

AUGUST 1945 – CHANGI POW CAMP

Sid didn't know who had first spotted the hole in the fence, but it didn't take long for a group of prisoners to assemble and discuss how to make best use of it.

Having placed himself in charge of all escape plans, Major Kirby was the most senior officer and believed his word was law. He'd approved their plan and thought it sensible that only three were attempting to burrow beneath the perimeter fence.

'Small parties fare better than large escapes. Now for a little advice. Your route is in direct line with the path to the rice paddy. We've all worked there when it was needed and we also know that the pigs are in pens on the other side of the road. This side. When we went out to work, we went along the road. But now, dear chaps, if we take advantage of this heaven-sent opportunity, we go through the jungle and get to the pigs before we sink knee-deep into the paddy field. There's usually a sow with piglets. Pinching one or two of them will keep us going.'

'Keep us going for what?' muttered Sid, his gaze fixed on two scorpions circling each other in a dance that would eventually end in death for one of them – perhaps both.

The major glared at him as though he was as lowly as the two fighters with their stings held high, each determined to land the first blow. 'What do you mean, Corporal?'

Sid couldn't remember when he'd first made the rank of corporal – probably here in the camp after all the others had died. He scratched at a red patch on his arm. Something had bitten him there last night. It was bigger than all the other bites – fleas, cockroaches. He didn't know what; perhaps a spider; perhaps a rat.

He made the decision to say what was in his head. 'If the hole's big enough, we should crawl out of it and escape.'

The major shook his head forlornly over his clenched hands and the swagger stick clutched beneath a sweaty armpit. The stick proclaimed he was an officer. An officer was not expected to do manual work, but the Japanese had had other ideas. He'd been forced to work alongside everyone else – especially when there were few lower ranks left to work and plenty of officers. Like the rest of them what was once plump flesh hung sparely on prominent cheekbones, eyes sunken beneath a bony brow.

The major had become more cautious about his men escaping of late. He was hanging on in there for rescue, willing to risk further starvation whilst relying on hope.

His bony brow lowered over sunken eyes and sallow complexion.

'Look. It's just a matter of surviving a bit longer. We need food, even if it's a village dog.'

Sid refrained from licking his lips, though in his mind he could still taste the last one they'd put in the pot. It had been dead when they'd found it, possibly the result of a fight with something wild. Anyway, they'd found it in time before it had turned green and become inedible – though they might still have chanced it. Hunger steels the empty stomach to smell and taste.

Heads bent and voices whispered.

'What's it saying on the radio?'

The officer dropped his voice and his eyes. 'The Yanks are beating the Japs. It won't be long before they're in Okinawa. That's what they're saying.'

Sid frowned. He couldn't help wondering what the camp guards would do once they learned that their homeland was close to being taken by the Americans. It might drive them mad and likely to take out their frustration on the prisoners of war. It would be bad enough if they found out about the illegal wireless set.

One man voiced what he was thinking. 'They'll likely kill us if they think their country is taken. Then kill themselves.'

The men looked at each other. The Japanese believed it better to commit suicide than surrender. Killing the prisoners before killing themselves meant they'd have nothing to lose.

* * *

When darkness fell and the heat of the day was replaced by the humidity of night, Sid met Alan and Tom, two chaps around his age who were as ragged and emaciated as he was.

The camp was asleep. The solitary footsteps of the guards sounded from inside the compound. Insects kept up a constant cacophony in the trees beyond the fence. Now and again, a night creature screamed a challenge to another of its kind or in response to being taken by a predator.

Midnight. They crept their way to the hole in the fence, keen to inspect it under cover of darkness.

'How does it look?' Tom whispered.

Sid got out a lighter – one bartered with another inmate for an extra bowl of rice. 'Gather round and we'll see. Even a lighter flame looks like a bonfire in the darkness.'

They did as he said.

Alan, whose sense of touch had become more acute when he'd lost his sight through lack of protein, felt around the ripped wire, lifted it and felt it again.

'Not a bad size,' he said when he let it drop.

'We need to plan,' said Sid. 'Food and a weapon of some kind.'

'A big stick?'

Sid grinned into the darkness. 'A sword would be better. Anyone got anything left to trade with one of the Koreans?'

The Korean guards hated the Japanese more than they did the prisoners and were more than willing to trade. They were both ill-waged and ill-treated by their Japanese masters. Some of them had been taken from their country by force and conscripted into the lowest ranks of the enemy invader. If the trade was good and they were able to steal a sword from a Japanese soldier, they would do so.

Alan revealed that he had a watch. 'I took it from a dead man when I was in hospital. An officer he was, so it's a good watch. I had it in mind to send it to his nearest and dearest when my eyesight returned – if it ever does.'

Alan had been a brave man back before they were imprisoned. Enduring terrible deprivations and cruelty had left him nervous and almost broken. Besides going blind, his hands shook. He was only just about hanging on – though most of them were only doing that.

Sid slapped him on the back. 'Well done, Alan. If we get out of here, I'll say a prayer for that officer every day for the rest of my life.'

Tom took Sid aside later. 'Do you think he'll be all right?'

'I think so. Getting through that fence will do 'im the world of good.'

The truth was that he couldn't say. Like Tom, he was a bit worried that Alan might fall apart at the last minute. And there was the blindness, of course. Sid had suggested he tie a rope around

Alan's waist and the other end around his own. 'Where I go you'll have to go.'

Alan had laughed then – a brittle laugh that sounded like it could shatter at any moment.

'Just one thing,' Alan had said. 'If I don't get through, I want you to have this.' After fumbling with what was left of the breast pocket of his shirt, he passed Sid a small pouch.

'What is it?'

'A ring. An emerald. I told the Korean who traded it that he'd been fooled. It was just glass.'

'But it's not?'

'No. It's not. My aim was to give it as an engagement ring to the first girl I came across when I got home. Keep it safe for me and if I don't get through, give it to your girl and when you get engaged then married, think of me.'

* * *

It took a few days to gather the supplies they would need to sustain them. Not that there was much. Sid hoped the sword would keep them fed. Monkeys, dogs, birds and even the odd wild pig. They all existed beyond the wire fence.

They chose a moonless night for their escape just before a fresh patrol came on. Each would pack his necessities and make their own way to the hole in the fence.

'See you soon,' Sid whispered to Maisie's photograph before he tucked it into his bundle. The weakness of his tired muscles seemed less severe after looking at her. The memory of her and the thought of being reunited had kept him going through this long imprisonment. He was desperate to see her again, desperate to get home.

It seemed the canopy of stars was doing its best to make up for the lack of moonlight.

Sid had fashioned a piece of rope to run from around Alan's waist to his own. It was pretty rotten – as things were in this blasted climate and thinning in the middle. He just hoped it would hold. 'No jerky movements,' he'd warned before they'd set off.

The three of them made it to the far side of a hut roughly twenty yards from the hole in the fence.

'How far?' whispered Alan.

'Twenty yards,' Sid whispered back. 'You OK, Al?'

'Does it sound stupid to say that I'm afraid of the dark? Seeing as all I ever see is darkness?'

'You'll be fine, mate,' said Tom and gave him a reassuring slap on the back.

Sid felt a trembling in the rope. *Please, Alan. Don't fall apart now*, he prayed.

His fears were further confirmed when he heard Alan whimper, like a puppy that wants to go out to freedom. *And that*, he thought, *is exactly what we want to do*. No more restrictions. Get up when you like. Go to bed when you like. Eat when you like – and indulgently, not ravenously gulping back a bowl of rice as though it was fish and chips from Hamblins.

Fish and chips! The very thought of it made him salivate. He needed to concentrate if escape was to happen. He needed to think for himself and for Alan. Tom could take care of himself and to some extent would have to.

Although pressed against the side of the hut, Sid managed to turn round and pat Alan on the shoulder. 'Come on, old mate. Get a grip. Tom? You all right?'

'I'm ready to go.'

'Sword at your side?'

'Yep.'

They were thankful that Alan's watch had clinched the deal. The Korean guards were always more than willing to supplement their income. In exchange, they'd gained a Samurai sword – one with the end broken off but enough sharpness left to supplement their diet with a small animal or bird.

'Right.' Sid turned to face the fence and the hole they knew was still there, the loose wire mesh pulled back into place so it seemed nothing was awry. Thankfully, none of the guards had noticed it. He badly wanted to make that fence, to push his way through and head for freedom and ultimately home.

He felt for the photograph of Maisie and smiled. In his mind, he was telling her that he'd pop the question the minute he got home. They would be married and live happily ever after.

A touch on the arm was Tom's signal to go, which he did, his belly on the ground, slithering forward like some of the big lizards they'd seen in South-east Asia.

Sid counted to twenty, the signal they'd agreed on, allowing enough time between Tom getting out through the fence and him and Alan following on behind.

Alan was still whimpering.

Sid didn't have the heart to urge him to be silent, though he was getting angry with him. If a guard did come that way, he was bound to hear him.

'Twenty. Right. Our turn.' His hand clenched Alan's shoulder in a reassuring shake. 'Right. Now!'

Sid took off, keeping low as Tom had done. The rope stretched between the two of them. Without looking round, he knew instinctively that Alan was staggering not crawling, whimpering more loudly now and murmuring far too loudly, 'I can't.'

As he dropped beside the hole, Sid felt the rope tighten around his middle. The only reason the rope would do that was if Alan had stopped dead.

'Bloody fool! Come on,' he hissed.

Nothing changed except he sensed the sounds they were

making had carried. Some way beyond the rank of huts, two guards were talking. He imagined them looking suspicious, gripping their weapons tighter, their fingers tickling the triggers.

He heard Tom hissing for him to crawl through the hole. 'If he won't come, leave 'im. For God's sake...'

Tom was right, of course. He had to move now if he was to get away at all.

'Sid!'

Sid thought of Maisie, of his mum and of home, of a pint in the London Inn, of a day out at Weston-super-Mare.

'Now!' came Tom's subdued voice.

Sid knew what had to be done. With hands frenzied by fear, he fumbled with the rope, struggled but finally had it undone and thrown in Alan's direction.

'Sorry, old chum.'

His chest ached. Sweat dripped from his forehead and into his eyes. Now it was him that wanted to whimper, but he constrained himself. He crawled through the fence, pulled it into place behind him and joined Tom.

For a moment, they stayed there feeling guilty and helpless. Thanks to the stars, they had enough light to see Alan wandering off, arms outstretched, feeling for the side of the hut, the rope trailing between his legs.

Hopefully, he would regain enough control to untie the rope from his waist. That way, he wouldn't have to explain why he was out there wearing it around his waist. Not that he seemed to realise where he was.

The whimpering became a wail and shouts of 'I don't like the dark. I told you I don't like the dark. I want to go home!'

The whimpering rose to a scream.

Sid felt Tom nudge his bony ribs.

'Come on. We've got to go.'

Reluctantly, Sid followed him into the undergrowth where they were hidden by total darkness. Their aim was for the three of them to head for the coast. Only two of them now. Somehow they had to cross an expanse of water to freedom. That was the advantage of Changi Jail. Escape was almost impossible, but they had to try, that's what Sid told himself.

They were some way from the camp when the unmistakeable crack of gunshots rang out into the night. They paused only for a split second, then carried on, not daring to stop whilst carrying the heavy burden that those shots had ended Alan's woes and also aware that they too would go the same way if they were caught. So, to that end, Sid struggled on despite tears stinging his eyes and wishing he had gone back to take Alan's hand and either drag him to safety or die with him. The guilt of not doing so would stay with him for the rest of his life.

9

Demobilisation of those no longer needed to serve in the military was speeding up. Phyllis had been released quicker than most because Mick's head injury necessitated her being on hand. He was conscious now but still in need of hospital care. The good thing was that she'd obtained a bed for him at a hospital in Bristol. She'd considered the merits of moving him there; was it the right thing to do? After all, she no longer had any relatives in the city. Her mother had moved up north and eventually intended moving with her husband of three years to Canada.

'But I do have friends in Bristol,' she'd informed the doctor in charge of her husband's case.

He'd smiled cheerfully. 'It's very commendable that you wish to look after your husband, but you also need to look after yourself.'

He was right. It was important to remain healthy and to keep her spirits up.

On arriving back at the farmhouse, the smell of Mrs Crane's cooking welcomed her back.

'So how is he?'

Mrs Crane liked to know how he was and cared about Phyllis as she might be a daughter she'd never had.

Phyllis told her what the doctor had said.

'He's right,' said Mrs Crane. 'You need a bit of joy in your life. A bit of a holiday or seeing friends.'

An idea had seeded in Phyllis's mind. 'I think I'll drop a line to my old friends in Bristol. I'd love to see them. We were all such good friends.'

The writing pad was pre-war and came with matching envelopes. Both had been lying in the bottom drawer of a chest of drawers in her landlady's bedroom. At mention of her needing to write to family and friends to tell them what had happened, Mrs Crane had insisted Phyllis have them.

'After all,' she said with a hint of sadness. 'I don't have anyone to write to any more. I lost my husband back in 1917 and my son two years ago in 1943 in North Africa. I've only got my sister to write to and have got enough stationery for that. You have it. Go on. Write and let them know what's been happening.'

Phyllis thanked her profusely, at the same time telling herself that there would always be people worse off than her. She and Mick weren't going to Australia as planned, but no matter where they were at least they were still alive.

On the morning when she sat down at the heavy old kitchen table to write, Mrs Crane made her excuses and said she would leave her to it.

'You don't have to. I don't want you to go out on my account.'

Mrs Crane smiled kindly. 'There's lots you might want to think about before committing words to paper. Anyway,' she added with a flourish of the immense willow shopping basket she favoured, 'I've got shopping to do. Fingers crossed the queues aren't too long.'

The old farmhouse-style kitchen creaked. It being summer, the huge black range was on low, but still it hissed as though keen to get to full heat again. Two cats lay still and content in front of it. A kettle hung from a trivet; the gently simmering water was soothing.

Pen at the ready, Phyllis sighed heavily. This was the first time she'd allowed herself to think seriously about anything and anyone except Mick.

Put your mind to writing. First, who will you write to?

The answer came readily enough. Maisie was the only person she knew for sure would be at the same address she had been for at least the past year. It had to be her.

Mrs Phyllis Fairbrother,

> *Back Lane Farmhouse,*
> *Little Wickham,*
> *Nr Stowmarket.*
> *Suffolk.*
> *Dear Maisie,*
>
> *I'm sorry I haven't written sooner, but Mick is in hospital. It's quite serious, so our plans for living in Australia have been put on hold. He's being transferred to a hospital at Frenchay in Bristol, so I'm coming up shortly to check on accommodation for myself, perhaps also for Mick once he's out of hospital.*
>
> *I'll be there next Saturday so thought I might pop in if that's all right. I know you don't have room to put me up, what with Carole and the baby being there, but there are lots of guest houses around that would suit.*
>
> *I've put the address at the top of this letter, but if you do reply, please bear in mind that the post is a bit slow crossing from one side of the country to the other.*
>
> *There is a phone box at the post office in the village where you can leave a message.*
>
> *The telephone number is 073902.*
>
> *Looking forward to seeing you.*

All my love, Phyllis.

* * *

That afternoon, she took a walk into the village to post the letter. The day was bright enough and the land a patchwork of gold and green beneath fluffy clouds rolling like sheep across the blue. If Mick had been beside her, Phyllis would have enjoyed this view. Mick would have compared the expanse of sky and land in East Anglia to Australia.

'Not nearly so hot, though,' he would have added.

In the village, a young man using a crutch raised his trilby to her. 'It's a good day to be alive,' he said cheerfully.

'Yes,' she said, smiled and walked on, back to Mrs Crane, a lady who had lost so much but still smiled and did what she could to bring cheerfulness into the world.

I've got to try and do the same, she told herself. *Mick and I are still alive – damaged but alive* – at least Mick was damaged, but she was still healthy and capable of helping him. In time, he might overcome his injuries and she would be there for him.

'Buck up,' she muttered to herself. 'You're going to get things sorted.'

* * *

Throughout the war, the country had been urged to put a brave face on things. That's what Phyllis was doing now as she packed a few things and prepared herself for travel. She was off to Bristol to check on the hospital and a place where she could stay.

Excitedly she'd filled Mick in on the details. He'd always been of a positive nature and it seemed that had helped him improve. The doctors had been surprised but refused to let him go just yet.

'We have to be sure.'

She respected their opinion. Mick on the other hand was less accepting.

Rather than wish her well in her quest to find them accommodation and work, he'd been morose at best and angry at times, accusing her of leaving him alone in his suffering and even suggesting that she wasn't coming back.

'Who'd want an old cripple like me?'

His raised voice had disturbed other men in the ward.

She'd lain her fingers across his mouth. 'Shh, darling. Here's one woman for sure who wants you. I'll want you forever. I'll never leave you.'

He'd grunted some kind of agreement but the morose look had remained.

'I must find us a house or rooms. Close to the hospital, if possible. We must do our best to make you better.'

Over supper she'd told Mrs Crane how it was. 'I'm doing my best, but it never seems good enough. All Mick really wants is to be his old self.'

Mrs Crane had sighed and got out the sherry bottle. 'None of us will be that after this war. It was bad enough after the other one. Here, have a drop of this. It'll help you cope. It certainly helped me.'

Phyllis wasn't sure how many small sherries they had. On reflection, it was probably enough to fill a half-pint mug. But at least her landlady listened and did speak from experience. She'd been good to her, helping in any way she could.

One aspect was clothing. During the last few years, Phyllis had rarely been out of uniform and would have enjoyed wearing civvies a lot more if she'd had something decent to wear. Clothes had been on ration for so long, it was almost impossible to buy anything new. All she had was years old, apart from a skirt and blouse she'd purchased at the village jumble sale and was relatively presentable.

Every woman at that jumble sale had grabbed anything in good enough condition to be cut into something wearable.

'Oh, but I look a fright.'

Her remark was overheard by Mrs Crane who had come to the rescue and made her a dress from an old pair of turquoise silk curtains.

'I trimmed off the faded bits. The amount I had left was quite surprising.'

Her landlady's little blue eyes had twinkled like dew-kissed bluebells and her expression was one of considerable pride.

Phyllis told her she shouldn't have, but all the same had thanked her profusely. The dress had a sweetheart neckline, capped sleeves and a nipped-in waist. The skirt swung and swished around her legs when she twirled on the spot.

'It's wonderful,' she had said as she'd twirled around the room, the fabric making a soft rustling sound with each movement.

'Those curtains must be ten years old, but it's good material. Good material lasts a lifetime.'

Phyllis had run her hands over the silky material. 'I'm truly grateful and never mind its age. My uniform is the only item I own that's less than three years old.'

Mrs Crane had fingered both jacket and skirt hanging on the back of the door. 'It's good material. Will they make you give it back?'

'They don't seem to care either way.'

Mrs Crane had brought her hand to her mouth. 'Well,' she'd said, 'I could cut that jacket and make it less obvious that it's part of a uniform. Air force blue is such an acceptable colour. Thank goodness you weren't in the army. Khaki is a very different matter. It has to be dyed to disguise what it once was. Nobody wants to wear khaki. It means mud, you know. Back in India.'

Phyllis had smiled. The comment alone was enough to tell her that Mrs Crane had already got her hands on khaki in the past and therefore spoke from experience.

The sound of rattling milk churns and the clop of hooves announced the arrival of Morris Hunt, a local farmer, who was on his way to drop off his churns for the train and had been asked if he could drop Phyllis off at the same time.

He'd responded that it would be his pleasure.

'Long as you don't mind the milk churns; even when they's full they rattles.'

She accepted the lift gratefully.

In an odd way, the sound of the churns and the horse's hooves was reassuring, that and Morris whistling 'Daisy, Daisy' and other old songs.

'Now you take care of yerself,' he told her as he helped her down from the front seat of the cart and handed her the cardboard suitcase Mrs Crane had given her for the journey.

'I will. Thank you, Morris.'

He winked and smiled before breaking into song again as he manhandled the churns onto the wooden structure from where they would be loaded onto the train for delivery to the dairy.

Phyllis paused for a moment to take in the fields of golden corn soon to be harvested, blossoming hedgerows and the heavy branches of old trees that had, according to Mrs Crane, been there since the Domesday Book.

'Goodbye for now,' she whispered. 'I'm going home.'

10
_____

August was a sublime month and the first two days of September were turning out the same.

Safe in the knowledge that Bridget's father was expecting her without her needing to contact Bridget, things in the short term looked plain sailing. As is the case when spirits rise, something happens to knock them back down again.

The last thing Maisie had thought to encounter in the factory that day was a boy on a red bicycle waiting for her at the entrance. Her legs almost gave way at the sight of him.

'Oh no.' It was all she managed to say as the colour drained from her face. Telegrams always meant unwelcome news.

She felt some relief that the boy was smiling as he puffed on his cigarette, as though nothing bad had happened.

'Miss Miles?'

She said that she was.

Wordlessly, he handed her the telegram, took his tip, tapped at his hat and was gone.

Maisie's hand was trembling but it reduced when she saw it did not refer to the War Office or indeed any other government department.

She would have read it then and there, but suddenly it was as if a riot had broken out at the factory. Women were running out of the building, shouting, crying laughing and cheering at the tops of their voices.

'What's happened? Have you all gone mad?'

'It's over!'

'What's over?' she asked.

'The war in the Far East. I heard it on the wireless this morning.'

'The king's going to make an official announcement tonight.'

'Japan's surrendered.'

'The king's going to proclaim two days of public holiday.'

'And it starts now,' someone shouted.

The army of women who'd been entering the factory had collided with those falling out of it. They joined the crowd, turned round and began dancing.

Before she got swept up into the celebrations, Maisie ripped open the telegram, her heart drumming against her ribs.

She read the first line.

I'm coming home.

'The pubs are opening,' shouted one of the latest school leavers to join the factory workforce. 'Are you coming?'

'I've got to read this. Anyway, you're not old enough to go drinking.'

'Nobody cares. Not today.'

'I'll be along shortly. I want to read the rest of this.'

'Good news, is it?'

Maisie smiled happily. 'It's from Sid. He was a prisoner of war but says he's coming home.'

'Blimey. That's quick. The war's only just over.'

It did indeed seem a bit odd. Maisie read the rest of the message.

Escaped. Got on boat. See you soon.

She broke into a broad smile, though her eyes filled with tears. Sid. Alive and on his way home.

She wondered whether he'd sent word to his mother. Just to make sure, Maisie dashed into the post office and asked to send a telegram to her. It was only a short distance so shouldn't cost more than sixpence.

Some of the crowd around her were waving Union Jacks. Men were kissing women. Women of all ages were singing and many were dancing.

For a while, she did too but after half an hour disengaged herself from the interlocked arms and dancing feet. She could understand them celebrating and celebrations would no doubt go on all night. Her biggest urge now was to go back home, to break the news to everyone on the way and eventually to Carole, who would be as excited as she was. Pleased as she was that although the war in Europe was over and likely to be declared so shortly in the Far East, her main concern was that very soon Carole would be marrying Joe and likely moving to Liverpool.

It had worried her to learn that Carole had met his mother, who had welcomed both her and Paula with open arms.

On the one hand, Maisie's heart was breaking. On the other, she had to let go, and besides, Sid had survived. He was coming home and she didn't doubt that they'd marry, but first she would have to tell Ted.

That was when she stopped in her tracks and went back into the factory. Loyal to his employers, Ted was still there finishing his shift, overseeing the reassembly of a machine that had broken down. He looked up and smiled when he saw her.

'I've got news,' she said pensively, determined to straighten things with him, to let him know that Sid was home. Her smile was weaker than his. She was about to hurt him and it wasn't something she wanted to do.

'Do you think I don't know,' he laughed, pulled her towards him and planted a big kiss on her lips. 'The war's over. At long last. All of it is over.'

He must have seen her hesitant expression, the downcast eyes that for now hid what to her was a great happiness but to him would likely bring disappointment.

She raised her eyes. 'I've received a telegram. Sid's alive. He's coming home.'

She felt bad to see his smile was much diminished.

'Your fiancé.'

She nodded. 'It was an informal arrangement, but...'

'You feel duty-bound to honour it.'

'I have to be here for him when he gets back. It's been a long time. He might not feel the same, but you do see, Ted.'

He looked at her silently and sadly before he nodded. 'Of course you do.' Then he turned and despite the giddy men and women tumbling into the factory and out again, still singing at the top of their voices, still weeping tears of happiness that the war was finally over, he went back to his work.

* * *

It took her over an hour and a half to get home. Some passengers on the bus expressed relief rather than joy, except for a drunk who was singing 'Land of Hope and Glory' at the top of his voice.

After what was possibly his tenth rendition, the bus conductor ejected him from the bus, suggesting he go home and sleep it off – or take singing lessons!

Maisie was still smiling at this and, keen to tell Carole all about it, rushed up the garden path as fast as her legs could carry her.

The moment she pushed open the front door, she knew no one was at home. The house was agonisingly empty. It occurred to Maisie that Carole had perhaps already heard the news and had gone out to join in the celebrations. Unless a kindly neighbour had offered to babysit, she would have taken Paula with her.

She sighed and, leaving the front door on the catch, went out knocking on the doors of neighbours.

Mrs Dander, their new neighbour two doors along, opened the door before Maisie even had chance to knock.

'Heard the news,' she said, beaming from ear to ear. 'I thought you'd be 'ome early. Everyone gone off to celebrate, 'ave they?'

Maisie told her that this was so.

Mrs Dander clapped her meaty hands. 'Over at last. My old man will be coming 'ome soon. Bin away for two years on and off. It's goin' to seem funny.'

'Yes. What a relief. I don't suppose...'

Mrs Dander jerked her head along the passageway behind her. 'Paula's sound asleep on the sofa. I said I'd look after her whilst Carole nipped to the shops.' Mrs Dander frowned. 'I would 'ave thought she'd be back by now.' Her face brightened. 'I bet she's got in with the partying.'

'I bet she has.'

The patter of tiny feet preceded Paula's appearance, her cheeks rosy and blinking her way into wakefulness. On seeing Maisie, she stretched out her arms. Her fingers were sticky, her hair tousled.

Maisie swung her up into her arms, thanked Mrs Dander profusely and, clutching Paula tightly, headed for her own front door.

Once the little girl's hands were washed and she'd eaten a bowl of buttered bread and sugar, Maisie made herself a cheese sandwich. After she'd finished, she allowed Paula to carry one plate and a spoon out into the kitchen, where she pointed at the back door and made demanding sounds.

'You want to go out into the garden?'

'Yeth,' Paula lisped.

Warm air and sunshine flooded into the kitchen. Paula stretched her arms as though embracing all the world had to offer.

Maisie watched her as she chased a butterfly or cupped a flower with both hands. Both acts made her smile and for a moment the world somehow seemed a happier place.

The old shed at the end of the garden was touched with sunshine, small consolation when her thoughts strayed to the fact that soon – very soon – Carole would be getting married and moving to Liverpool.

The sun was drawing her out and if they took the right route they might run into Carole. She'd certainly been gone long enough.

'Shall we go to the park?' Maisie asked.

Paula clapped her hands.

'We'll take the pushchair.' Although Paula could walk, the park was some distance and she was likely to tire.

'Walk!'

Maisie shook her head. 'Oh no, young lady. I don't want to end up carrying you.'

Paula made a whining noise.

'We'll take the pushchair and your reins. You can walk there, but only if you wear your reins and hold onto the pram. No doubt you'll want me to wheel you back after you've run around. Right?'

The little girl nodded.

'That's settled. Come on. Let's get ready.'

Biscuits and a cold drink made with sherbet and water were

placed in a carrier bag, the handles fastened onto the handlebar of the pushchair.

The walk there was slow, even though Paula skipped most of the time. On the way, Maisie's eyes searched amongst groups of revellers. If there were parties going on, Carole was likely to find them and join in. It would be just like her, and why not? She was still young and deserved some happiness.

I'll miss her, Maisie thought. *I'll miss her bubbly personality, her youth and having her in the house – even though she puts too much onion in her cheese and onion pie.* Yes. Maisie would miss Carole.

Children played on swings and roundabouts. Mothers sat on benches chatting. Some knitted. Every so often, a motherly hand would reach out to rock a pram where a baby had begun to cry.

There was no sign of Carole and the groups of revellers had melted away. Maisie guessed those who wanted to really celebrate the big occasion were making their way to the city centre.

It wouldn't surprise her if Carole had made her way there, though it did seem a bit odd she'd leave Paula with Mrs Dander that long and she wasn't to know that Maisie would come home early.

Set free from her reins, Paula ran through the grass, sniffed at flowers, patted dogs and interacted with other small children. As Maisie had guessed, she was tired out by late afternoon. Maisie grimaced as she pushed the sleeping child back home through clouds of insects and lengthening shadows. The little girl looked so like her mother and thinking of their first meeting made her smile as she brushed the midges from her face.

When Carole had first begun work at the tobacco factory, she'd been an outright flirt and too mouthy for her own good. Maisie had thought that she'd mellowed since giving birth to Paula and become more responsible than she used to be. Judging by the length of time she'd been out today; it might not be so.

The instant she pushed open the front door, Maisie knew that the house was still empty. There was no one to greet their homecoming, no laughing eyes accompanying an apology and plea for forgiveness. Carole was not home.

The evening shadows lengthened. Between feeding Paula and eating a small supper after the child was in bed, Maisie went backwards and forwards to the parlour at the front of the house, peering out of the window for the sight of those bouncing blonde curls.

Joe had gone back to Liverpool to go through the demob process before coming back to claim his bride.

Hoping for music, Maisie turned on the wireless. There was some music, but mostly the BBC were broadcasting details about the Americans dropping an atomic bomb on a Japanese city. She left a second cup of tea to go cold and was just about to take it into the kitchen and pour it down the sink when someone knocked at the front door.

For a moment, her spirits lifted until logic broke in. It wouldn't be Carole. Carole had a key. Unless she'd lost it. Otherwise it had to be Joe, returned from Liverpool and looking for her.

She opened the door wide, ready to give Carole a right dressing-down for causing her concern. 'Where do you—'

Her words were cut dead by the sight of a dark blue uniform with silver buttons. The police constable standing on the doorstep held a notebook in front of his face.

'Is this where a Miss Carole Thomas lives?'

An unseen pair of hands were gripping her throat and forcing the breath from her body.

'Yes.'

Her voice was barely audible.

'What's happened?'

The moment he took off his helmet and asked to enter the house, Maisie knew that something bad had happened. He declined tea but suggested she sit down. He was an older man, possibly one of those who had retired but called back when younger colleagues had been called up for military duty.

'Is she in hospital?'

He looked down into his notebook as though the answer was written there, then he turned his eyes to her. 'I'm afraid there's been an accident.'

'Is she badly injured?' Even to her own ears, her voice sounded higher pitched than it normally was; almost verging on a scream.

'I'm afraid she's dead.'

'How?' That high-pitched voice again, the feeling that she was drowning in ice-cold water.

She vaguely heard him say something about the shattered walls of a war-damaged house giving way, her buried beneath it, the long time taken digging her out – all to no avail.

'I'm sorry it took us so long to get here. Does she have family?'

'A child. She's asleep.'

Maisie didn't bother to mention Carole's mother or her being related to Eddie Bridgeman.

'Her ID was in her bag. Everything checks out. No need for you to go to the morgue and identify her.'

No need. Maisie knew enough of injuries to realise he was telling her she'd suffered injuries that made her unrecognisable.

She barely noticed him leaving the house. She just sat there staring into the distance.

It was still fairly light when the His Majesty King George the sixth began his speech. Such was Maisie's despair that it took a while before she tuned in to words that echoed in her heart.

'Our hearts are full to overflowing, as are your own. Yet there is not one of us who has experienced this terrible war who does not realise that we shall feel its inevitable consequences long after we have all forgotten our rejoicings today.'

'Amen,' she said softly, for indeed she would remember this day, but not for the same reason as the king. Paula had lost her mother and Joe had lost the woman he planned to marry. Personal prices would be paid for a very long time thanks to this war. 'Let there never be another one,' she said to herself. 'Never, ever.'

11

The house in Marksbury Road was Bridget's first stop before joining her friends at Maisie's house. She sat like a queen on a throne surrounded by her family, who were all fascinated by Lyndon's tiny fingers, the way he eyed them all in turn as if trying to work out who they were.

She noticed her father fidgeting, his guilty look, the fact that he'd fallen to silence, his eyes heavy with tears as he gazed on his grandson.

'Your mother would have been over the moon,' he said at last.

He lowered his gaze. The way he did it and his fallen shoulders made Bridget think he had something more to say but for her ears only.

The opportunity for just the two of them to talk came when Lyndon fell asleep. She asked the girls to keep an eye on him whilst she followed her father into the back garden.

His unlit pipe dangled from the corner of his mouth. He looked thoughtful.

Bridget rubbed her hand up and down his arm. 'Don't be sad,

Dad. Mum's here in spirit. She can see her grandson. I'm sure she can.'

He nodded. 'I do hope so. Your mother loved babies.'

His eyes strayed to the far end of the garden where he burned garden rubbish. Bridget recalled with a shiver something else burning there too. A miscarried child wrapped up in newspaper. Years ago now.

'I've been lonely,' he said, still looking away from her. 'I've got a lady friend. Ethel's the name. She's had a lot of trauma in her life. She became ill when her husband was away fighting. Some of her kids got taken away from her. She don't know whether she'll ever see them again. Then she got the telegram saying that her husband was killed. In the meantime... well... we give each other solace. I hope you understand.'

His statement had come sudden. Should she regard it as a confession? The death of her mother had hit him hard. The children were growing up and leaving home. She herself was relocating to the other side of the Atlantic. Once she'd left, goodness knows when she'd see him again. If only she wasn't going. This was where she'd been born. This was where she really belonged.

After thinking about it, she finally said, 'Dad. You have a right to be happy.'

He reached out and gave her hand a squeeze.

'I'm so glad to hear you say that. I know how close you were to your mother. You loved her. I loved her.'

'But she's gone, Dad, and I don't begrudge you your happiness.'

An increased warmth seemed to enter the atmosphere between them once she'd said that. She guessed how much he'd worried about her reaction.

'You're not the only one who's been worried.' Her face creased with emotion. 'My first duty is to my husband. I love him, I really do. I thought I would have no hesitation in following him to the ends of the earth if I had to. Leaving you, my family and my friends has proved harder than I'd ever imagined.'

The kind man she'd always called Dad sighed. 'I can't say I won't miss you. I will. Though I'm not your natural father you're a true daughter of my heart. I'll not deny that I'll miss you.' He shook his head mournfully. 'Truth be told it's going to take some adjusting for all of us. But each generation must make their own lives. You'll adjust – we'll all adjust. Just think of me in the quiet moments, the same moments when I'll be thinking of you.'

It was with an air of sadness that Bridget left her family and summoned a taxi. With tear-filled eyes, she looked back at her father waving her goodbye at the garden gate. *Such a small house*, she thought, *but full of love*. She could not deny her father his new chance at happiness. Now the war had ended, there would be many more like him. However long it lasted, whatever turns it might take, life was for living.

* * *

Bridget fed Lyndon in the privacy of her room at the Royal Hotel and shed a few tears for her father. By the looks of his clothes and the fact that he hadn't lost weight, his lady friend was looking after him.

'Right,' she exclaimed once Lyndon had finished feeding and had fallen asleep. 'Bridget O'Neil, this is no time to be glum. The world is finally at peace and you're off to see Maisie tomorrow. I think a celebration is in order.'

With that in mind, she thought about taking Maisie a present and ordered a hamper from the hotel reception. Maisie would appreciate that, Phyllis too if she got there. She hoped she would. The three of them back together and in the mood to celebrate. She certainly hoped so.

* * *

The following morning saw Bridget sitting in the rear seat of a taxi, Lyndon in his carry cot and a large hamper strapped to the front seat.

On the way to Maisie's house, they passed land where houses had once stood. Like London, the process of rebuilding took time, though there were signs of it happening. Men lately returned from war were swinging pickaxes, laying bricks and driving heavy machinery, which was needed to clear the rubble-strewn ground.

The houses in upper Totterdown showed little sign of bomb damage, their flat-fronted facades curving down the hill from Wells Road at the top to Bath Road at the bottom.

Curtains twitched and women stared as the taxi drew up outside Maisie's house.

The driver helped Bridget out and tagged along behind her carrying the food hamper.

Magic, she thought as the front door opened without her needing to knock.

'I saw the taxi. You're the only person I know who uses taxis.'

Paula peeped shyly around Maisie's leg.

Despite Bridget having Lyndon in her arms, they hugged.

'Maisie, you haven't changed a bit.'

It wasn't quite true. The redness around Maisie's eyes suggested she'd been crying. Not that Bridget would say that. If something was wrong, it was best not to pry but to wait until that person was ready to divulge what the problem was.

Maisie looked her up and down, the plain coffee-coloured jacket, the spotted skirt in the same shade. 'Well, you certainly have. That's a smart outfit you're wearing.'

'From America,' Bridget explained. 'The in-laws sent it over. They know things are hard over here despite the war being over.'

Bridget followed Maisie into the living room and the taxi driver came in behind her carrying the hamper. She paid the cabby and thanked him.

'Well, this is grand,' she said. 'Mind if I kick off my shoes? My feet are killing me. You don't happen to have a spare pair of slippers, do you?'

She couldn't quite understand why Maisie squeezed her eyes shut and swallowed as though a plum stone was stuck in her throat.

'These should fit you. Let me take Lyndon while you put them on.'

There was something quite odd about the way Maisie glanced at the slippers and in a very deliberate way kept her attention fixed on Lyndon.

'What a beautiful baby. He looks like you.'

'You think so? My dad insisted that all babies look like Churchill.' Her voice fell to a whisper.

Awake now, Lyndon was gazing around him, with wide-eyed curiosity. Maisie's head was nestled against his and her eyes were closed.

'And this must be Paula. Am I right?' she asked the little girl. 'Is your name Paula?'

Paula nodded, but Maisie remained tight-lipped.

Bridget was confused. Maisie always had plenty to say. She'd expected her to at least report on the visit she'd made to her father at the house in Marksbury Road. She convinced herself that all Maisie needed was a bit of cheering up. She waved a finely manicured hand at the hamper. 'I brought this to cheer us all up. Look. Seeing as you wouldn't know for sure what time I'd be arriving, I got the chef at the Royal to make me up a hamper. Cakes, sandwiches and champagne.'

'You shouldn't have.'

Maisie's low-key response troubled her. 'Of course I should,'

Bridget countered. 'This is a big day. It's been ages since the three of us got together and we've been through a lot. I presume Phyllis is coming?'

'I'm not sure.'

'Of course. Things are difficult. The trains are packed – or not running at all.'

She sat down on the settee and eyed her old friend, trying to work out the reason she seemed so down in the dumps.

'Oh Maisie. It's so good to see you.' She sprang to her feet and enveloped both Maisie and her son in as big a hug as she could.

Once they'd disengaged, Bridget began unpacking the hamper, setting it out on the table like a little girl at her first birthday party. She was positively bubbling.

She stopped unpacking and laying things out simply to say, 'Oh Maisie. You can't imagine how much I've been looking forward to seeing you.'

Maisie kissed Lyndon's head.

Paula, not wishing to be left out, reached up her arms.

'Baby,' she said.

'You want to hold the baby,' Bridget asked her.

Paula nodded.

'Then sit down in this chair and I'll put him into your lap.'

The tip of Paula's pink tongue poked out from the corner of her mouth.

'You're very quiet,' said Bridget.

'And you look wonderful. Those clothes... very London.'

'Thank you for saying so.'

'I should think heads turn when you walk by.'

'Nonsense.'

'You know it's true. My best outfit is a pink gingham dress that's now at least three years old.'

'And look at this lovely little girl,' said Bridget, bending down so she could better see into Paula's inquisitive face. 'Do you like holding my baby, Paula?'

Paula eyed her shyly and managed a faint nod.

Bridget stroked her face. 'You look like your mother. Isn't that wonderful.'

There was meaning in the look she threw over the little girl's head at Maisie; Paula did not look like her father – and thank goodness for that.

'Come along. You've cuddled Lyndon enough. Let's put him down to sleep here at the end of the settee.' She took Lyndon and lay him down.

Paula continued to be fascinated by the baby.

Bridget whispered in her ear, 'I've got something special for you. Chocolate. Do you like chocolate?'

Of course she did.

Bridget took a bar from the hamper, broke off two squares and gave it to Paula. 'Goodness, I've just swapped a chocolate bar for my son.'

She laughed and had expected Maisie to do the same. She barely smiled.

There could be only one explanation. Sid. She must have received unwelcome news. Bridget's stomach churned at the thought of it.

As the possibility sank in and she got up the courage to ask, she busied herself, making her sleeping baby comfortable, puffing up the pillow, tucking in the blanket.

'Have you heard from Sid?' Bridget kept her eyes lowered and continued to fuss with the baby. When she did look up, she saw the tension had fallen from Maisie's face.

'He survived. And he escaped. I don't know the details, but he reckons he's on his way home.'

'That's good.'

'Yes.' Maisie smiled a little sadly. 'Not everything is good, but that is.'

'Maisie? I can see that something is wrong. What is it? Tell me. Please.'

Maisie sighed, but just before she began to explain, the sound of the doorknocker reverberated through the house.

'Mummy,' shouted Paula. She ran out into the passageway after Maisie, a square of chocolate still in one hand. 'Mummy.'

The door opened to reveal Phyllis standing there, her auburn hair bright as sunshine and complemented by a turquoise silk dress.

Phyllis swept from one pair of welcoming arms to another, her tears and muted cries of joy breaking onto Maisie's shoulder and then onto Bridget's.

Paula, meanwhile, kept asking for her mummy.

'Let's get more chocolate,' Bridget said to her.

Determined that this moment would be enjoyed, Bridget directed them to the table. At least half of the contents were out of the hamper and she fetched glasses from the sideboard for the champagne, seeing as Maisie hadn't bothered.

Phyllis was bubbling, excited that she'd made it.

'There's so much to talk about, but first let's get that food on the table and open that champagne. I've never drunk champagne before. I'm looking forward to it. We'd better save some for Carole – hadn't we?'

She saw the colour drain from Maisie's face, the wide-eyed horror, the strangled gasp that escaped her lips.

Silently and with an air of total despair, Maisie collapsed into a chair and buried her head in her hands. Paula ducked beneath her arms and tried to bury herself in Maisie's lap, her sweet little face hidden from view and her shoulders heaving with sobs.

'Mummy. Ma, ma, ma...'

Gently, eyes brimming with tears, Maisie cupped the sweet little face with both hands. There was an appealing look in the innocent eyes and her pink lips were pursed like a small rosebud.

Bridget and Phyllis exchanged worried looks.

'What is it?' she asked, all signs of jollity vanished.

She exchanged another brief look with Phyllis.

Phyllis shook her head, completely confused about what was going on here.

'Let me look at you. What a pretty girl you are. I'm your Auntie Phyllis. Can you say my name? Phy-llis.' She tapped the small shoulder that was tucked beneath Maisie's desperate arms. 'Paula, isn't it?'

The little girl turned her head only slightly, unwilling to escape the protectiveness of Maisie's arms.

'Do you have any flowers in your back garden?'

The big eyes focused on her as she nodded.

'How about you show them to me.'

At first, there was wariness, but seeing Phyllis smiling warmly, Paula began to emerge from behind Maisie's protective arms.

Slowly, she took hold of Phyllis's proffered hand.

Phyllis smoothed the blonde hair from Paula's face, caressing it as she might have done for her own baby – if it had reached full term. It wasn't quite true to say that she hadn't thought about the miscarriage in a while because it was something she'd carry forever. A little girl. How would she have turned out? Regret and reminding herself did no good, and although she was worried sick about Mick, she knew from what the child said and Maisie burying her face in her hands that something very dreadful had happened. Maisie needed to voice whatever it was, but not in front of the child.

There was conspiracy in the look she threw in Bridget's direction. 'Tell me later,' she whispered and, under Paula's guidance, headed for the back door.

Bridget dragged the toddler-size stool used by Paula over to where Maisie still sat with her head in her hands. When she finally raised her head, Bridget could see her tear-filled eyes.

She waited. It was for Maisie to convey what was wrong, but difficult matters took time converting into words.

Maisie came out from behind her hands. 'Carole's dead. The one remaining wall of a bombed building fell on her. She was buried alive for a time – so I was told.'

'Oh no.' Now she understood. No amount of jollying would have raised Maisie's spirits.

Bridget sat quietly whilst gathering her thoughts. She'd always been the serene one, unruffled by mishap, her positive nature always seeking the best way out.

'When did this happen?' she asked softly.

'A few days ago.'

'A few days! Why didn't you get a message to me?'

Maisie shook her head. 'I haven't been thinking straight. In fact I haven't been thinking at all. It's all too much to take in.' Concern creased her brow and tightened her jaw. She swallowed. 'I forgot that losing someone could be so painful. It's more painful than when my mother died. There seems so much more to do and think about.'

'Like Paula for instance.'

'Yes.'

Bridget got up, poured a glass of champagne and handed it to Maisie. 'I wish I'd brought something stronger.'

Maisie knocked the lot back, then shook her head. 'This is fine. Anyway, I must keep sober for Paula's sake.'

Together they sat looking at each other.

'What will happen to her? Paula, I mean.'

Without Maisie noticing, Bridget poured a little more into Maisie's glass.

That forlorn shaking of head again. 'I don't know. I'm not sure where I stand about adopting her, but it's what I want to do. I've looked after her since she was small. I love her,' she said, looking up with tears in her eyes. 'Surely it must be the right thing to do?'

Bridget sighed and patted Maisie's shoulder. 'I'm sure everything will be fine. It doesn't have to be arranged now, does it? It can wait until after the funeral.'

Bridget poured herself another splash and watched as the bubbles rose to the top. Maisie had always been the courageous one. Nothing had fazed her and she would stand up to anyone. But this. She had seen from the moment she'd entered the house that she was stunned.

'I'll help you in any way I can. I don't know much about adoption, but we can find someone who does.'

Maisie blew her nose and dabbed at the wetness around her eyes. 'I worry that the authorities might take her away from me. I couldn't bear to lose Carole and Paula.'

'Cross that bridge when you come to it. Get the funeral out of the way first. How about Carole's mother? Does she know?'

'I sent her a telegram. She's coming down for the funeral next Friday.'

Bridget had always regarded Maisie as the toughest of the three Ms, the girl who could cope with anything. Small in stature but big in words and deeds, she had a heart full of courage and could stand up to anyone. In this sad moment, she crumpled. Tears welled in her eyes and ran down her face.

'She was going to be married. They were going to live in Liverpool when they got married. That's where he's gone. He can't face seeing a coffin and knowing that Carole's in it. Can't face being in Bristol. It's too painful.'

'What about her mother? Didn't she marry somebody with a house up north?'

'Yes. She married a man a good few years older than her. I think that suits her fine,' she said with a grimace. 'It doesn't sound as though he's capable of stopping her doing whatever she wants. Still, at least she's coming down for the funeral.'

Bridget hesitated to ask whether Maisie's mother would take Paula back up north with her, but it did seem the most likely thing. Much as Maisie might love the child, she did have blood relatives – a grandmother at least.

'I love Paula,' Maisie murmured. 'I can't bear the thought of her not being with me. What if she wants to take her with her? What will I do?'

Bridget felt her pain, reached out, took her hand and held it between both of hers, rubbing it as though to do so would help erase her anguish. 'Oh, Maisie, I feel your pain and I can see that you love her dearly. On the other hand, you have to accept that she does have a blood relative who has rights over her in law. If her grandmother insists she go and live with her, there's little you can do about it.'

Maisie threw her head back and cried out, 'Oh my Lord. What am I going to do? I can't bear to lose her, Bridget. I can't bear it.'

The moment Paula came running in from the garden, closely followed by Phyllis, Maisie brushed at her eyes and pasted a smile on her face. 'Hello, poppet. Have you been running?'

'My, but she's a livewire,' said a breathless Phyllis, a loose strand of hair flopping over her face. 'I could barely keep up with her.'

She laughed as she said it, but at the same time her eyes flicked between Bridget and Maisie. She wanted to know what was going on and why it was that Maisie looked so downhearted.

Fascinated at the sight of the sleeping baby, Paula snuggled up next to him, and although she didn't fall asleep straight away her eyelids were flickering as though closing them was not far off.

Bridget handed Phyllis a glass of champagne. 'To celebrate us getting back together. Perhaps for the last time, seeing as we're shortly going to be scattered to the winds.'

There was sadness in her voice, though she couldn't be entirely sad. She had Lyndon – both her husband and her son. Soon, they would be reunited in America.

She'd expected that Phyllis would second her toast and comment that she too was leaving everything familiar to live on the other side of the world. It surprised her to see the puckering between Phyllis's eyebrows and the way she looked from one to the other of her very best friends. 'Well, I won't be going so far as I thought I would.'

She went on to tell them about Mick having received a blow on the head when they'd been in Malta and a bomb had exploded close to him on their wedding day.

'He was allowed back on duty too soon. Went up flying, went on doing everything he had been doing. But, as they say, pigeons come home to roost. He has blackouts. He's banned from travelling. The doctors said it could be dangerous. So we're grounded here, along with our plans for going to Australia.'

'Will he never be allowed to go home?' Maisie asked.

'It's in the lap of the gods – cruel gods, if you ask me,' said a sad-voiced Phyllis. She bit her lip and looked down into the glass before downing the lot in one gulp.

Bridget adopted the gentle voice she'd used when dealing with patients back when she'd been a nurse. 'Don't give up hope. Medicine has marched on with the armies. It's improving all the time. Have the doctors given any prognosis in the long term?'

'They made it sound as though he'll always be in danger from the injury. They sounded so final – so sure of what his life would be from now on. No travelling, certainly not all the way to Australia.' She shook her head disconsolately. 'All our hopes wiped out. This bloody war! This bloody, bloody war!'

Neither Bridget nor Maisie made comment, though both agreed with her. There was no glory in war, only a limping along from one frightening episode to another.

The three of them sat there silently. The bottle was soon empty, but they ate little of the delicious food Bridget had brought with her. Each was remembering how the world was before the war and the death and destruction that had touched their lives since then.

Bridget, always aching to help in any way, dared to be practical. 'He'll have a pension. That should help – until things improve. Give it time. In the meantime—'

Not wishing to hear more sympathy, Phyllis cut her off. 'I might go back to work in the tobacco factory, though possibly only part time.'

'You'll live in Bristol?' Bridget asked softly.

'We all make a choice, don't we. I made mine.' She shook her head. 'I don't regret it. As long as I'm with Mick.'

'This war,' Maisie muttered as she eyed the sleeping children.

Phyllis too looked at the sleeping children and managed a sad but sincere smile. A small tear threatened from the corner of one eye. 'They sleep so peacefully, as though they don't have a care in the world because they know they are loved.'

'She would have been.' Maisie stifled a sob.

Phyllis cocked her head inquisitively. 'Am I missing something here?'

Maisie filled her in.

Phyllis gasped and shook her head as she attempted to take it in. There was an obvious comparison with her own experience, except that Mick was still alive, albeit in a bad way. But Carole, the mother of a three-year-old girl, was dead and Paula had been made an orphan. And Maisie? Maisie was there to pick up the pieces.

Sad-faced, she jerked her chin to where a mass of white curls spread over a dark green cushion. 'What will happen to her?'

'I want her.' There was no doubting the defiance in the way Maisie looked at the child and at them. 'Much as I love the tobacco factory, if I become her mum, then I'll leave it without a second glance back. That's how strongly I feel. That's how much I love her.'

Phyllis and Bridget exchanged amazed glances. Yes, Maisie had always been strong-willed, but never had it shone so brightly as it did now.

'But how will you keep yourself?'

Maisie shrugged. She wasn't quite sure how, but somehow she would win through.

Bridget voiced what was on her mind. 'You're the only one of us not married. If you were and seeing as Sid does consider that you're engaged—'

'I couldn't force him, Bridget. I will explain and give him the option, but I tell you now, I'll fight tooth and nail to keep Paula. Tooth and nail! And if Sid walks away, then so be it.'

Deep down, Maisie knew that what she had said was indeed what she would do. Nothing else mattered but Paula. There was no one or nobody she cared about so much.

The party had not worked out the way that Bridget had envisaged. There was not endless jollity. 'So much has happened since the beginning of this war.'

'Yes,' said Maisie, her eyelids fluttering with what looked to Bridget like embarrassment. 'It's funny as well as tragic how things turn out. What people do... what happens...'

Paula got up, tottered over to Maisie and threw herself into her arms.

'My darling,' Maisie said more softly, burying her face into the downy soft curls.

Phyllis fingered the little girl's curls. 'What a shame,' she whispered. 'I'm so sorry, Maisie. Really I am.'

Bridget touched Maisie on the shoulder. 'Me too, Maisie.

Anything I can do to help, just say the word. Let us know what happens, won't you? You know, regarding the grandmother and...' She bit her lip when she found she couldn't finish the sentence. 'Let me know,' she ended.

'You said the funeral is next week?' Phyllis enquired.

Maisie said that it was, the words like sawdust in her mouth.

'I'd like to come if I may. I'll run it past Mick.' Her brow furrowed as she considered the probable consequences. 'He clings to me. It took a lot of persuading to get here today.'

'You don't have to, but if you can, it would be much appreciated. I could do with the support.'

Phyllis promised Maisie she would let her know her address when the move to Bristol was complete.

'I'll leave the food,' said Bridget. 'Take what you want,' she said to them both.

Phyllis was visiting the Housing Department the next day to check if they could find her somewhere to live. 'It's not easy. There are so many people bombed out from their homes.'

Maisie offered her a room. 'For however long you need it.'

'I was going to look for a rooming house, but nothing could compare to your hospitality.'

It was exactly what Phyllis wanted. She needed company and it looked very much as though Maisie did too.

Bridget fed Lyndon his bottle before bundling him into her arms once the taxi had arrived, the driver tooting his horn in the street outside. Maisie guessed curious neighbours would be looking on, either from their doorsteps or from behind their curtains.

Helped by her friends, Bridget got into the same taxi that had brought her. A tipsy Phyllis handed Lyndon into her arms whilst Maisie stood at the front door holding on to Paula.

They waved Bridget off with an air of sadness, both feeling slightly envious of the future she would have in America. And

Bridget herself who would have what sounded an idyllic life, though part of her would always be here in Bristol.

Once the taxi had disappeared down the steep hill leading to the Bath Road and ultimately Temple Meads Station, Phyllis turned to Maisie and said, 'I understand how you feel about Paula. I wouldn't give her up either. Looking back now, I would have kept my baby. Even if Robert had found out he wasn't the father, I would have kept her.' There was a hint of despair in the way she shrugged her shoulders. 'Who knows if I will ever have other babies? It's my punishment if I never do.'

Back inside, she poured herself the dregs of the champagne and looked a bit sorry for herself. Never had Maisie seen Phyllis look so despondent. Up until the war, she'd always been the glamour girl, the one who'd landed herself a husband before the rest of them – albeit not such a great catch, as it turned out. Reassurance was needed and Maisie did her best to supply that.

'But it wasn't your fault. It just happened. Miscarriages happen all the time.'

Phyllis shook her head disconsolately. 'I don't know for sure whether it was just one of those things. What if I hadn't gone walking all the way along East Street that day? I might not have lost my baby and she'd be older than Paula by now.'

Maisie gripped her friend's shoulder. 'Oh Phyllis. You couldn't know that a long walk would cause problems. It seems to me it was that dreadful mother-in-law of yours implicated in that! The woman was out of her mind. Anyway, it's all water under the bridge and you still have your friends. You always will have.'

Phyllis sighed. 'I'm going to try to be here for the funeral.'

'Phyllis, I would love you to be here, but you've got to be there for Mick. He's your husband and gets priority. Anyway, I think it should be a good turnout. I've got good friends at the tobacco factory and so did Carole.' She managed a tight smile that felt it might crack her face. Ted had visited and offered his condolences. He'd also told her he would make enquiries at the factory regarding paid time off.

Maisie couldn't recall whether she'd expressed her gratitude. The world had turned to a blur of talk and conversations. Just thinking about burying Carole was heartbreaking. This period and situation was the worst thing she'd had to contend with in her life. More devastating than losing her mother, more soul-destroying than growing up in a home devoid of love and ripe with poverty and neglect.

'Old friends should always be there for each other,' said Phyllis. 'No matter what.'

'The Three Musketeers, that's what Bridget named us.'

They laughed at the memory.

Replete with food and drink, Phyllis was still thinking about this comment as she fell asleep in Maisie's spare room. The war had changed their lives forever. Nothing would ever be the same again – except for their friendship. Come rain or shine, peace or war, that would never change.

12

The next day Phyllis had left for her appointment at the Housing Department when Eddie Bridgeman, supposedly Carole's father, arrived on the doorstep.

He stood with hat in hand looking distinctly distraught.

'I can't believe it,' he said, shaking his head, the corners of his wide mouth downturned. 'How's the nipper?'

'Fine,' Maisie replied.

'Can I see her?'

She didn't feel she had any choice but to let him in.

He wandered into the back living room, where Paula was playing with a rag doll and a cardboard box. One of the cushions from the sofa had been stuffed into the box, the doll lounged against it tucked in with a tea towel.

He bent down so that his face was level with that of Paula. 'You looks just like yer mother,' he said to her. 'Do you know who I am?'

Paula eyed him warily and shook her head.

The crocodile smile almost split his face in half. 'I'm yer grandfather. Anything you want, you tell yer Auntie Maisie and she'll tell me. All right?'

Although too young to understand, Paula gave a shy nod of her head. Her blue eyes were as round as glass marbles, more so when he held his arms open, inviting her to give him a hug.

She won't do that, thought Maisie, so was surprised when she did, her little arm entwined around his neck whilst she eyed him warily.

Eddie measured her surprise over the little girl's shoulder. 'In case yer wondering, I used to call in now and again when you were at work.'

Maisie held in her surprise. On reflection, she should have known. Carole and Paula were always well looked after. There was always a larder full of food and she realised that not all of it had been bought by her or the housekeeping she gave Carole. Eddie had been giving extra.

'Give me all the bills,' he told her. 'Funeral directors, flowers, everything. I've already booked for refreshments at The Three Lamps down the road. Them that ain't got a car shouldn't find that too far to walk from Arnos Vale Cemetery.'

She agreed it was a good option, in fact she'd been considering it herself and having gone in there the day before to make arrangements, the landlord at the pub had told her so.

'Eddie Bridgeman's paying,' the landlord had said with the air of someone who felt honoured to oblige the one-time criminal who was now rumoured to be standing for councillor. 'Anything for Mr Bridgeman. Anything at all. You related to 'im are you?'

She'd shaken her head and left the pub, trying not to think of the coffin, the hearse and the wake that would follow. The tobacco factory had been informed of what had happened and that she wouldn't be in until she'd finalised everything that had to be done – including looking after Paula.

Over a cup of tea in the back room adjacent to the kitchen,

Eddie shook his head in disbelief and vowed that whoever was responsible for leaving a dangerous wall in situ would pay.

Remembering the time a body had been discovered on a bomb-site, the man who'd attacked Carole, Maisie panicked. 'No. Carole wouldn't want you to do that. All she would want is for someone to look after Paula.'

Eddie looked surprised. 'I assumed you'd be the one to take over that job,' he declared. 'She knows you and you knows her.'

His faith that she was the right person touched her deeply. 'I want to adopt her.'

Eddie took a hip flask from his pocket and poured a drop of its contents into his tea. 'Have you looked into it?'

'I need to see Carole decently buried first. In the meantime, it's a worry. I can't sleep, I don't eat...'

Her forehead felt hot beneath the palm she'd placed there.

'If it's money you want—'

'No. It's getting rid of these worries that I want.'

'I wish I could do more to help. I ain't been much of a father to Carole and I'm too long in the tooth to take on a little kiddy.'

'Of course you are.' She shook her head. 'I despair that Carole's mother will take her. Paula doesn't know her.'

'Mavis? I doubt that. Not now she got a new bloke in 'er life.'

His eyes narrowed. He no longer looked the crocodile. There was calculation in his eyes and the tip of his tongue flicked along his bottom lip. Like a snake, still and silent but eminently deadly.

'I know how much you love the little mite.'

'You're right there. I'm beside meself about what's likely to happen next. I know what I want to happen. I want her to stay with me, but Carole's mother might have other plans.'

'Leave it with me,' he said. 'I'll make enquiries. I know some blokes in the council. One of them's a judge. I'll see what I can find out about you adopting the little 'un.'

* * *

Arranging a funeral for such a vibrant young woman was heartbreaking. Both Joe and Carole's mother had been informed by telegram. Joe had written to say he couldn't bear to come. Maisie guessed it was his mother who'd written the note, Joe too devastated to put pen to paper.

I'm going to send the biggest wreath of roses I can find.

Maisie didn't doubt it.

For some reason rather than replying direct to her, Carole's mother had phoned the Three Lamps and asked them to convey that she would be there. 'But not 'er 'usband,' said the pub cleaner who had brought the message. 'Said 'e 'ad too much business to deal with.'

It wasn't entirely unexpected that Ted would take the opportunity to call. He came visiting on Sunday evening, his big silhouette framed in the doorway. He took off his trilby as she opened it and stood there nervously, twirling it around in his fingers. Obviously he had something to say but was finding it difficult to find the words.

Finally, once he'd finished mulling it over, his eyebrows beetled just before he said, 'You won't be able to keep your job if you must look after her. Unless you get a childminder, and the good ones don't come cheap.'

Maisie had already considered this. One of her neighbours had told her of one who lived in one of the big houses up on the Wells Road. Another had warned her not to go there. The story had been hair-raising.

'My friend's daughter Fanny took her little 'un there when she went to work at the cotton factory down in Barton 'Ill. When she got there to pick 'er up at half six, the poor little mite was tied to the highchair. Fanny went mad, she did. Told the woman she'd be reporting 'er to the authorities for child cruelty.'

'And did she? Report her that is?'

Her neighbour had shaken her head. 'There was nowhere else to leave the kid so she 'ad to back down and carry on as she was, though did warn 'er that she didn't want to see 'er kid tied to the chair. But there, you 'ave to do what you 'ave to do.'

Maisie had reluctantly agreed. Desperation made people more accepting. Ted was right about the good ones not being cheap and those that were affordable had questionable standards.

She was resolute. 'I've got enough money to manage until I can sort something out.'

The fact that she had money in the bank earning interest was most definitely to her advantage and all thanks to her grandmother. If all else failed, perhaps she could take in a lodger? She voiced none of this.

Ted, one of the kindest men she'd ever met, was telling her what steps he'd taken so far to help her out. 'I've put in your request for leave. They're giving you part as paid holiday and the rest on compassionate grounds.'

'How long for?'

'Two weeks.'

She sighed. 'It's not long, but I can manage until I can sort things out.' She smiled wryly as a random thought came to her. 'Do you know what, I'd completely forgotten that I can afford not to work, at least in the short term. But I love my job. Wills's has been my life for a few years now. All my friends are there – even though Bridget and Phyllis have left, I still feel a connection with them when I'm at the factory.'

She poured Ted a cup of tea.

He didn't reach for it but looked at it thoughtfully.

The pause was palpable, like the perfume of roses on the summer air, and somehow she knew what he was going to say.

'You could get married, then you wouldn't 'ave to work.' He looked up at her. 'You know I'm willing. And in case you're thinking it, I don't care about her not being my kid.'

Maisie rubbed at the ache she felt in her forehead.

Ted ran his finger around the edge of his saucer. 'I know your bloke's coming home from the war and you've got an understanding, like, but in case he sees things differently and ain't so keen on taking on a ready-made family...I'm willing to marry you. Whenever you want.'

Although she'd half expected his offer, she took a deep breath. Ted was a likeable chap, but she had to let him down gently. 'It seems I've got a lot to think about. But first... there's the funeral.'

There was true affection in the gentle pat he gave her shoulder. 'Anything you need, just say so.'

'Thank you. That's very kind of you.'

He got to his feet. 'I'll sort everything out at the factory and tell everyone the date of the funeral. There's a few there who knew Carole.'

Her downcast eyes remained fixed on her lap. 'That's very good of you.' She heaved a heartfelt sigh. 'I can't wait till it's come and gone.' She finally managed a weak smile. 'Thanks for the proposal, Ted. I know you mean well and I know it makes sense. But I need to think about it. I need a little time, what with all that's going on.'

With an air of finality, he reached for his hat. 'I quite understand. You've got a lot on yer plate. That's why I want to take care of you. I know I can.'

She felt guilty saying she would think about it, but it was all the hope she could give him. Paula occupied her thoughts. So did Sid.

'Well. I suppose I'd better be going.'

'I'll see you out.' She got to her feet.

When they reached the front door, he kissed her gently on the cheek, placed his trilby on his head and pulled the brim down, shading the hope that resided in his eyes.

'Think on what I said.' A smile burst like sunshine on his face. 'I'd be a proud man, Maisie, and I think we'd be happy.'

An air of sadness came upon her as she watched him stride off down the street. The war in Europe and in the Far East was now over, yet nothing was straightforward. A time of peace seemed to be throwing up as many problems as the war itself. People had been scattered, buildings blasted to rubble, the world turned upside down at the whim of a madman.

There was also another reason she'd refrained from accepting his offer. A message had arrived from Sid that morning. Luckily it was short. She couldn't have concentrated on a long letter, but in the years of incarceration Sid had always been straight to the point.

She took it from behind the clock on the mantelpiece and read it again.

Dear Maisie,

I'm on the way home. The long wait is over. Can't wait to see you. Get married. Speak soon. Love Sid.

The long wait was indeed over. Three years in a Japanese prisoner-of-war camp where cruelty and starvation had been the order of the day. She had prepared herself for the change she would see in him. Would he see change in her? Who knows?

Nothing was very certain these days, but what she did know was that no matter what happened, she would do her best by Carole's little girl. Whatever it took, she would keep Paula under her roof.

13

Bridget was surrounded by luggage. Packing had begun over a week ago. She would be leaving England and all that she'd known behind.

Lyndon had not been prepared for her to wait until the New Year and a berth on a ship carrying many other mothers and children to their husbands in the United States. He sent tickets for both his wife and son for passage on the next liner to cross the Atlantic to New York.

Few men who'd married British brides had the money to reserve a luxury suite on one of the few liners that hadn't been requisitioned for war duties. Most war brides and their children had been told they had to wait, there were other more important considerations that took precedence. Ships requisitioned for the war effort were still ferrying the fighting men home. Women and children were last on the list and would only get passage to join their husbands once the ships were free to do so, their passage paid for by the United States government.

Lyndon declared her one of the lucky ones.

I can't wait until next year, he said in a letter. *I can't live without you and my son. I'll be waiting at the dock.*

She knew he meant every word and would move heaven and earth to have her and the baby by his side. He'd been on one of the last operations of the war when she'd given birth and had barely had time to see the little scrap of new life before being ordered home. *I can afford to pay to have you here with me, so why shouldn't I?*

For the first time since knowing him, Bridget shrank from what she couldn't help thinking of as flamboyant and unfair. She'd written back and told him she was quite happy to wait. The letter that came back told her in no uncertain terms that he could afford to send her on a liner that was still luxurious, its patrons well-heeled enough to afford the extortionate fares and he would not be dissuaded from doing so.

Like many others who had fought for their country, Lyndon had been released from duty and gone on ahead, opting to travel on one of the many troop ships. It seemed there were a lot of husbands waiting on the other side of the Atlantic for their wives and children to arrive and catch up where they'd left off. There were also American in-laws apprehensively waiting to see their son's choice of wife and the grandchildren they'd only ever seen in a photograph – if at all.

'I'm still under orders,' he'd told her before he'd disembarked. 'Anyway, I need to see how the plantation is doing. Besides which...' He'd looked mighty pleased with himself, a look that bordered on triumph. 'There's a chance of a government post. As you know, I had a taste of it during the war but wanted to be an active fighting man. Now it's all over I've had a chance to reconsider. You know, babe, I really think it might suit me. Who knows,' he'd said laughingly. 'I could end up a senator. Or even president.'

Having not long given birth, making love before he left was both rushed and necessarily unsatisfactory. It had to be enough to hug, kiss and promise so much more the next time they saw each other. As fleeting as it had been, that night would stay with her forever.

Now here she was, all alone and reeling from Phyllis's and Maisie's predicaments. In contrast she was truly fortunate.

Phyllis had mentioned the prospect of moving to Bristol, which she thought a good idea. Phyllis and Maisie could and would give each other support.

She sat on the bed, hands folded, eyeing the mountain of tan-coloured luggage, the clothes that still needed to be packed. They had so much compared to some people, certainly more than she'd grown up with, though she fully accepted that the house back in Marksbury Road had been filled with love. Material possessions had been a bit thin on the ground.

The trip to see Maisie had reminded her of who she really was and where she came from. It went deeper than she'd thought. On wandering through London, she'd browsed in a bookshop on Baker Street. In such a place, Sherlock Holmes was the obvious character who came to mind, but she also alighted on *Treasure Island*. Long John Silver and the Bristol harbour, King Street and the Llandoger Trow that had been the basis for Long John's Spyglass. How often had she stared at the black-and-white timbered building situated in the same street as the Bristol Old Vic? How often had she imagined a man with a peg leg limping over the ancient cobbles, a jaundiced eye on the main chance, greedy to sail away and find the hidden treasure of long-dead pirates. Thinking of the pub brought to mind work colleague Aggie Hill who had run the old place with her husband, Curly – the man who hadn't had a hair on his head. Aggie had dominated the stripping room in the East Street factory of W. D. &. H. O. Wills.

A lot of those old work colleagues were gone now – Carole being the latest to die. Others had been uprooted by war, either bombed out of their houses or having joined the armed forces and been posted overseas. She doubted any of them had found their own chest of gold – the pieces of eight mentioned in the story of Robert Louis Stevenson's *Treasure Island*.

And now you're going, she thought. *You've found your chest of gold.*

It struck her that it was unfair to compare Lyndon with a chest of gold. That wasn't how it had been. Their love was genuine, and yet... she couldn't leave England without standing with her old friends one last time. Both Maisie and Phyllis were going through challenging times. She hadn't known Carole that well but felt she should be there at the funeral to offer her condolences. Besides, Maisie might not admit it, but she did need to be surrounded with friends. Bridget felt guilty to be so happy and to be leaving this country. She had everything, or it seemed that way on the outside. Inside, she harboured her own guilt. Leaving the family was the hardest thing she'd ever been faced with. Oh yes, her father told her she had her own life to lead and not to worry about him. Still at least he had a lady friend, but in a strange way Bridget resented her.

And what about Phyllis?

It had saddened Bridget to hear that Mick's injuries had resurfaced after the doctors believed him fully recovered.

'Anything else you'd like me to pack, Mrs O'Neill?' A knock at her bedroom door had preceded the voice but she'd barely noticed it.

Flossie was the maid Lyndon insisted she had to help her with the packing. Despite having a withered arm, she carried out her task with great efficiency.

Roused from her musings, Bridget blinked. Her gaze wandered over the trunks and suitcases. 'I think I've got enough.'

Some of the items filling the cases had been sent over by her in-laws. They'd heard about the rationing and sprang into action, sending her far more than she could make use of. The clothes were straight from Fifth Avenue and packed in cardboard bags and boxes, some with gilt writing on the sides.

Bridget took a deep breath. Her mind was made up.

'In fact, I think I'm going to lighten the load. Can you make use of that underwear? It's still wrapped in tissue and I've certainly got enough.'

Flossie's jaw dropped. 'But, Mrs O'Neill, I couldn't...' Even as she said it, she was fingering the soft silk, the lace edging of a negligee, and knickers – three pairs of exquisitely embroidered cami-knickers.

'Take them.'

'Are you sure?' Her surprise was a joy to behold.

Bridget pressed them on her with both hands. 'I wouldn't offer them to you if I wasn't.' She frowned as once again she eyed the proliferation of luggage. It occurred to her that a lot of people could make use of the excess clothes that had been sent to her. 'When is your sister hoping to join her husband?'

Flossie's sister had married an American back in 1943 and they had two children. Just a brief time after the end of the war in Europe, he'd been repatriated. Flossie's sister was waiting for the signal to join him.

'They told her it should be some time next year. She's desperate to go. It's not easy coping with two kids and in temporary accommodation. Nissen huts have been converted to married quarters for them still waiting to go to America. If that's how the women and children are treated after their men have won a war, well I don't think it's right. In fact, I think it's an outright disgrace!' Flossie pronounced the last comment whilst rolling up the silk items and shoving them into a spare carrier bag.

'I totally agree with you.'

Bridget wasn't one of those who had to wait – the pile of luggage was testament to that. The guilty feeling remained with her.

The leather straps on the travelling trunk, a splendid affair of pigskin reinforced with wood and metal bands, had been fastened securely. The travelling trunk would have kept the contents safe and secure all the way across the ocean. That in itself increased her feeling of privilege, that money and status dictated she could have more than others. Her discomfort brought her to a snap decision. 'Give me a hand, Flossie. You undo that one. I'll undo this one.'

Once they'd undone the straps, they heaved up the lid between them. Bridget eyed the contents, the clothes for both her and for her son. Some of her husband's clothes were also in the trunk: a lounge suit in a light cream, a tuxedo complete with crisp shirts and four neckties. What had his mother been thinking sending him four neckties? How often did she think the opportunity arose for him to get out of uniform?

Flossie was still talking. 'I said to 'er, there's no need to rush. You've got the rest of your lives to look forward to. Some ain't got anything like that. No husband, no home, no...'

Bridget murmured her agreement. There was a great deal of simplicity to Flossie's comments and a lot of truth. The outpouring of words drilled into her mind. This funeral might be her last chance to be with her friends, both of whom were going through personal crises, one that might end in tragedy or at least in great sadness.

They need you to be there. That's what she told herself. *They're in dire straits. Lyndon will understand. I'll send a telegram first thing in the morning.*

A little more time in England was needed before she made her way across the Atlantic Ocean to where her husband waited for her.

The sound of the telephone ringing broke into her thoughts. Flossie got to it before she did. When she'd first come to help her with the packing, the telephone had represented a thing of fear to a girl who'd never had the chance to use one. After a while and with a bit of encouragement she'd got over her silliness. Now she pounced on it with weird fascination, totally converted to something of the modern age that she didn't have at home.

She put her hand over the mouthpiece as she'd been instructed to do. 'It's a man. He says he's the forwarding agent and wants to know when it would be convenient to pick up the luggage.'

Bridget walked over to the window and looked down at the traffic cruising up and down Oxford Street. 'Tell him the reservation will no longer be required. I have unfinished business to deal with in this country before I can possibly leave.'

In a decidedly plummy voice put on for the occasion, Flossie repeated what Bridget had said. On replacing the phone in its cradle, she said, 'He said he can cancel the luggage, but you'll have to deal direct yourself with the cruise line.'

'Give me the phone.'

Bridget rang the number of the shipping line that would take her across the Atlantic. Although her heart was thudding and a vision of an angry Lyndon flashed in front of her eyes, she went ahead and cancelled her passage. Once that was done, she had Flossie help her unpack everything and pack it in smaller cases – even in carrier bags with Harrods printed on the side.

'I want some kept here.' She pointed to a few others. 'These are the cases I want forwarded on and this is the address I want them sent to. Can you manage to do that?'

Flossie beamed. 'Oh yes, Mrs O'Neill.'

Bridget eyed her appraisingly. 'You're very good on the phone, Flossie. I dare say whoever you work for in future will appreciate your skill. Ladies like their maids to be well spoken and efficient on the telephone.'

Flossie tossed her head indignantly. 'I'm not going to be a lady's maid once you're gone, Mrs O'Neill. I'm going to get a job as a telephonist. They're crying out for them. I've got an interview next week. Can't wait.'

14

'Have you found somewhere in Bristol?' The matron was a kind soul, her manner honed to her vocation over a period of thirty years.

Phyllis caught a glimpse of her reflection in one of the many windows lining the ward. Her paleness was obvious, even to herself, and her glossy head of auburn hair didn't look as vibrant as it had once been. Unwilling to accept that she looked tired and full of woe, she turned away, faced the matron and replied as best she could.

'Not yet, but I am there again next week. It's so difficult finding anything. There are so many people in similar circumstances.' The fact was that she'd been offered two rooms at the top of a tenement in Montpelier – an area of Bristol not far from the city centre. She had it in mind to take it even though it could do with a lick of paint and some serious cleaning. Still, if that was all there was...

What matron said next broke her plan in two.

'Well, I must warn you we can't possibly discharge him unless he's in a suitable home with no obstacles.'

'Obstacles?'

'Steps, stairs – that sort of thing.'

'I see.' So much for the rooms at the top of a tall building.

'I don't say it's going to be easy, quite an uphill struggle to get accommodation, so I hear. So many houses have been destroyed. The sooner this new government begin building new dwellings, the better.'

'Yes.'

'Staying with relatives, are you?'

Phyllis smiled a little wanly. 'With a friend. I'm going to a funeral.'

'Oh, I'm sorry.' The matron peered through one of the circular windows in the double doors that opened into the ward, then remarked, 'He's finished having his bed bath. You can go in now.'

The soles of her shoes squeaked on the shiny brown lino as Phyllis made her way to Mick's bed. There were at least twelve beds in the ward. His was roughly halfway along.

She'd been told that the worst was over and that from now on it was a case of wait and see. 'Whilst he remains here he'll be closely monitored. We must be sure he can cope before we let him back into a normal life.'

Phyllis didn't enquire what the matron might mean by normal. From what she'd seen and heard so far, Mick would be wound up in cotton wool for the foreseeable future.

Phyllis leaned over and kissed his forehead and tasted salt. She took in the fact that his natural tan was fading, that his skin was taut across his cheekbones. But his jaw was no less square and firm than before. At the touch of her lips, his eyes opened.

The matron had followed her in and now stood at the end of his bed checking his notes and signing something before taking hold of his wrist and checking his pulse. She announced that everything was as well as could be expected, then went on to state yet again that he needed as much rest as possible.

Before leaving, she touched Phyllis's arm and whispered, 'Take a tip from me and look at one of those prefabricated houses that are being built. They're single storey. No stairs at all, but they do have gardens. If you're lucky enough to find one, make sure there are no steps in the garden. Choose carefully.'

'What's she on about?' Mick asked grumpily after the matron had left.

'About a house, darling.'

'Have you brought me in some clothes?'

'No I have not.'

He looked grumpy and he sounded grumpy.

From the moment he'd regained consciousness and some of his strength had returned, he'd been demanding to be allowed to leave the hospital. The amenable man she'd known had become bad-tempered.

'I'm too bloody healthy to be cooped up here.'

He'd been saying the same things for a while. It was like a toothache that wouldn't go away.

'They won't sign you off yet. You have to be patient, Mick.'

'I'm not good at being patient.'

She pulled a face at him. 'So I noticed.'

He rolled his head on the pillow, an action that made her want to shout out that he shouldn't be doing that, but she didn't. He'd retaliate, his words the harshest he'd ever made – at least to her.

Tightly clenched fists thudded the bed on either side of his hips. 'I don't know what all this bloody fuss is about. I'm fine. Just look at me.'

His voice was loud, his manner demanding.

She did her best to placate him. 'They're still carrying out tests, Mick. They won't let you out until they're satisfied.'

'Tests!' He almost spat the word.

Phyllis sighed. 'No need to get huffy.'

'I'm not being huffy!'

'You're shouting.'

'I'm not shouting.'

During his time in hospital, his grumbling had become more frequent than it had ever been. In fact, even in the darkest of days dodging bombing raids out in Malta, he'd always maintained a bright devil-may-care disposition.

Mrs Crane, her landlady, to whom she confided the events of her visits told her that the old Mick she'd known was still there beneath the ill temper. 'It's a case of waiting. It'll break through – like fresh air into a stuffy room. It's like opening a window.'

'Or smashing a pane?'

They'd laughed at that.

Now Phyllis was no longer in uniform and back in her civilian life, it was possible to visit him almost every day. Her lodgings weren't that far away but being stuck in hospital had taken its toll.

He grumbled about her going away to visit Maisie in Bristol.

'I wasn't gone for long,' she reminded him. 'I couldn't help that the train journey took so much time. I could have stayed longer but I didn't. I got back here to see you.'

He glanced thoughtfully at the hand that patted hers, then looked darkly into her face. 'Off gallivanting, leaving me to my own devices. How do I know you haven't got a fancy man, seeing as I'm far from being my old self? Stuck in bed here. All alone.'

His accusation was like a slap across the face. She reeled at the very thought of it. She'd been honest about her past, the father of her baby, the man she'd married and her running away from it all.

Being confined to bed and told what he could or could not do was the reason he lashed out – thankfully only verbally.

Despite his outburst, she clung on to sharing a future with him and to that end, she needed to revisit Bristol.

'I'm going there again next week to look for somewhere to live. I did find a place, but from what matron says, it wouldn't be suitable.'

He eyed her fiercely. 'There's no need to do that just yet is there?'

He'd become very possessive, but she had to do what had to be done and had rehearsed her excuses. 'I'd be killing two birds with one stone. I'm going for Carole's funeral.'

'I thought she was Maisie's mate, not yours.'

It would have been easy to give in, to feel sorry for him and shroud him in sympathy. But she dare not.

'Maisie needs her old mates to be there. She's heartbroken. Besides Bridget, I'm her best friend and Bridget can't go because she's setting sail across the Atlantic. Her husband's waiting for her in America.'

The face that had once been so cheery, always smiling or grinning and winking whilst making a cheeky comment, was now warped with a scowl. 'That doesn't mean you have to go. What about me, Phyllis?' He raised his voice. 'What am I going to do lying here all by myself?'

This was all too much. Phyllis began to lose her temper. 'I've just told you it's also about getting us a place to live that's close to the hospital and suitable for your needs.'

'I'm not a bloody invalid.'

'Nobody said that you were. Your doctor said he was transferring there too...'

'For whose benefit,' he shouted, the yellow of his eyes showing with his fury. 'He might be saying it's for mine, or is he moving there to be close to you? Is that what this is all about? He fancies you and you've made plans to be together!'

'That's preposterous! And you know it!'

'How do I know that?' His look was morose – gloomy in the extreme.

'Well,' she exclaimed, feeling angrier with him than she'd ever felt with anyone, 'the sooner I get a place for us to live, the sooner you'll be out of here.' Taking a firm grip on her handbag, she got to her feet. 'If you don't trust me to do the best for your future – our future – then say so now and I won't bother to call again.'

Her face was hot with anger and although she could have fallen apart and cried her eyes out then and there, she held them back.

His chin jutted out and the corners of his mouth were down-turned. Everything about his expression conveyed that he was feeling hard done by. 'So whilst you're down there I have to lie here all by myself.'

'That's about it. You'll be lying here ungrateful for what everyone tries to do to help you. I'm doing my best for you, Mick. I was not responsible for the bomb exploding in Malta. I was not responsible for you insisting on becoming operational the moment you got back here. There's nothing I can do about it. You're hospi-talised here. There's nothing I can do about that. You can't go back to Australia. There's nothing I can do about that either.'

She'd listed all that was relevant. Up until now, she'd been totally sympathetic. Today had been a turning point, a realisation that if she didn't stand her ground and state the facts, he would walk all over her. Not only that, but he wouldn't get a grip on his self-pity, which she felt had to be controlled if his health was ever to improve.

Holding back tears of anger, she flounced out, her shoulders rigid and his voice ringing out behind her.

'You can't just leave me like this.'

Some other patients complained that his shouting had woken them up. Another shouted at him to shut his bloody trap.

Phyllis shouted back at him over her shoulder. 'You're a bad-tempered bully and anyway visiting time is over. I'll come back at the same time tomorrow.'

It was all she was prepared to do. He could enjoy her company until she travelled down to Bristol. She would not allow him to control her as Robert and his mother had done, to have her live in isolation from her friends.

Nurses, their linen veils floating behind them, passed her in the corridor, smiling and saying they'd see her again tomorrow. She would indeed see them tomorrow. It wouldn't hurt leaving Mick to stew but she couldn't abandon him completely. She would bend whilst she could. However, on the matter of attending Carole's funeral and giving Maisie moral support, she would not be moved. Because she had both the funeral and some house hunting to do, she determined to stay longer than a day. She favoured a five-day stay, though that depended on Maisie being able to put her up.

Before going back to Mrs Crane and a hot supper, Phyllis went into the post office and asked to send a telegram, the quickest way she could to let Maisie know she was coming. The words were to the point.

```
Dear Maisie, I would very much like to
attend Carole's funeral. Can you provide me
with a bed for at least three nights? Your
dear friend, Phyllis.
```

15

LYNDON O'NEILL

Rigid with anger, Lyndon pressed his foot down on the gas pedal hard – very hard. His jaw was locked in an iron grimace. The wheels screeched as he braked outside the Waldorf Hotel. He got out, slammed the door behind him and almost threw the keys at the valet who would park it for him.

He didn't usually treat the guy like that. Aaron had been there for years, was always willing and smiled when he said, 'Good day, Mr O'Neill. Nice to see you again.'

Lyndon grabbed his room key from the astonished receptionist and barked, 'Any calls for me?'

'I believe your mother called.'

'Any telegrams from England?'

'No, sir.'

Although bitterly disappointed, he gritted his jaw. If only he could use the telephone to talk to her, but as yet the transatlantic phone line was still hot with military traffic. The public didn't stand a chance of getting through, even someone like him with friends in high places.

Radio traffic from shipping was also still tied up with military traffic. Another year and things might be different, hence the reason for postponing the transfer of civilians – war brides included – until the following year.

On receiving the telegram she'd sent, he'd chanced his luck, using the hotel phone to get through to her. It was a long shot and turned out to be useless. Joe Public didn't stand a chance.

She would have had the same trouble from her end, but once on the ship bringing her across, she could have used the ship-to-shore radio – when they were within a few hundred miles of New York. He'd genuinely expected a call.

No ship-to-shore message came through. Angry and disappointed, he had to accept that she wasn't on the ship. She hadn't got on it!

Once up in the penthouse suite where the skyscrapers of New York could be viewed in all their glory – literally scraping the sky – he poured himself a whiskey, slumped into a chair and brought out the latest telegram she'd sent him.

> Darling, something terrible has happened. One of my workmates, Carole, has been killed. I think you met her. She leaves behind a little girl, no more than a toddler. I feel duty-bound to go to the funeral. I also need to visit my father again. He's all alone in the world. I will write in more detail again. Darling, please don't be angry. Love, Bridget.

Angry? Of course he was bloody angry.

Such was his anger – and his disappointment – that his first thought was to screw it up and throw it in the wastepaper basket. He didn't. The day was a long way off when he could phone the flat in London where they'd lived so happily – despite the war – the telegram was all he had for now. All these things combined to exasperate him as he'd never been before.

So he awaited her letter, dreading what it might say. He didn't doubt that some tragedy had occurred. Bridget wasn't the sort to lie or betray him in any way. He'd always accepted she'd have difficulty leaving her family but hadn't really taken on board how difficult it might be. The Milligans lived in England, but they were a typically Irish family, absolutely devoted to each other. He felt guilty about her father, left alone after her mother died. Nobody could deny how hard that must be. All the same, he wanted his wife here. He missed her. He missed their baby who he'd only seen for a brief time before travelling back to America.

The measure of whiskey proved an ineffective deterrent to his self-induced melancholy. He would have poured another but didn't fancy drinking alone.

To forestall a deeper depression, he picked up the phone and asked reception if he could speak to Aaron. He'd learned from his father how wise it was to remember the names of those employed to be of service. In turn, they tended to remember yours.

'Aaron. Sorry I was a bit brusque earlier. I had things on my mind.'

'No problem, Mr O'Neill. I guessed you were a bit out of sorts.'

'Thank you. I don't think it a clever idea to keep to my room tonight. In fact, I fancy a drink. Could you recommend a decent bar nearby?'

'Depends on your taste, Mr O'Neill. There's the Skyline bar on the top floor of this grand hotel you're staying in.'

'Yes, I know that. But I could do with something more grounded. An Irish bar for preference.'

'That would be the Four-Leaf Clover, just a short cab ride away, or you could walk there if you feel up to it...'

'I'll walk. I could do with clearing my head. Thank you.'

On his way out, Lyndon slipped Aaron a five-dollar bill, buttoned his jacket and stalked off into the early-evening crowds.

The Four-Leaf Clover was trying to pretend it was an authentic Irish bar, though the shiny clover etched onto its front window suggested its prices were above those of anything ordinary or authentic.

The atmosphere was warm, due in no small part to the lighting provided by green-shaded lights of the kind found above a pool table. The bar ahead of him was of dark wood, the green lighting reflecting off the bottles lined up on the back bar in front of a huge mirror with barley twist spindles.

The waiter asked him what he was having.

'Whiskey. Irish. Double.'

'Of course, sir. We only serve Irish whiskey, sir. Spelt with an "e", that is. We're not so mean with our measures or spelling as the Scots who don't include an "e".'

Lyndon smiled sardonically and didn't comment that Americans too spelt whiskey in the same way as the Irish. Like the overly lavish surroundings, the barman's accent was too polished to be real. The management, it seemed, was going all out to emphasise the Irishness of the place. The bartender wore a green striped vest, as an American would say, called a waistcoat by anyone from the British Isles, whether Irish or not. An olive-green bowler hat worn at a jaunty angle finished the ensemble. Lyndon had seen nothing like it in Ireland. Nothing like it in England either. Only in New York could it exist.

'Are you visiting the sites of New York, sir?'

It seemed the barman had also been encouraged to be friendly.

'No.'

He swigged back the drink. Without him asking, the barman refilled his glass.

'Business then?'

Perhaps the whiskey was stronger than he'd thought, but he found himself wanting to talk.

'I came here to await the arrival of my wife from England. But I've been let down.'

'Is that right?' The barman's eyebrows rose in surprise. 'Got held up, did she?'

'That's right.'

'Just come back yerself, are you?'

'Yes. I flew bombers in England.'

'And met her over there?'

'Yes.' Lyndon looked down into his glass and realised he'd already drunk too much.

'And she hasn't turned up as promised?'

'No. She has not.'

He clamped his mouth tight shut. He'd so been looking forward to seeing Bridget and his son. He'd planned to show her the sights of New York, just as she had shown him the historic places in Bristol.

'Met her in London, did you?'

'No. Bristol.'

The barman shook his head. 'Can't say I've ever heard of it.'

'It's in the West of England. John Cabot, the explorer, sailed from there to discover North America – not the West Indies like Columbus, but America proper. It's also where William Penn's father is buried. You've heard of William Penn, I'm sure. Had Pennsylvania named after him.'

'I didn't know that. But there you are. The States is a mighty big country and nothing like the old one. Never been there myself.'

'How about Ireland? Have you been there?'

The bartender looked agitated and a little embarrassed. 'Hell no. I mean, it's a long way away. My family are here in New York. My grandfather came from the old country. Always moaned that he wanted to go back and see his family again. Said he missed them. Never did get to go back, but there you are. He cut the ties and made a new life. There's no going back. What's left behind is left behind. All in the past.'

'No going back,' repeated Lyndon. Too many good men would never be coming back. Many young men, their average age around twenty, had been buried in France. A field of crosses and Stars of David would be created where cows had once grazed.

'I've had enough,' Lyndon said when the bartender was about to refill his glass.

Whether the bartender realised that his customer was becoming irritated by his presence or was annoyed that he had refused more drink, he moved away. A customer came through the door and grabbed his attention. The old Irish stuff resumed, the bit about the difference between Scottish and Irish whiskey, the barman spilling it out like a gramophone record played over and over again.

Lyndon fingered his glass as he thought about what he'd just said about Bristol. On his first visit, he hadn't known much about its history, especially regarding the American connection. All thanks to Bridget and her interest in the history of the city she was born in. He smiled at the thought of that day when she'd taken him around St Mary Redcliffe Church and parked him in front of the tomb of Admiral Penn. He'd been taken totally by surprise and touched by her telling of everything she thought would interest him.

The bartender's comments about cutting ties bit deep and made him realise just how much his wife was sacrificing. Bridget was leaving the place where she'd been born and giving up everything for him. She was leaving behind friends and family, familiar places, where even the air held something ancient and traditional – like memories.

There was no getting away from the fact that he'd been bitterly disappointed when she'd sent the telegram saying she would not take passage on the *Aurora* as planned.

His heart was heavy and thanks to the drink so was his head.

Was it selfish to want her here with him? He'd never regarded himself as a selfish man, but he did now. Leaving everything was a massive wrench for her. New York and the United States of America would be alien to her, but she wasn't coming here for the country. She was coming here for him.

Yes, she had their son with her and she had him, her husband, but would that be enough? Only time would tell.

The anger he'd felt on receiving the telegram was less now, but the disappointment lingered. She had promised she would write to him. He reckoned the letter, no doubt sent by air mail, would be with him within two weeks. He would be patient. He would give her time. And, in the meantime, he would pursue enquiries regarding posts in the Virginian legislature or even Washington. He had served his country in war and perhaps now he might serve it in peace.

16

On the day of the funeral there was only intermittent sunshine coupled with a chill wind. Both added to the sombre mood of the occasion, the prospect of sadness and the silence of tearful friends gathered at the graveside on the following day.

Phyllis came to stay with Maisie for the funeral and although Bridget could have booked into the Royal Hotel with her son, she changed her mind at the last minute and joined her two friends.

'I don't mind sleeping on the sofa and I've brought his carry cot.'

'No need. I've got three bedrooms. Paula won't mind sleeping in her old cot in my room with me if Lyndon doesn't mind sleeping in his carry cot.'

Bridget confirmed that would be fine.

'How's your father?' Maisie asked.

'Happy. And that's all that counts.'

'You're right about that.'

Maisie sensed that despite what she'd said Bridget was thinking ahead of the time when she'd be living in the United States.

Like the others she was wearing black. Unlike her friends her clothes were new. Some of the more upmarket London stores were refilling their clothes racks.

There was a sad atmosphere at Maisie's house, though all three of them did their best to hold back their emotions for the sake of the children.

Bridget eyed the lovely little girl who was a miniature version of Carole. 'Does she ask about her mother?'

'Yes. I've told her she's got wings now and flown up to heaven. She wants to know when she'll get her wings so she can go there too. I told her that won't be for a very long time, but eventually she would get them.'

All three took big sips of their drinks. Silence followed until Bridget remarked that it was a very good answer.

'She's coping well. I have read that even babies can sense adverse atmospheres.'

Maisie rolled her eyes in mock consternation. 'Goodness me, but you still sound like a schoolteacher.'

Bridget ignored her and turned to Phyllis. 'So how long do you think it's going to be before the council give you somewhere to live?'

Phyllis sipped at the tot of sherry Maisie had given her – something to fortify them for the ordeal ahead. 'I'm not sure. They've got a long list. So many houses were destroyed and the rebuilding is going to be slow.'

'How about one of these prefabs I've been hearing about?'

'I wish I could get one. They're single storey, so there are no stairs. As yet they're a bit thin on the ground and nobody knows what they'll be like. Hopefully they won't blow away in the wind or turn soggy in the rain.'

Bridget was glad to see that, despite everything, Phyllis was bearing up, though she did seem a bit thinner and her freckled expression lacked its natural warmth. But then it would do. Responsibility was lying heavy on her shoulders. East Anglia was a long way away and, from what she'd said so far, Mick was an impatient patient!

She made an offer anyway. 'It's quite a task for you. If I can help in any way, I will.'

'Time to go soon,' interrupted Maisie, smoothing down her skirt. She got to her feet, which she slipped into a pair of black suede court shoes. 'The cars should be here shortly.'

Bridget and Phyllis also got to their feet, both uttering deep sighs. Funerals were always difficult and this one, Carole being so young, would be even more difficult.

One of the neighbours had volunteered to look after Paula and Lyndon until they got back. Breakfast had been taken before the sherry and so far none of them were lightheaded, just warmed and braced to face the day.

The hearse was crammed full of flowers surrounding a light-coloured beechwood coffin. Stately and refined, it glided to a stop outside the house. Following it was a shiny black limousine. A solitary figure, black and difficult to identify, sat in the back seat. As they approached the car, they realised who it was. Carole's mother Mavis had arrived.

Maisie showed surprise as she opened the door of the limousine. 'I thought you were staying at a guest house.'

A cloud of cigarette smoke poured from her mouth along with her explanation. 'I was but thought it my right to be in the funeral car. After all, I am her mother.'

The three of them, Maisie, Phyllis and Bridget, climbed into the back with Carole's dry-eyed mother. Two sat alongside her, Maisie sat opposite, preferring to be as far from the tobacco smoke as possible.

From this vantage point, she espied another car following behind and couldn't stop turning her head, trying to work out if she'd ordered two cars by mistake. Surely she'd ordered only one car from the funeral directors.

'You're going to crick your neck if you keep doing that,' pronounced Carole's mother. 'Someone following, is they?'

'Just shadows.'

Maisie blinked at the passing scene; the soot-coated buildings, the tired look of a city attempting to breathe again. Looking through the gap between Carole's mother and Bridget, she saw the car, one she had seen before. Eddie Bridgeman with one of his henchman at the wheel was following. Eddie was no more than a silhouette in the back seat of the car but she knew it was him. Eddie Bridgeman, who claimed to be Carole's father.

A few neighbours who had known Carole, if only for a short time, were making their way steadily down the steep inclines of Totterdown to the Bath Road. Once they got there, it was a flat journey between Arnos Vale Cemetery and its small chapel on the Bath Road and the Three Lamps public house some way along.

Maisie much appreciated their attendance and lost count of how many people she thanked for coming.

'Poor girl. Had to come.'

'What a shock.'

'She was a lovely girl. Bright and full of fun.'

'And that dear little girl. All alone in the world.'

Her response was straight from the heart. 'She won't be. She has me.'

The vicar conducting the service had asked her what hymn she thought Carole would like sung. 'Nothing too gloomy. Something bright and full of life.'

The vicar had suggested 'All Things Bright and Beautiful'.

'Like her,' she'd said. 'Carole was bright and beautiful.'

He'd smiled in understanding, asked if she wanted a second hymn. She'd told him that she did not.

It was obvious from the way the congregation belted it out that they knew the words by heart. They'd probably learned it as children – one of those old classics that had stayed with them no matter the passing of the years.

There were more kind words after the service was over.

One thing her neighbours remarked on was that it would be harder walking back up the hill than walking down.

The sky was mostly overcast, though the sun did deign to come out just as the coffin was lowered into the ground.

The three Ms huddled together, each of them dabbing at their eyes, Maisie holding in heavy sobs that made her shoulders shake.

Carole's mother was standing expressionless at one end of the grave. Phyllis found it strange that neither she nor Eddie exchanged even the slightest sign of recognition yet they were supposed to be Carole's parents. It made her wonder.

It was Eddie who dabbed at his eyes. Mavis remained stiff as a poker, though she frequently glanced at her watch and rubbed at her arms when the wind gusted.

Once the earth was falling in on the coffin, the friends, Carole's mother and the neighbours from Totterdown and work colleagues from the tobacco factory began to drift towards the tarmac path leading to the exit. A tram rattling along the road outside disturbed the perfect peace of Arnos Vale Cemetery.

Maisie wasn't sure whether the wind was as cold as it seemed. Funerals by nature lacked warmth. Happiness was left at the gate. Amusement banned until the end of the event or rejuvenated by a drink at the pub.

Neighbours and friends walked with bent heads, preferring to look at their feet, as they contemplated what they'd just witnessed and the tragedy that had occurred.

In a few days, it will all be forgotten, thought Maisie. The realisation left a bitter taste in her mouth.

Eddie stood, inviting everybody along to the pub for refreshments.

'This is a sad day,' he declared, hands in his pockets, his jaw set like iron and his voice ringing out. 'I've shed tears with the rest of you. Now it's time to drink to my girl's memory. The drinks and refreshments are on me.'

Faces brightened. Steps quickened. Carole's mother cheering resulted in a look of condemnation from Eddie. To Phyllis's mind, he looked as though he could kill her. That look sent shivers down Phyllis's spine.

Mavis gave him a haughty look. 'Chilling me to the bones this is.'

If Eddie had heard her comment, he took no notice.

Seeing she was getting nowhere with him, she tagged on behind the three Ms. 'Mind if I come with you, girls?'

Nobody objected or responded at all.

Taking it as a yes, Mavis hugged her coat around her. 'And me feet are soaked, 'aving to stand around on that wet grass. I could catch me death.'

It was very doubtful that she noticed Maisie gritting her teeth or saw the look of pure contempt that passed between Carole's three friends. Her attention was wrapped up in herself, the only person she felt any affection for.

She trailed along behind them to the car.

'Well, that's that over,' she pronounced. 'I don't know about anyone else, but I could do with a brandy. A double brandy.'

The driver had gone off to relieve himself so they had to wait a bit.

Mavis lit up cigarettes like there was no tomorrow. 'Now it's the sorting out. Are there any of her effects for me to take back up north with me? You know, clothes, jewellery, money.'

Maisie was close to exploding. She gritted her teeth and her eyes blazed with anger. 'There are the funeral costs to pay.' Her mouth was dry and her teeth hurt. She took deep breaths as she tried to bring her anger under control.

Deeply sympathetic for what she was going through, Bridget patted Maisie's arm. 'Come on. Let's get a cup of tea and a sandwich at the Three Lamps. That should put us right.'

'I could do with something stronger meself,' said Carole's mother, so thick skinned she failed to notice their antagonism. 'Hats off to Eddie splashing out on a spread and a free bar.'

'Well, he is her father, so I suppose it's only natural, isn't it,' said Phyllis, who, like her friends, would quite happily shove the woman out of the car given half the chance.

It was only minutes by car between Arnos Vale Cemetery and the pub where the wake was to be held.

'I wouldn't mind walking there,' Maisie said pointedly. The thought of being in a confined space with Mavis Thomas and her unending cigarette smoke made her feel sick. 'I could do with a bit of fresh air. How about the rest of you?'

Carole's mother wouldn't hear of it. 'These bleedin' shoes are killing me. I'm going by car.' They were bumped aside like skittles as she grabbed the car door and made herself comfortable. Like a queen, or the lady mayoress about to progress through a waiting crowd, she sat there in the absolute centre of the back seat. It seemed almost likely for her to start waving to the crowds. Not that there were crowds. Those that hadn't left the graveside were already at the wake.

'I'll walk too,' said Bridget.

'Likewise,' said Phyllis.

'Suit yerselves.'

With Maisie between them, the three friends set off, their arms linked and their spirits rose once the limousine carrying Mavis had passed them.

Bridget stated what they were all thinking. 'What an awful woman. Poor Carole having a mother like that.'

Phyllis added her opinion. 'I'm surprised she came at all.'

'She wants to check out Carole's belongings and take charge of what's valuable.'

'She would,' Phyllis exclaimed.

They shared a sigh before Bridget asked, 'Does that include Paula?'

Maisie barely suppressed a shiver when she said, 'That's what I'm afraid of.'

Bridget lay her head on Maisie's shoulder and hugged her arm more tightly against her side.

'I want to adopt her.'

'Is that possible?' On seeing the hurt look on Maisie's face, Phyllis followed her question with words of reassurance. 'Paula knows you. I'm sure those who deal with adoption would see that.'

Bridget said nothing but it did cross her mind that Carole's mother, being the hard woman she was, might indeed have other plans; especially if money had anything to do with it.

By the time they got to the pub, the funeral car had departed. Rather than going inside as they'd expected, Carole's mother was standing outside, a fresh cigarette held in her nicotine-stained fingers.

'Oh Lord,' muttered Phyllis under her breath. 'She's not waiting for us, is she?'

Maisie felt a tightening in her stomach. At some point today, she would have to broach the subject of what would happen to Paula. It didn't really matter when, except that she needed to compose herself before she felt able to do so.

Carole's mother stood in front of the pub's double doors. 'I'm going in there first if you don't mind.' She jerked her head at the stained glass of the pub doors. 'Seeing as I'm mother of the deceased. I takes precedence. Better powder me nose before I do though. Got to look me best.'

'It's not a wedding. It's a funeral,' snapped Bridget.

Bridget's words were water off a duck's back. Mavis totally ignored her. Woodbine hanging from the corner of her mouth, she opened a powder compact and began dabbing tan-coloured powder on her face. Once she'd finished, she exclaimed that she was well and truly ready for a drink.

'What's a funeral for except to get roaring drunk,' Phyllis hissed under her breath.

Cigarette still hanging from the corner of her mouth, Carole's mother made her entrance and seemed totally unaware of the impression she was making. Some of those who had attended the funeral looked surprised. As the truth circulated, the looks of surprise turned to condemnation. Members of the respectable working class knew a tart when they saw one.

Maisie seethed. Carole's mother was more atrocious than she recalled – and thoughtless. Not once had she seen her shed a tear or murmur that she regretted her daughter's death, and neither had she mentioned Paula. Just a desire to go through whatever valuables Carole had left. Paula was obviously not valuable and that alone made her bristle with anger.

Eddie was circulating, greeting people and thanking them for coming to Carole's funeral.

'I'm gutted,' she heard him say. 'Right gutted.'

He frequently blew his nose and his tone of voice seemed genuine.

'Glad you could come,' he said to almost everyone, though he knew few of those that were there.

On spotting Maisie, he made a beeline for her and gave her a kiss on the cheek.

'Oh Maisie. This is a terrible day. I'm dead gutted. The bloody war over and the wall of a bombed building fell on 'er. I'm going to bring it to the attention of the council. All unsafe remains should be brought to the ground.' His jowls drooped and his tough demeanour had been replaced by a heavy sadness.

'Yes, it is,' Maisie said softly, a little embarrassed by the kiss on the cheek. It was out of character. She couldn't recall him ever having done it before. The thought that Eddie Bridgeman had a heart was touching and, on past history, somewhat surprising.

He asked after the whereabouts of Paula and she saw genuine concern in his ink-black eyes.

Maisie reassured him. 'A neighbour offered. She's being well looked after. I wouldn't even be here if I wasn't sure about that.'

It was impossible to believe that those ink-black eyes could get any darker, but when Carole's mother sidled up close, elbow resting on the bar and what looked like a port and lemon in hand, his look darkened.

'Managed to drag yerself away then.' There was a barely concealed sarcasm in his voice.

'I ain't completely 'eartless,' she retorted, her peroxide-blonde hairstyle shrouded in a cloud of cigarette smoke. Did the woman never stop smoking?

Bridget and Phyllis watched from a distance.

'Eddie doesn't look too pleased,' observed Phyllis.

'And Maisie looks as though she wants to cough. She hates cigarette smoke. Funny really for a girl from the tobacco factory.'

Both watched Maisie wave the smoke away. To anyone else, her action would be obvious and the smoker would apologise and move away. Mavis appeared not to notice.

When Bridget and Phyllis joined Maisie, Eddie moved away, his expression sour and a look of pure hatred on his face for Carole's mother.

Bridget, always the peacemaker, asked her how was she getting on up north.

'Well,' Mavis began. 'Some of the 'ouses up there ain't no better than pigsties. Ours is all right though. Derek owns our place and a few more besides. Collects the rents and that's what we live on. Don't need to go to work. We're almost gentry.' She spoke the last words through thick smoke, accompanied by a toss of her head.

Phyllis nearly choked but managed to say, 'Sounds as though you've got plenty of money then.'

'Oh yes,' said the former Mrs Thomas. 'Derek makes sure the rents come in on time. Don't take no nonsense about 'aving no wages or moaning about the roof leaking. Tells 'em they're lucky to 'ave any kind of roof over their 'eads. There's them more unfortunate got to live on the street.'

Bridget swallowed her disapproval but exchanged a look of quiet disgust with Phyllis.

Maisie's shoulders stiffened in consequence and she felt as though she was swallowing iron particles and choking. 'You don't have any sympathy for them being poor?'

The look she got was sneering. 'They're only poor 'cause they don't work 'ard enough.'

'Not like you.'

Maisie's insinuation was lost on this dreadful woman.

Phyllis wanted to mention that most of Mavis's work was carried out when lying on her back – and, under her influence, Carole might have gone the same way. She told herself this was neither the place nor the time.

Carole's mother was swigging back another port and lemon. Along with snide comments, it might turn her difficult and Maisie didn't want that. She had other fish to fry, one very important fish.

Her stomach churned at the prospect of pinning Mavis down regarding the question of Paula. It would neither be easy nor palatable. The first thing was to keep things low-key, probe gently until the moment was right to ask her bluntly whether she was willing to give her granddaughter a home with her up north or make other arrangements.

To that end, Maisie furnished her with a double port and lemon – a tart's drink if ever there was, and there was no doubting the woman was a tart. She'd entertained loads of men whilst Carole was still a girl and had even had plans to have her daughter follow the same path. Getting a job at the tobacco factory had finished that. Carole had been well paid and there'd been a free issue of cigarettes to look forward to. Won over by such luxury, her mother had dropped the plan in favour of having a packet or two of free cigarettes every week.

'Softening her up?' whispered Bridget.

'If possible,' Maisie whispered back. 'I need to know what she intends for Paula.'

She informed Phyllis there was a plan in the offing. 'Making her a bit tipsy might also make her more malleable.'

Free drink provided by Eddie; Carole's mother was looking like the cat that got the cream.

She asked for more – far in excess of everyone else.

'Ooow, ta very much.' Half the drink was soon gone, swiftly followed by the rest and a refill.

Phyllis had something else to think about other than Mick and their problems. Maisie needed all the help she could get. Finding out a bit more, getting her to give answers to pertinent questions, could be useful. A fixed smile was a prerequisite to gaining Mavis's trust. Phyllis knew how to be charming. 'So where are you staying?'

The remaining drink was gulped back before the answer came.

'Guest house along the road. Someone I used to know way back.'

On the way here, Phyllis had noticed several guest houses, large and forbidding, ranged along the main Bath Road. In Victorian times, many of them had been grand houses with servants. They'd fallen on tough times since the Great War, each floor split up into separate living quarters.

When Carole's mother was exchanging saucy comments with the pub landlord, Maisie exchanged whispers with her friends.

'I've got to find out her intentions. I need to know.'

A rude intimacy was developing between Mavis and the pub landlord – until his wife appeared on the scene.

'The barrel needs changing. I'll take over 'ere.'

The jut of her chin and the steely hardness in her eyes was more than enough to convey her displeasure.

The landlord bustled off. The landlady, her purple perm clinging to her head like dull metal, took his place.

Undaunted, Mavis turned away, her eyes searching the customers for a likely replacement for the man with whom she'd been having an enjoyable tête-à-tête.

Seizing the opportunity, Maisie stood with Mavis at her front and Bridget and Phyllis behind her.

'Can I have a quiet word?' She kept her voice low and as friendly as she could manage. Every fibre of her being wanted this to work.

Carole's mother sniffed and there was a slyness in the way she looked at her. 'Once I've had another drink. Need to warm me cockles. That's a chilly wind blowing out there. I don't know where it comes from, but I bloody well know where it's going.' The breath of her laughter was flavoured with tobacco smoke and she laughed as though she'd stated the most original joke in the world.

It was obvious to anyone that she'd had enough, but as the drinks were free, there was nothing Maisie could do to stop her. A firmer approach was needed. On top of that, her patience had run out and her anger was likely to explode if she wasn't careful.

'Let's go outside, shall we?'

Phyllis and Bridget made a move to follow. Maisie signalled them with a slight shake of her head. This was something she wanted to do alone.

Maisie wasn't that far removed from the slight person she'd always been, but she'd always been strong. Determined to see this through, she grabbed Mavis's arm and guided her through the pub doors and into the vestibule, the small hallway just inside the main double doors. The door off to the right said public bar and the one to the left said saloon. Directly ahead was the shutter that when knocked provided service from the off licence. Ignoring all this, Maisie bustled Mavis through the double doors and out onto the pavement.

A bus passed on its way into the city centre at the same time as another passed on the other side of the road on its way back out. A few lorries carrying a variety of goods made the windows rattle as they went past. A brewery dray, a steam roller, its heavy giant wheels making ruts in the tarmac road, a handful of cars plus horses and carts, men on bicycles, women congregated in the shop window of a haberdashery on the same side of the road as they were but further along. The other side of the road was open, the vista of the city easily visible between the trees, a yellow gauze mixing with the blue of the sky resulting in a sickly washed-out pea green.

Mavis's behaviour was unchanged. Although one cigarette had just been stubbed out in the ashtray, out came another packet of cigarettes, swiftly opened, red-tipped fingers selecting one from the box of five.

Maisie awaited the offer of one for herself but it didn't come. Not that she would have smoked it anyway.

The smoke continued – thick and eye-watering. *She's like a train pulling out of Temple Meads*, thought Maisie as plumes of smoke rose in a cloud to be sucked outwards and then blown sideways by a passing van.

Considering what to say next wasn't easy. This woman was not a great conversationalist. Best, Maisie decided, to keep things simple and tread very, very carefully.

Her voice shook with emotion when she uttered the words, 'I'll miss your daughter. She turned out a wonderful mother.'

'I suppose you will. I'm grateful you took 'er in,' came the swift response.

The sudden hint of gratitude took her aback. It was not what she'd expected.

'I was fond of Carole. It was like having a younger sister. I'm fond of Paula too.'

'You would be. Poor little bugger. She'll grow up barely remembering 'er mother.'

Maisie thought of the sliver of hair she'd cut from Carole's head before the lid had been placed on the coffin. Her plan was that it would remain sealed in the silver locket that had once belonged to her grandmother. For the most part, it would be kept safely until Paula was grown. But she would allow her to see it, touch it and hold it. She would talk about Carole, how she looked, her exuberance; she'd even try to describe her laughter. Carole was gone but, for Paula's sake, Maisie would do everything possible to keep her memory alive.

She gulped down her fear and forced herself to form the question to which she most desperately wanted an answer. 'I was wondering what your plans are for Paula – after all, she is your granddaughter. Will you have her live with you?'

Eyes bleary with drink regarded Maisie through the smoke and Mavis tilted a bit, like a ship thrown off balance by the sea. Only it wasn't the sea.

No answer being immediately forthcoming, Maisie pressed on, her heart hammering in her chest. 'Have you given it any thought?

A brittle laugh joined the fug of smoke. 'She's an orphan.' One hand rested on her waist. Her other hand waved in a careless manner. 'And I'm too old to cope with a kid.' The high-pitched, drunken female voice carried on, devoid of emotion and any hint at responsibility – certainly not of love. 'There's only one place for orphans. An orphanage.'

Maisie's eyes opened wide in horror as she swallowed the shock. Surely she couldn't be contemplating putting her own grandchild in an orphanage. Perhaps she had heard wrong. She needed clarification and a hook of hope for the little girl's future.

'You can't mean that. She's your granddaughter.'

Mavis shrugged. 'Yeah but look at the circumstances. No father and now 'er mother gone and on top of that she's a bastard.'

Astounded, Maisie sucked in her breath. She couldn't believe what she was hearing.

A man who'd been drinking in the public bar chose that moment to come out and pass between them. 'All right, me beauties?'

He tipped his hat drunkenly at them both. Carole's mother smiled at him. Thankfully, he went on his way before Carole's mother, who was preening like a cat, could make any headway with the second man she'd tipped her hat at that day.

'I'm willing to adopt Paula,' Maisie blurted, determined to get her proposition over with as quickly as possible. 'Please let me do that.'

She felt as though her heart was trying to thump its way through her ribs. The sound of her own blood racing too fast sounded in her ears and made her feel dizzy.

Whether she'd said it a bit too sudden and a bit too loud, Carole's mother was taken by surprise. Her jaw dropped enough to expose her yellowed teeth between gaping red lips. 'So that's it, is it? You think you can dictate to me about what to do with my own granddaughter?'

It was now Maisie's turn to be amazed. This was not at all the response she'd expected until she reminded herself that the woman was drunk.

She shook her head. 'I've known Paula since she was born and she knows me. I love her dearly. Why would you put her in an orphanage when you've got me willing to adopt her?'

The hard, over-powdered face was clouded by smoke, but still Maisie perceived the look of calculation. It occurred to her then that Mavis was enjoying the feeling of power it gave her. It was her choice and she was relishing upsetting her, dangling her emotions and Paula's future like a puppet on a string.

There was a lofty toss of the head and a contemptuous arrogance. 'I'm the kid's grandmother. It's up to me what I decide is the best for her. She's nearly three now, ain't she?'

'She'll be three next spring.'

Maisie's heart seemed to go into free fall, like she'd heard airmen did when their parachutes didn't open. That's what was happening now, hoping against hope that there would be no injuries when she crash-landed.

The heavily made-up eyes narrowed. 'Well, you might think I don't care about the kid's future, but I 'ave made enquiries. Australia takes them once they turn three. She'd 'ave a new life out there where nobody would know what 'appened, 'ow she came to be. I went along to Nazareth House last week. The nuns told me she'd 'ave a good life out there. A fresh start. The best of everything.'

'You would take her out there?' Maisie couldn't contain her surprise.

Mavis shook her head and laughed derisively. 'Oh I wouldn't be going. It's just kids. They all get to 'ave a ride on a boat and then get taken to the people who'll look after them.'

It seemed to Maisie that the world was spinning around her. Her anger finally spilled easily. 'A three-year-old travelling alone to the other side of the world! You'd do that?'

'It's for the best.'

'It's barbaric! How could you? How could you send your grand-daughter to live with strangers thousands of miles away? Have you no feelings at all?'

Mavis shrugged. 'Up to me, ain't it. You can look after her until the spring. I can't be bothered with a kid. Did my bit with Carole.' She looked down into her empty glass. 'Unless we agree on a price for her. Pay me the right price and she's yours.'

Maisie's jaw dropped. 'Money? You want me to give you money for her?'

The cruellest and most calculating look came to Mavis's face. 'That's exactly what I'm saying. Three hundred pounds should do it, otherwise she's off to Australia. I know you've got yer own 'ouse. Sell it and buy the kid. Your choice.'

'But where would we live?'

Mavis shrugged. 'Couple of rooms, same as everyone else.'

'No.' Maisie shook her head so hard her jaw hurt. 'No. I will not do that on principle.'

Mavis tossed her head. 'Up to you, dear. It's my decision and that's the way it is. I'll get a few bob for sending 'er there and I wouldn't' ave the trouble of bringing 'er up.'

Maisie's head was reeling. Her legs felt so weak that for a moment she leaned against the wall. Without that support, she might have crumpled to the floor. A life without Paula was bad enough, but living knowing she was on the other side of the world? It would be torture for her and she didn't doubt for Paula too.

For a while, she stood there, immovable, staring at the passing buses and other vehicles without really seeing them. Her thoughts were with Paula and the plans Carole's mother had made for her. She had to do everything she could to stop this happening, but catering to Mavis's greed was anathema to her. She made her mind up that she would not – under any account – give the woman money. It wasn't right. Her principles wouldn't allow her. Then a thought came to her.

'Surely Eddie Bridgeman has a say in his granddaughter's future?'

Carole's mother tossed her head and blew a cloud of cigarette smoke into the air. Pursing her lips to the size of a threepenny piece, she said, 'He might think that she's his granddaughter, but it ain't necessarily true.'

'But you said—'

'What I said and what's the truth is two different things.'

'You're saying that Carole isn't Eddie's daughter?'

'He liked to think she was and my Carole did well out of it.' Another cloud of smoke shrouded a self-satisfied smirk. There was a message in that hard gaze and her smile held no kindness.

'You said three hundred pounds.'

She laughed. 'That's the least I'll accept. Top bid wins.'

Had she heard correctly? 'Let me get this right. You're selling her?'

'To the highest bidder. By the way, I don't 'ave time to go through Carole's things. Parcel them up and send them on to me. I'll give you the address.'

Before Maisie had chance to respond the double doors swung open and there was Bridget, Phyllis behind her. Her glance at Mavis was disdainful, her more caring look was reserved for Maisie. 'We wondered where you'd got to.'

Back in the bar, Phyllis had been sharing her concerns for Mick and the future with Bridget and Eddie Bridgeman, who was doing the rounds again, saying goodbye to those who were off home and thanking everyone for the flowers and commiserations.

Bridget had added input about cancelling her passage across the Atlantic just to be here, just to be with the Three Ms one last time. On seeing that Maisie had not returned from outside and wondering what was keeping her, they had come to find out.

Mavis headed back through the double doors.

Bridget's look of concern was matched by the tone of her voice. 'Maisie. What is it? You look shell-shocked!'

Phyllis was also concerned. 'Was it her that upset you? Carole's mother? What did she say?'

It wasn't easy but Maisie got a grip, rebounding from her shock and shaking herself back into the present. Haltingly, her words hesitant and seemingly sticking on her tongue, she told her friends all that had been said.

Both Bridget and Phyllis looked shocked and sick at heart.

Bridget shook her head. 'I don't understand how she could be so heartless. Sending her granddaughter to the other side of the world? It's terrible.'

'Bloody cow,' Phyllis exclaimed.

'Oh my darling!' Bridget folded Maisie in her arms. Phyllis did the same, wrapping her long arms around the other two, drawing the three of them as close as if they were one.

There was great reassurance in the act of them huddling there together, an antidote to dismay that was fleeting but badly needed. There was no need to say much. They were sharing their affection and their support just as they'd always done. A flood of tears trickled down Maisie's face and her shoulders quaked with heart-felt sobs.

When they went back inside the pub, Carole's mother had adjourned to the public bar, where several men had gathered straight from work to have a few pints and she'd joined them. The sound of her brittle laugh threatened to crack the etched glass of the door. Her comments were ribald and slurred. More drink had been poured down her wrinkled gullet and likely more would follow.

It occurred to Maisie that even being put into an orphanage might be a better option than Paula living with her grandmother. She'd experienced something of that lifestyle herself as a child. Drink and violence were a way of life for a lot of people. She didn't want it to be so for Paula.

Back in the saloon bar, Eddie Bridgeman offered them a lift back up the hill to Maisie's place. 'I can't come meself, Maisie, but my driver Jim will do the honours. But you'll be seeing me on a regular basis. Got to keep an eye on that baby girl of mine.' His jet-black eyes turned from Maisie to Phyllis. 'And I'll be in touch with you too, Phyllis, about what we talked about. I'm sure I can come up with something.'

They said their goodbyes to Eddie and others who had attended the funeral. The air outside was still warm and the evening sun was throwing a reddish glow over the grey granite of the stoutly built houses.

Bridget pulled on a pair of black net gloves whilst Maisie pulled her black hat from her head.

Jim, Eddie's driver, opened the door for them. He wasn't a tall man but what he lacked in height he made up for in width. Either his shoulders were extremely wide or the tailor who'd made his suit jacket had inserted overly large shoulder pads.

As the car travelled up the hill, Bridget remarked on their meeting with Eddie Bridgeman back in the bar.

'Eddie Bridgeman was friendly. More kind than I'd ever known him to be. Not that I knew him that well. He really seemed to be listening.'

She kept her voice low in case the driver should hear and report back.

Phyllis sighed. 'He was surprisingly kind.'

'So it seemed.'

She knew from Maisie that Eddie was, or at least, had been, a man who operated outside of the law.

Maisie voiced the fact that he wasn't known for being kind, though he had been to Carole and the baby.

'He's hoping to be a bigwig in the council.' She chuckled. 'From crime to council in a couple of years.'

Phyllis chuckled too. 'I know what you mean but I'm not dreaming about his offer, am I. Bridget heard me telling him about Mick and us wanting to move back here to be close to the hospital, but needing to find somewhere to live, preferably one of those new prefabs. It's best we live in something without stairs. He said he might be able to help.' Her worried expression was tempered with a hint of hope in her eyes. 'I don't care if he was a bit shady. If he can help us I'll thank him till the end of my days.'

Maisie pulled a so-so expression. 'Well, I don't know anything about prefabs, but he does own a few properties here and there.'

'He claims he's making a name for himself on Bristol City Council. Said to leave it with him and he'll swing me and Mick a place to live. They're single storey – ready-made factory-built houses. There's going to be thousands of them built during the next few years to replace all the ones destroyed in the war. He reckons that thanks to Mick and me serving in the forces he can swing us one of the first ones to be built.'

'That's wonderful,' exclaimed Bridget.

'Lovely,' added Maisie, more subdued but just as happy for her. 'Just make sure he don't have any ulterior motive. Eddie always did like the ladies.'

'Young ladies, if I remember rightly,' said Bridget. 'And I mean younger than us, if what you told us is anything to go by.'

Maisie had to admit it was true. Eddie had always liked his women as young as possible. At one time, she'd been in his sights but that was a few years ago and perhaps his tastes had changed. He'd got older and she'd heard nothing detrimental in that regard, but then, she didn't live in the Dings any longer and neither did he. He had a posh house along Coronation Road. She'd been there once. No young women had been present and he hadn't made any untoward advances. In fact, he'd seemed obsessed with Carole and having so recently acquired a daughter and then a granddaughter. Perhaps that was it.

Once back at the house, Phyllis expanded on what she knew and hoped for. The prefabricated houses would have two bedrooms. There was an inbuilt kitchen and bathroom and the coal house was in a bunker out back. There was also an outside shed for keeping gardening things and suchlike.

'Sounds lovely,' said Maisie. She was genuinely happy for her friend, though she sensed unease born of the disappointment of she and Mick being unable to pursue their dream. It was tempered with her worries about Paula and the intentions of Carole's mother. She loved Paula so much. She couldn't imagine living here without her and she didn't trust the child's grandmother.

Both children, Paula and Lyndon Junior, were fetched from the neighbour. Paula was presently tucking a shawl around Lyndon, who was sound asleep on the settee.

Nobody was keen on more food or even tea. Maisie went upstairs to read Paula a night-time story. Bridget fed Lyndon and got him ready for bed.

Once the children had been put to bed and were asleep, the conversation went back to where their lives were going and what might happen next.

'How long will it take before you move in?' asked Bridget. Her elbow rested on the arm of the chair, her chin on her hand.

Phyllis wound her arms around her knees, hands tightly clasped. 'Two weeks, so Eddie reckons. One month at the most.'

'Where will they be built?'

'Out of town a bit. Airport Road is one of the places mentioned. The airport there is due to be closed now the Yanks have gone and it's no longer needed. That's what he says anyway. Homes for Heroes. If he can swing it, then hats off to him. He said he'd ring the housing department tomorrow. Says he knows the people in charge and that I wasn't to worry.'

'Then here's to Eddie Bridgeman,' said Maisie, who had poured each of them a measure of sherry.

'Full marks if he can swing it,' added Bridget.

Phyllis raised her glass. 'I shall be eternally grateful.'

Maisie couldn't help but smile. Never, ever had they raised a toast to Eddie Bridgeman, who had been leader of a criminal element, but now, perhaps because he was older, seemed to have turned a new page.

'Eddie Bridgeman! Man of the moment. He still puts himself about as though he's Rudolf Valentino.'

Bridget laughed behind the hand that she raised to her face. 'I did notice that he's losing his hair. Perhaps that's the reason for his change of direction.'

Phyllis laughed too, but Maisie barely smiled.

'Excuse me a minute. I just must check on Paula. I thought I heard her call out.'

Bridget and Phyllis looked at each other as she dashed up the stairs.

'It's as though she's likely to vanish into thin air,' Bridget remarked.

'She's very worried.'

Maisie reappeared. 'She's fine. I must have been hearing things.'

Bridget put down her glass and looked directly into Maisie's chocolate-brown eyes. 'It's been an exhausting day, hasn't it. And you're worried about Paula.'

Maisie lowered her eyes and nodded.

Phyllis exchanged a quick glance with Bridget.

'You know we're here for you. Aren't we, Bridget? But things might yet turn out OK.'

Maisie's bottom lip trembled before she spoke.

'I'm hoping so, though quite honestly I can't believe that Carole's mother could possibly...' The rest of the sentence stuck in her throat. She looked down at her fine long fingers that had so easily stripped the tobacco leaves. Now they were tightly inter-twined, twisting this way and that.

To Phyllis's mind, the prospect of Paula going to Australia was both cruel and unfair. It should have been her and Mick. She refrained from pointing this out and instead left it to stab at her heart. 'It doesn't seem right. I can't think that it is. There must be some mistake.' She looked across at Bridget. Her eyes narrowed in the way they did when she was seriously concentrating, finding a worthwhile prognosis.

It was finally as though she'd reached an important conclusion. She tossed her head determinedly, firmly committed to whatever destination she'd arrived at. 'I'm in London for a while yet. Whilst I am, I'll visit Australia House and find out what's going on. I cannot believe what she said and did wonder whether she was trying to frighten you.'

'Yes. That's it,' Phyllis exclaimed, looking from Bridget and then to Maisie. 'She was just trying to frighten you. Who's ever heard of sending a three-year-old across the world all alone. It's unbeliev-able. Ridiculous!'

Bridget frowned at what was left of the sherry as she swirled in her glass. 'Whatever's going on, leave it to me. I'll go along there and find out if what she's saying is true.'

Phyllis divided the last third of the bottle between the three of them. 'To the Three Ms. All for one and one for all.'

Bridget did the same. 'With thanks to Alexandre Dumas!'

'The author of *The Three Musketeers*,' said Maisie in response to Phyllis's questioning look.

* * *

The following morning dawned overcast but dry. Goodbyes were said and tears were wiped from overflowing eyes. A taxi arrived to take Bridget to Temple Meads Station where it would also drop off Phyllis.

Bridget whispered into Maisie's ear as they hugged on the doorstep, 'I won't let you down.'

'Chin up,' said Phyllis into her other ear.

They waved from the cab and Maisie waved back with one hand whilst holding onto Paula with the other. At the same time, she vowed she would not cry again. Too much could be wasted on grief, too much strength. During the next few months, she had to do her best to make Paula's life as normal as possible. Her mother was gone. All that mattered now was to give her a happy life – as long as they were together.

* * *

As usual, Temple Meads Station was full of people. The air smelt of coal, the paintwork on wooden panelling was peeling and, overall, there was an atmosphere of tired neglect.

Initially Phyllis had intended staying longer but Eddie

Bridgeman had given her hope. He'd told her to leave everything to him and he would be in touch.

Her concern for Mick was incentive enough for getting back. It was a long journey back to Suffolk through the centre of England with changes at two stations en route. She was anxious to get back to Mick but couldn't help admitting to herself that she'd been glad to see her friends.

Bridget was also travelling on the train to Paddington, where Phyllis would change to the route that would take her to East Anglia. Conversation about their present circumstances and those of Maisie might very well last for the whole journey. It began over a cup of tea in the station canteen. Phyllis asked Bridget how Lyndon was feeling that she had put back her departure from England.

Bridget pulled a face as she thought about it, her eyes focused on the milky surface of her tea. She was divided, of course, but at times thought herself selfish for letting him down. It wouldn't hurt to try to explain.

'The telephone between here and the US isn't brilliant, so I've written him a letter that explains everything. I mentioned the funeral, of course, and my dad being by himself. The funeral's over and my dad isn't as lonely as I'd expected. He's got a lady friend,' she added with a cheeky smile. 'That should have been it, but this with Maisie...'

Her grey eyes were as serene and full of inner wisdom and unselfish kindness as they'd always been. That was the way it seemed to Phyllis anyway.

Bridget went back to the subject of Maisie and Carole's little girl. 'We both know that Maisie will be heartbroken if that child gets sent halfway around the world.'

'That cow,' growled Phyllis. 'How could she do that to her own grandchild. She's totally selfish.'

'We can both agree on that. I'd take her on myself if I thought it would do any good. And I've seen the look in your eyes, Phyllis, enough to know that you were thinking the same. I did offer Maisie money so she could pay her off, but Maisie is stubborn. She finds the whole idea grotesque. It reminds her of the time Carole was contemplating letting some adoption agency take Paula when she was just a baby. Luckily, Carole changed her mind. I fear her mother is determined to stick to her guns. Awful, awful woman!'

Phyllis took a cigarette from out of a silver-plated cigarette case Mick had bought her some time back for her birthday. She'd been considering giving up smoking at the time, but on receiving his gift she'd relented. It seemed such a waste otherwise, not just of the item in question but his thoughtfulness.

She blew a cloud of smoke into the air. 'But what to do? How do we stop Carole's mother from sending her to an orphanage on the other side of the world?'

'I need to think.' Bridget held out her hand. 'One of those might help.'

She pulled a cigarette from the open case Phyllis offered her. The flame from Phyllis's cigarette lighter sprang into life. The lighter was even more ostentatious than the silver cigarette case she'd already flashed between them.

'Mick gave them to me,' said Phyllis, though Bridget had not asked her.

'Lyndon bought me a gold cigarette case and a gold lighter. I barely smoke these days except at social events. I can't quite get used to being able to afford anything I want.'

'Lucky you.'

There was no malice in Phyllis's tone, but it did concentrate Bridget's mind. 'Wealth is a great facilitator.'

Phyllis shook her head and frowned. 'What does that mean?'

'It means I can use it for whatever I want and at this moment in time I want to help Maisie in any way I can. She refuses to accept money or pay for the privilege of adopting Paula. But I do believe I can do something.'

There was warning in the way Phyllis pulled in her chin. 'You could be hanging around over here a long time if you get heavily involved in this. What's Lyndon going to think about that?'

Bridget contemplated her sleeping son, caressing his face as she settled the shawl around him, content because he was content, warm and smelling of babyhood.

'He won't be pleased. But I must do something to help. One look at my own child and I feel Maisie's pain. Carole's child is the centre of her universe and if in some small way I can help her adopt the dear little soul, then I will do what I can.'

17

SID

'Did you see them flying fish?'

Gordon Brent was leaning on his crutches, face as excited as a kid at a sweet shop.

'*On the road to Mandalay, where the flying fishes play...*'

Sid and the rest of the prisoners of war joined in the singing. It was pointed out that they had long passed Mandalay and were heading towards Ceylon, an island that hung like a huge teardrop at the southern point of India.

Debriefing back in Malaya had consisted of a shower, a medical inspection and a new uniform. The latter hung loose and baggy on the men who had until recently been inmates of Japanese prisoner of war camps where food was scarce and death a daily occurrence.

Sid smoked as he leaned over the guardrail, feeling the sun on his face and smelling the saltiness of the sea.

'Do you know what, Sid. I don't know what I'll do if Gwen ain't waiting for me at home. We were only married for six months before I got posted out 'ere. Didn't even get chance to have some kids.'

He sounded wistful, erring towards downhearted.

Sid slapped him on the back and winked. 'Better make up for lost time when you get back then, Gordon.'

Gordon had been a wreck when they'd first taken his leg. He'd been injured prior to the surrender of Singapore and might have kept it if he hadn't ended up in a camp. Leaving his wounds to fester led to gangrene, and despite having little in the way of anaesthetic, the surgeon had done what he could. Gordon, only twenty-six years old, now depended on two crutches to keep him upright and walking. His wife knew and she had written, but it was hard to read between the lines, to know whether she would adapt to being married to a cripple. Gordon worried about it incessantly. Sid had heard him cry at night and had once joined him on the ship where he was staring at the wake, arms supported by the guardrail and crutches thrown aside.

The wake of the ship had churned white, a long streak of surf disappearing into the distance where a bank of cloud hovered above the horizon.

He'd grabbed Gordon's arm. 'Dropped yer crutches did you, Gordon? Here, let's get you sorted.'

It was as though he'd awakened him from a dream. He'd blinked and looked at Sid as though he was a stranger.

'Come on,' Sid had said again. 'Let's 'ave a chat, shall we?'

They'd had several chats since that first time on this voyage home when he'd prevented Gordon from throwing himself overboard and the strain was beginning to take its toll. The thing was that at times he found himself taking on Gordon's doubts and asking himself whether Maisie would be there waiting for him.

Gordon and Sid shared a bottle of brandy they'd acquired from a quayside tavern. He swigged brandy straight from the bottle. Sid did the same.

'Do you think my Gwen's strayed since we been away?'

Sid laughed as though he wasn't trying to make light of it. The truth was, neither of them could possibly know whether she had. The same applied to Maisie.

'I had a dream the other night that she'd be waiting there when I got 'ome and had two kids. Twins. Both black and speaking with American accents.'

Sid laughed. 'Leave it alone, Gordon. Your girl will be there.'

'But what if when I get 'ome that she does 'ave a kid? Not necessarily a black kid or twins, but any kid? With somebody else... that's what I mean.'

'The bottle's empty,' said Sid, his head spinning from the effect of the liquid it had contained – all gone now – swishing around inside him. He didn't want to respond to where this conversation was going, though, truth be told, he'd had a similar dream, Maisie with a kid that wasn't his. Maisie unfaithful in his absence. The dream had left a nasty taste in his mouth. It was entirely possible. He'd been away for years and clinging on to the prospect that she would be waiting for him had helped him get through it all. Home and Maisie was all he wanted and the sooner he got back and was reassured, the better.

But the journey was long. From Ceylon, they were heading towards East Africa. In peacetime, they would have passed through the Suez Canal, but mines had been laid during the war. They were only now being removed, which necessitated the ship travelling south around the Cape of Good Hope. After heading west, they would turn north up the west coast of Africa and finally the west coast of Spain, France and then the Western Approaches to their final port, Southampton.

Gordon voiced what Sid was thinking. 'This journey's taking too much time.' His face was long with misery, his eyelids drooping and bleary with tears. 'I want to go home. I want to put my arms around Gwen.' He stared at Sid, his eyes wide with fear. 'What will I do if she's not there for me? What will I do, Sid, me, a man with no legs and no wife!'

When Sid spread his arms, Gordon fell into them, his head slumped onto Sid's shoulder and his body quaking with sobs.

Sid saw the others looking. Nobody condemned their embrace as they might have done in peacetime. There was tension in every face, sadness in everyone's eyes. Some hung their heads. Some sobbed into their hands. Sid was one of them.

18

True to her word, Bridget visited Australia House, leaving Lyndon in the safe hands of a nanny recruited from a London agency. It had taken some getting used to, but it was the way it would be as part of Lyndon's family in their New York penthouse or on their estate in Virginia.

The quiet of pre-war days pervaded the entrance lobby of Australia House, footsteps and the sound of closing doors echoing with the hollow coldness of an underground cave. It made her shiver, made her fear that as a woman her demands would not be met – and she did intend to demand. This was for Maisie. She fully intended doing what she could.

The officious man behind the main reception desk wore spectacles with thick black rims. His suit was dark too and his shirt blindingly white, a study in monochrome, she thought. An insincere smile, one that looked trained to appear rather than spontaneous, crept like frost across his thin lips. There was an autocratic air to the way he lifted his chin, as though whatever she wanted wasn't necessarily a given; it was up to him.

'Good morning, madam. What can I do for you?'

'I've a question to ask. One that I can't believe I need to ask.'

The stiff expression remained etched on his features as though speaking to a woman who dared to ask a question was beneath him. 'I am here to help, madam.'

'Is it true that Australia accepts orphaned children?'

The question seemed to take him off guard. He blinked and the thinly smiling lips became nothing more than a hard slash in his face. 'In what capacity are you asking, madam?'

'As a person who wants to know. I have a vested interest.'

It sounded and was vague, but that's how she wanted it to be. At this point, she wanted to give nothing away until she was facing somebody who might answer her question and not dismiss her as of no account.

'I'm not sure I can help you.'

'Then get me someone who can. Now, if you please. I haven't got all day. My husband is in Washington and I'm expecting a call from there.' She wasn't, of course.

It was for a moment as though she'd slapped his face. His jaw dropped, though the rest of his features stayed the same.

'May I ask your name, madam?'

'Certainly. Mrs Lyndon O'Neill the third.'

Mention of her husband being in Washington might have been enough to impress him by itself. Adding the epithet 'the third' seemed to do the trick.

'If you would like to wait a moment, I'll get someone to speak to you. Please take a seat.'

The chairs provided were made of wood and highly polished. Crossing one leg over the other, Bridget prepared herself to wait, watching as he whispered with a colleague before disappearing through a door.

All around her, the echoes continued. Even whispered conversations sounded as though they were being blown through a loudhailer.

Ten minutes or more went by before he returned, accompanied by a pompous-looking man with a florid complexion and a black moustache. The top of his head was pink, a band of hair running around the back of his head from behind one ear to the other.

He extended his hand. 'Mrs O'Neill? I'm Roger Shawcross. Pleased to meet you.' His smile was more fluid than his underling, but she sensed an air of suspicion. She took a guess that whatever he said would be guarded until he was sure of her intention. 'I understand you're enquiring about the children's emigration scheme.'

'Yes.'

'And you're American?'

'My husband is American. He's in Washington at present pursuing a political career.'

At mention of Washington, the suspicious look disappeared to be replaced by one of respectful fear. 'How very interesting. Please.' He indicated another door on the other side of the reception desk. 'I expect you'd like to discuss the issue in private.'

The office she was shown into held a desk and two chairs, one either side of the desk. Daylight filtered through the top half of a single window, the lower half frosted and wired.

Whilst Bridget sat clutching her handbag in her lap, Mr Shaw-cross busied himself opening a buff-coloured file into which he placed half a dozen sheets of paper. Once satisfied with the arrange-ment, he took a fountain pen from the breast pocket of his jacket.

'Excuse me for being presumptuous, Mrs O'Neill, but a woman sporting an Irish name must be a representative of one of the Catholic children's charities. We've already had dealings with several such charities, though never one with an American connection.' He beamed at her in a conciliatory manner and looked very pleased with himself as he awaited her reply.

Quick as a flash, she decided to play her cards close to her chest; that way she might find out more than she would otherwise. 'You're right. I'm Catholic. Perhaps you could give me further information about the scheme.'

At first, he fiddled with his pen as though unsure whether to divulge anything else until he was sure of her provenance. Deciding it could do no harm to impart further information, he lay down his pen, being careful to align it perfectly with the top of the folder. Finally, he folded his arms and outlined what was going on.

'Western Australia is virtually uninhabited and rather than see it populated with Asians, the aim of both us and the British government is to populate it with good British stock. Many children have been orphaned by war. Orphanages are overflowing with unwanted youngsters. Australia can provide a home for these children, who, in time, will become well-acclimatised citizens. There are many organisations taking part in the scheme...'

She'd heard enough to be appalled. 'Unaccompanied children travelling to Australia, some only three years old.'

Mr Shawcross blinked. Her sudden outburst had taken him by surprise.

'I cannot confirm that,' he snapped. Frowning, he now eyed her with deep suspicion. 'Who did you say you represent?'

If the hands that held her handbag so tightly had been around his fat neck, he would have been gasping for breath. 'Where do the children end up when they get there? Are they adopted by a family?'

'They are looked after. We don't arrange where they live. The trustees of the various charities involved deal with that.' His face reddened.

'So they don't end up adopted by families, they're more likely to end up in Australian orphanages run by anyone who cares to earn money from taking them in?'

'I didn't say that,' he shouted, getting to his feet. 'Now, who is it you represent, Mrs O'Neill?'

Feeling sick to her stomach, Bridget kicked back at the chair as she got to her feet and made for the door. In a flurry of anger, she left the office door swinging open behind her, aware that Mr Shawcross was standing in the doorway shouting at the man behind reception that she was never to be allowed in again.

* * *

The horror of what she'd heard was still with Bridget when she was sat at home that evening, baby Lyndon cradled in her arms. It was beyond his bedtime, but she just couldn't bear to set him down for the night. She held him tightly, so tightly that he whimpered in his sleep.

Her thoughts were reeling. Children sent thousands of miles away from home. Orphans, yes, but that did not mean to say that they didn't have relatives who might have taken them in. And what about Ethel Ellard? She'd been ill in hospital and unable to care for her two eldest. They weren't orphans.

How best to warn Maisie and what would Maisie do when she knew Paula's fate for sure?

Once her baby was asleep, she gratefully poured herself a whiskey and stood looking out of the window at the tall buildings surrounding the one she lived in. What could she do to help the situation? She felt torn in two. Lyndon wanted her to join him. She'd let him down but had been considering arranging a passage shortly. Now she sorely wanted to help Maisie.

There was no option but to write to Lyndon and inform him of the situation. To that end, she went to the bureau, picked up a pen and began to set out what she was up to.

Dear Lyndon,

As you know Maisie has been left with Carole's daughter, Paula. The mother is threatening to have the child sent to an orphanage in Australia. Somehow I must be there, to support Maisie in her hour of need and see what we can do to prevent this happening.

I do hope you understand. I'm missing you. I want to be with you, but I feel duty-bound to help Maisie in any way I can. I only have to look at Lyndon and my anger gives me wings. I want to help her.

Can you forgive me?

I'm sending my love to you, and in time will make it up to you.

All my love, sweetheart.

Your loving wife, Bridget.

The prospect of leaving her family weighed heavy on her mind and so too did this situation with orphans being sent miles away from where they were born. Perhaps it was because she herself was the offspring of an illicit relationship her mother had had prior to marrying her father. What might have happened if Patrick Milligan hadn't come along? Her mother had been struggling to keep body and soul together. What if she too had ended up in an orphanage? Because of all that Bridget had a great urge to find out more. The only person who might give her that information was Ethel Ellard.

19

Maisie could not believe she was doing this. Sleep had been elusive the night before, disturbed by thoughts of leaving the workplace she loved so much. Every fibre of her being was committed to adopting Paula. Three hundred pounds was a lot of money and she couldn't possibly sell her house. She'd miss the money she earned, but she did have money in the bank. So here she was sitting in the office of Mrs Prince at the tobacco factory, giving in her notice and trying not to cry.

Mrs Prince had replaced Miss Cayford, who had taken Maisie on in the first place, shortly after leaving school. Mrs Prince was a bespectacled woman with snow-white hair and soft brown eyes. Someone had told Maisie that she was a member of the Salvation Army and had lost her husband during a bombing raid.

'Miss Miles, I have to say here and now that W. D. &. H. O. Wills will be sorry to lose you.'

'I'll be sorry to leave, but it can't be helped. I've been left with a young child to care for. Her mother was killed. A wall fell on her. Perhaps you read about it in the newspaper.'

'I am so sorry.' Mrs Prince shook her head sadly, her expression one of genuine compassion. 'If there's anything I can do, you have only to ask. You can either find me here or at the Salvation Army tabernacle in City Road. It helps to have supportive people around you, and God of course. He's always there, my dear. You have only to ask.'

People like Miss Prince meant well, but Maisie couldn't conjure up the same enthusiasm for the unseen that some could. Singing hymns and saying prayers at school hadn't resulted in making her life at York Street easier. God had been left behind at the school gate. In York Street, her stepfather had held sway with his own commandments.

'Thank you,' Maisie murmured. 'But there's nobody else to look after her. It has to be me.'

She made no mention of Paula's grandmother, because she didn't want to face next year, next spring, when she could lose Paula forever.

'I presume the father died in the war?'

'He died back in 1943.'

It sounded as though Carole's attacker had indeed died in the war, not been killed and buried by persons unknown – or at least unknown to the authorities. Carole had known who was responsible. So did she. Eddie Bridgeman had meted out his own code of justice. That's how it was with those who made their own rules.

'You have my heartfelt sympathy.' Mrs Prince sighed as she eased herself back into her chair. She raised her eyes and regarded the view beyond the window, where a sliver of sky showed above the rooftops of the shops in East Street. Like a stone saint, thought Maisie, though perhaps the stone part was unfair. Perhaps all of it was.

'I truly believe that a child should be brought up with both a father and a mother. My concern at present is, of course, that we have lost many men in battle and women will be required to take over as head of the household. Commendable, of course, but a woman alone cannot possibly fill the shoes of both adults. They don't have the strength of purpose, the aura of a patriarch which a child so respects. Mothers they love. Fathers they respect.'

Maisie had so wanted to get this over with, to give in her notice, sort out the money she was entitled to and leave the building – never to return. That was the worst bit to accept – never to return, though if she lost Paula, she would be back. Since her first day, she had loved it here, but weighed up against keeping the child and keeping her job, Paula won every time.

'My fiancé is on his way home from the Far East. He was a prisoner in a Japanese prisoner of war camp, but now he's coming home.'

'Are you hoping to marry?'

'It's very likely.'

Mrs Prince stirred a little in her chair, as though there was something unpleasant she might be considering. 'It's my opinion that men traumatised by war will be defensive, irritable and possessive. Has it occurred to you that he might not wish to take on another man's child?'

Maisie sat bolt upright; her face flushed. The comment was unexpected. 'He's got no reason to be suspicious. It's not my child. I haven't been with anyone else.'

Mrs Prince shook her head sadly. 'I'm sorry, my child, but as I've just pointed out to you, war changes a man, especially one that's gone through what your fiancé has gone through. He might just leave you to it.'

'I don't care,' Maisie responded hotly. 'If he walks away, then I'll bring her up by myself.' Somehow she couldn't believe that Sid would walk away and leave her to cope. Sid wasn't like that. Sid was down to earth and kind as could be.

'Look,' said Mrs Prince, elbows resting on the desk, eyes gazing kindly over steepled fingers. 'I'm not saying he will definitely be changed, but what I will say is that if it does turn out that he won't accept the child, then the Salvation Army is there for you. We can arrange adoption with a caring family or we can place the little girl into an orphanage until suitable parents come along.'

Maisie stared at her hands; her fingers interlocked so tightly that her knuckles threatened to burst through her taut, white skin. She just couldn't believe she was hearing this. 'No!'

Mrs Prince was so taken by surprise that her head jolted backwards.

Maisie sprang to her feet. 'No! Paula is not going into an orphanage.' She shook her head vehemently and kept shaking it, determined to push away something she could not countenance.

'Miss Miles...'

Maisie raised her hand, palm facing Mrs Prince, a signal that she would not, and could not, listen any more. The words engraved in her heart poured from between her trembling lips. 'I've loved Paula ever since she was born. I have to do what's right by her and I ain't having her put into any orphanage – not if I can help it.'

Having recovered from her surprise, Mrs Prince leaned back in her chair and eyed her appraisingly. 'You're a very selfless human being, Miss Miles. What do you think the mother would have wanted? Does she have no relatives?'

'A grandmother.'

'Surely she's first choice to be her guardian.'

'No,' stated a grim-faced Maisie. 'She's not the kind of woman who takes on young children – even when it's her own kith and kin. Blood is said to be thicker than water, but in her case, there's no love lost. She's too busy spending her husband's money and concentrating on herself.'

* * *

Maisie felt numb on leaving the factory.

I won't look back. The same words ran through her mind, and although determined to stick to her guns, she felt sick to her stomach. So much of her life was wound up in that building and with the people she worked with.

Her back facing the factory, she stood on the pavement trying to place one foot in front of the other and walk away. She'd taken only one step when a familiar voice shouted her name.

Ted came dashing out and appeared at her side. 'I couldn't let you go without saying something.'

'Goodbye would be a suitable word,' she said. Her smile was crooked and her tone slightly sarcastic.

'I can't say it. I don't want to say it.'

He stood beside her, staring across the road at the shops the same as she was doing.

Maisie sighed. 'I'm sorry. I didn't mean to be unkind, it's just that this was so hard to do.' She turned her head just enough to look up at him. 'Thank you for everything, Ted. I did like you.'

'But not enough to marry me!' It burst out of him like something tight held in his chest for too long. 'I still would marry you, despite the kid. It don't matter to me. And before you say it, I do know that Sid is coming home and you have an understanding. But the offer still stands – if he don't step forward and do you the honour.'

Maisie smiled down at her gloved hands. She spread her fingers. They were unusually sore today, a condition inherited from the years of stripping tobacco leaves. In time, they would heal and so would she. 'Ted, if I change my mind, you'll be the first to know.'

A moment of silence ensured before he said, 'Can I kiss you goodbye? As a friend.'

She looked up into his hazel eyes, usually so warm but today a little misted. 'As a good friend,' she said. 'A very good friend.'

His kiss was gentle, his lips warm and soft as velvet. For a moment, she regretted having refused his offer, but only for a moment. Sid was coming home and Paula needed a mother. They were her priority until the fates decreed otherwise – if indeed they ever would.

20

The council official showed her around and pointed out, with justifiable pride, that it came complete with running hot and cold water in the kitchen and bathroom.

'And the fridge runs on gas. Same as the stove. And don't mix them up or you'll have fried lettuce and frozen eggs!'

He laughed at his joke, though his jollity disappeared on seeing only a hint of a smile on Phyllis's face.

'There's a nice little garden front and rear,' he added in the hope that might cheer her up a bit.

She'd already seen the front garden. Now he opened the back door and invited her to take a look.

'Big enough for flowers and vegetables,' he said, still brimming with enthusiasm. 'Once it's dug over. You married?'

The question took her by surprise.

'Yes.'

Of course she was. This little house was for her and Mick but worlds and oceans away from what they'd planned.

'Army, navy or air force?'

'Air force.'

'I bet he'll have this dug over in no time.'

She didn't contradict him. She didn't want to explain. In her mind, she could see the expanse of mud that existed at present covered in grass. A nice lawn surrounded by flowers. Mick might just about manage that, though she thought it more likely that he would recline on a deckchair, at least at first.

She'd been staying with Maisie, each supporting the other with their distinctive problems.

'So how did it go?' asked Maisie when she got back.

'Fine. For a tiny little place it has everything.'

Deep inside she worried about Mick's reaction. His dream had been for the wide-open spaces of Australia and a rambling house set within acres of vineyards. The prefabricated dwelling was a long way from that but in the circumstances was really all they could hope for.

Sensing her friends confused emotions, Maisie suggested they go to the park.

'We could do with the fresh air. It'll clear our heads.'

Phyllis agreed. The little house was lovely but what would Mick say?

Together they went to the park, with Paula playing chase around a sycamore tree after they had shown her how to make the seeds fly in the air.

'Just a little blow... They're like little aeroplanes. See?'

After tiring herself out, Paula demanded to be picked up.

Maisie picked her up. 'Paula Thomas, you're getting too heavy to be carried.'

Afternoon shadows were falling with the first leaves from the trees as they made their way along the narrow path that led to the exit.

Maisie sank onto the wall that formed the boundary of the park.

'Let me take her,' Phyllis offered.

Paula was passed from Maisie to Phyllis, her head flopped against her shoulder, eyes tightly shut and cheeks still pink from exertion and the blessed peace of sleep.

Maisie took a deep breath and stretched her neck, turning it from side to side to ease the ache. 'Peace is going to take some getting used to,' she said.

Phyllis kissed Paula's forehead. 'The younger generation will be grateful for that. The sooner all this is put behind us, the better.'

'I think we'll have to get the bus back. That hill is a devil to walk up even without carrying Paula.'

'Let's get our breath first.'

The road that ran in a straight line beside the park was empty of traffic until a black limousine entered at the top end. They were sitting on either side of the gap between the stone wall separating the expanse of grass and flowerbeds from the road. At one time, there had been iron railings on top and a pair of gates in the gap. They'd all been taken as part of the 'scrap iron drive' along with pots and pans donated by patriotic housewives. The official stance was that it would be used to build aircraft. It had been rumoured that most of it was rusting away in piles at various corporation yards, never used and never, it seemed, needed.

As it came level with them, the car stopped. The rear window wound down and Eddie Bridgeman's face appeared.

'Can I give you a lift?'

At one time, Maisie might have declined, but that was back when Eddie had had designs on her. Eddie had once worn menace like a sharp suit. Ageing had softened its edges and there was almost a cherubic look on his face when he smiled at Paula.

'Oh, look at that little sweetheart. Sound asleep. Now we don't want to disturb her, so you two get in the back with her and I'll go in the front.'

His driver stayed at the wheel whilst Eddie got out and opened the back doors of the car, ushering Maisie and Phyllis in, suggesting they gave Paula room to lie flat on the back seat.

'Thank you, Eddie. We do know how to look after a child.'

'Yeah,' he said, looking a bit crushed, which for Eddie meant admitting he knew nothing. Maisie exchanged a secretive smile with Phyllis. A milestone indeed!

On their way back to Totterdown, he bragged about having moved up in the world.

'An important man then,' said Maisie. 'And still not married?'

'I'm thinking about it. But I'm moving in respectable circles so she'd 'ave a lot to live up to.'

Maisie almost choked. It was noticeable that his speech was more refined, though he did drop the odd aitch in places.

'Now, about that prefab, Phyllis. I've made enquiries.'

It turned out that his enquiries had borne fruit. He insisted on a date she come down on next and there would be a prefab waiting for her.

'You'll jump the list,' he told her.

* * *

A week before Mick was due to arrive, Phyllis stood in the middle of the living room of her own little house with the keys in her hand. Somehow, she didn't know how, Eddie had also got hold of some furniture – 'from a bloke I know who's got a shop in Old Market'. A green moquette-covered three-piece suite, a dining table and chairs, a sideboard, a bed, curtains, bedding and just about everything else she needed.

He'd been there at Maisie's house when they'd returned from seeing the furniture moved in and setting it into place.

'Anything else you want, just let me know. There's nothing too good for a war hero. Especially an injured one. Brave man,' Eddie said, nodding his head in time with his words. 'Brave man.'

As she told Maisie, whilst Eddie was in the bathroom and Paula slept on the sofa, there was no doubt about her taking it. 'We've nowhere else we can go.'

'I'm so sorry. Things haven't gone easy for you and Mick.'

Phyllis forced herself to be positive. 'At least we're still alive.'

'True.'

'Have you heard from Carole's mother?'

Maisie shook her head. 'I've written trying to persuade her to change her mind. But she's got this fixation on sending Paula to Australia.' She shook her head. 'I just can't understand it.'

'Out of sight, out of mind?'

'Selfish bitch!'

Phyllis had heard Maisie being forthright before but never with such vehemence.

* * *

Eddie Bridgeman had returned unnoticed. Quietly listening to other people's conversations had been a necessary skill when he'd been operating on the wrong side of the law. Listening was information and information gave you the advantage. In this case, however, he'd only learned enough to leave him wanting to know more.

'Language, Maisie Miles. Somebody's upset you. And what's all this about Australia? What's this about my Paula?' His facial expression had turned dark.

Maisie took the silver locket from the mantelpiece, opened it and fingered the locket of hair. 'I wasn't going to get you involved.'

'Involved in what, Maisie? Come on, if it involves my granddaughter, then I deserve to be told. She's my flesh and blood, ain't she?'

'I got the funeral directors to cut this lock of hair from Carole's head. I've got a few photos too, but I thought Paula would appreciate something more...' She sought for the right word, thought of past conversations with Bridget and finally said it. 'Tangible. Something that was part of her.'

Eddie's eyes narrowed. 'And?'

Phyllis sat down at the far end of the sofa next to Paula's feet. She felt for Maisie and knew what was going through her mind, why she'd been reluctant to disclose Carole's mother's plans for Paula to be sent to an orphanage in Australia. The man who had raped Carole had been found half buried in rubble on a bombsite. His head had been smashed in. Though there'd been no evidence, it was rumoured that Eddie had a hand in the killing. If he could do it once, he could do it again. Such an occurrence would be difficult to live with.

He stood at the back of the sofa and looked down on the sleeping child. 'I'd do anything for her. Anything. Same for her mother.' He looked up and caught Maisie's hesitant stance, the fleeting thought darkening her eyes.

Maisie sat down; hands clenched in front of her. Her frightened eyes strayed to the sleeping child. 'Carole's mother won't hear of me adopting her. She's planned for her to go to an orphanage in Australia unless I pay her three hundred pounds, which would mean selling the house, but then where would we live? How would we live?' She shook her head.

'Don't ever worry about money. I'll give you an allowance. I won't 'ave my little girl in rags and starving. And neither will you. I'll see to that.'

'You don't 'ave to. I'll manage somehow.'

'I bloody well do 'ave to. The kid's my responsibility. Leave it to me to sort Mavis out.'

She knew the moment she said it that Eddie would be true to

his word. The only thing she feared was if Mavis told him to his face that he might not be related to the child at all. Unless...

'I've tried all ways to get her to see sense, but she wanted payment. Imagine,' she said, 'selling your own granddaughter. I cannot – will not – pay her a penny. It's not right. I asked my solicitor if it was against the law. He said that so long as the legal guardian agrees, there's nothing I can do.' She shook her head. 'I'm hoping she'll change her mind, keep asking myself how she could do something so cruel. How could she do this to her own flesh and blood?'

Eddie's lips clamped in a grim line and his pupils were like dark pools beneath his heavy brow. He turned his back and stood at the window looking out, his shoulders rigid and boxlike.

Suddenly he turned round and nodded. The way he did it reminded Maisie of the late Italian dictator, Mussolini. He'd had that same defiant way of holding his head high and making his face and jaw look as though it was made of iron.

'So that's it. She's forgotten that the kid is my flesh and blood too. Australia, eh? Selfish bitch!'

Maisie almost smiled when he used the same expletive as she had done, though grimly, wishing that a good fairy might yet come along and make things right.

'I suppose that, as grandmother, she does have certain rights,' commented Phyllis.

'So have I,' returned Eddie, rage in his eyes and his voice a deep growl in his throat. 'Leave her to me.'

Maisie felt her breath catch in her throat. 'You won't do anything...'

Silently he looked down at the floor, his hands clasped behind his back. He raised his head and there was almost a smile on his face when he looked at her appraisingly. 'I never knew Mavis could sink so low, though I should 'ave done. Money is all she cares about, but don't sell your house, Maisie. The kid and you need a roof over your heads and I'm all in favour of you adopting my little darling.' He looked down at Paula, then glanced at his watch. 'No blood of mine is being sent to the other side of the world. You've got my word on that. Time I was going.'

Maisie frowned at her hands and the fingers reddish through years of tearing tobacco leaves. Her thoughts returned to when a man was found dead in suspicious circumstances on a bomb site. The man was Carole's attacker; there had been no hiding place from Eddie. Just a shallow grave amongst the weeds and the rubble. Now someone else had dared upset him. Maisie disliked Mavis and wanted Paula but was concerned that Mavis too might end up on the other side of life.

'You'll offer her money?' Maisie asked.

Eddie put on his hat and made to leave. At the door, he turned round and answered her question.

'She likes money. Oh, and don't bother sending 'er Carole's stuff. Keep it for the little 'un. A few things to remember her by.'

'Do you think Mavis will accept money from you?'

His eyes were dark pools beneath his black eyebrows. 'She likes money and she fears me. It's a good combination.'

21

Determined to make Mick happy as she greeted him into their new home at number twelve Airport Road, Phyllis donned her best dress, which almost matched her eyes and complemented her auburn hair.

As yet, there was nothing much growing in the garden to pick for a flower display. Driven by a need to have everything perfect, she'd gone out with half a crown in her pocket. She recalled seeing an old cottage set some way back from the road, its garden brimming with late-summer blooms. The mild weather had continued and even now, at the beginning of October the smell and colour of roses, daisies and dahlias was holding up well.

On earlier occasions, she'd seen an old man, his hair as white as dandelion down, bending over a spade or forking at the earth. He'd always seemed very intent on his tasks and only once had he looked up and signalled an acknowledgement with a curt nod of his head.

She'd nodded back, her smile a little hesitant, impeded by the weight she was carrying on her shoulders, her concern for Mick and planning for him coming down here.

Today she saw he was clipping spent roses, cutting others, which he placed on the ground to join other blooms.

'Excuse me.' She waved. Both hands resting on top the ivy-covered wall, she leaned forward.

It didn't seem that he'd noticed.

'Excuse me,' she called again. The waving of her hand was more vigorous this time. The old man saw her.

He wore a puzzled look on his face from beneath that snowy white hair, a doubling of his wrinkles as he stepped carefully between bushes and clumps of flowers to gain the red-brick path that led from gate to door.

She prayed he was coming her way, not going back into the house. In a moment of panic, she took the half-crown from out of her pocket. 'I'd like to buy some flowers – if you could sell me some.'

The look on his face was unchanged as he came towards her. 'You wants flowers?'

'Yes. If you can spare some. I have some money.'

The silver coin glinted as she held it up, keen for him to see that she really did have some money.

''Alf a crown?'

'Yes.'

His puzzled look lessened, though he was tenacious with his need to know more. 'Special occasion? Is that what you wants 'em for? Getting married are you?' He cocked his head to one side so that he was perusing her with one eye only. With sudden shock, she realised the reason was his other eye was glass.

'No.' She shook her head as if doing so would help him see her better. 'I... We... My husband and I... we've just moved into one of the prefabs. He's coming home from hospital today. I wanted...' She swallowed back the sob that threatened.

'Injured in the war, was 'e?'

She nodded silently.

'And you wants to make it look nice for when 'e arrives?'

'Yes,' she whispered.

He cupped his hand around ear. 'Speak up. I was in the artillery in the first lot. Lost an eye to shrapnel and me ears to being close to the barrage. Load 'em and fire 'em.'

'Yes,' she said, louder now. 'I want it to look nice for him.'

His one good eye narrowed. 'Wait there. I'll fetch a bit of newspaper.'

She watched him disappear into the house before returning, then bend down and lift the pile of cut flowers by his feet and wrap it in a sheet of newspaper, then a second one.

'Them thorns are sharp,' he said as he handed her the impromptu bouquet.

Perfume filled her nostrils and colour almost blinded her eyes. There were roses, gladioli, moon daisies, dahlias and feathery grasses that tickled her nose.

'I grows these in the green'ouse. It's still warm in there and they're clinging on.'

She gasped at their beauty and thanked him profusely. 'Here,' she said, handing him the half-crown. 'It's all I brought with me, but if you want more, I can go back home and get...'

He held up one hand, palm facing her. 'No, no, no! You make your house look nice. Give your bloke a homecoming he'll remember for the rest of his life.' Sadness came to his eyes. 'My missus planted most of this garden whilst I was away serving. She reckoned all the colours and smells would help me forget what I'd been through. We 'ad a good life together. The garden 'elped put it all behind us. She's gone now, but I'll never forget that day. Never!'

* * *

There were enough flowers to fill two vases. Phyllis set one display in the centre of the dining table, the other in the kitchen window. The sight of them gladdened her heart. She hoped they'd have the same effect on Mick. Mr Hargreaves had kindly provided her with a few late blooms after she'd explained she wanted the house to look and smell nice for Mick's homecoming. He'd also come along and tidied up the front garden though there wasn't enough time to tidy up the back garden. 'I'll be back to do that as soon as I can.' He went on and gave her the benefit of some advice.

'A bit of lawn and some nice borders of mixed flowers, fruit and vegetables. Rome weren't built in a day.'

At the sound of the ambulance pulling up outside, she took a last glance in the mirror, tidied her hair with her hands and took off her apron.

Mick had suggested he come down on the train. The doctors had insisted otherwise.

'The slightest jolt from another passenger, a suitcase falling down on your head…'

They'd listed a whole range of possibilities, and although Mick had pooh-poohed them, he'd given in once they'd warned they wouldn't let him out unless he went home by ambulance.

A lump in her throat and a smile on her face despite her misty eyes, Phyllis threw open the front door.

It had been three days since she'd last seen him. His face was drawn and he looked older than his twenty-eight years. In the past, his eyes had lit up the moment he'd seen her. That sparkle had disappeared. He looked morose and fed up with life.

She couldn't let him know that she'd seen. Everything she could do to cheer him up she would do.

Cushions were patted into place behind his back as the ambulancemen set him into a chair.

'Home at last,' Phyllis said brightly. 'I expect you could do with a cup of tea. And I've made a cake. Your favourite. Apple cake and made with fresh apples too.'

Once they were alone, she suggested he look round. 'So you know where everything is.'

He grunted an acknowledgement. Phyllis handed him his walking sticks.

'I don't need those,' he snapped. 'It's my head that's injured, not my legs.'

Using both hands, he pushed himself up from the chair, straightened and took careful steps whilst she hovered behind him.

'This is the kitchen...'

'This is the bedroom... the biggest so I've made it ours.'

'This is the second bedroom...' She didn't mention that it would serve as a nursery – if they ever had children.

'This is the bathroom...'

'Leave me a moment. No need to wait.' He closed the bathroom door in her face.

Feeling helpless and desperate, she made her way to the kitchen. Her hands shook as she put the kettle on the gas. The teapot and cups sat waiting on the work surface. She took the cake out of the fridge and set it on the table. Out of everything else in the house, the fridge was the one thing she couldn't help staring at. In all her life, she'd known nobody who'd owned a fridge. Never again would butter melt and milk go off in the summer heat.

Hearing the flush being pulled, she made the tea and carried the tray – cake and all – into the living room, setting it down on a small side table.

When Mick came back into the room, she stood apprehensively, taking a step towards him, one hand reaching out, just in case he stumbled.

'Stop fussing!'

His anger surprised her. She stepped back from the arm he

flung at her. Some women would have run scared. But she wasn't going to do that. They had come this far and she had every intention of soldiering on. She found the courage to say, 'I'm not fussing. If you fell and hit your head—'

'It might be just as well if I did.' He leaned on the windowsill, facing the front garden, his back to her.

'Mick, you can't mean that. We've survived the war. We've still got each other.'

'Yeah,' he grunted. 'Two small people in a small house living on an air force pension with no prospects of ever doing anything else.'

His comment was like a sword to her heart, but she had to remain calm. She would not raise her voice.

'They told you to have a rest first, then apply for a job – something in an office or—'

'Me. Sitting at a desk? Passing pieces of paper from one file to another?' He spun from the window and even though he pretended otherwise, she knew spinning around so fast had made him slightly dizzy. He groped for the windowsill again. She reached out to save him, then retracted her arm, mindful of his response when she'd done that earlier.

'It's early days, Mick. Getting a job would help you adjust... they said just take it easy. Take up a hobby...'

'Like what?' he snapped.

There were jobs he could do, but she knew instinctively that in his current state of mind he wouldn't take up any of them. She searched hard for some things that might at least give him food for thought.

'Swimming. It would mean catching the bus, but...'

He shook his head in disbelief.

'Gardening. It's not a big garden, but it's not that small either. How about planting vegetables and some fruit? Apples. Raspberries. Rhubarb.'

When he looked at her, it was with ire and smouldering grief. 'I was going to plant a vineyard. Now I'm reduced to planting bloody rhubarb!'

* * *

Their bedroom walls were the standard colour of every room and every prefabricated unit. Pink sprigs of blossom patterned the matching curtains and she'd decided that in time she would paint the walls a soft mint green. Even as it was, she was content with how it looked and had easily imagined her and Mick snuggled down together beneath the pink satin eiderdown. How wonderful it would be to feel his arms around her again, to trace his shoulder and chest muscles, feel the knotted strength in his neck.

It was easy to believe that he would want the same, especially considering the amount of time gone by since they'd lain together. Yet here she was lying beside him, wide awake and nervous. She wanted to reach out and touch him yet couldn't find the courage to do so. If he'd wanted her, he would have taken her into his arms by now. He lay there still and silent beside her. Perhaps it had something to do with the prescribed medication that was mostly for pain relief and known to cause drowsiness.

She lay awake for a long while, finally dozed off but was disturbed when he got up during the night and went to the bathroom.

He got into bed and turned his back on her.

'Mick. Are you all right?'

'Yeah.'

The room was dark. She sensed, rather than saw, the tension in his shoulders. Did he want to reach for her as much as she wanted him to? Or did he fear the blood that would rush to his head, the physical process that might threaten his head injury?

Over tea earlier, she'd tried to get a decent conversation out of him, not just about his health, but about the hospital and, beyond that, to the memories they shared. She'd mentioned Malta, then his past life in Australia. His face had come alight and that old sparkle she'd known so well had come back to his eyes. But only momentarily, only until he'd reminded himself that the man he had been was not the man he was now.

He'd kept his temper until she'd mentioned Eddie Bridgeman getting this place for them and how grateful she was. It was the worst thing she could have said.

'You think we should be grateful for this bloody rabbit-hutch?'

His attitude had stung. But, for all that, she was glad he was back. She was also determined that they would get through this. To that end, just to set the ball rolling, she reached out in the darkness. He was wearing pyjamas. She was wearing a nightdress. Her fingers traced a path from his neck to his shoulder. It was sheer bliss to feel his muscles knot beneath her touch. She dared ease herself a little closer.

'I'm tired,' he said, and jerked his shoulder away.

Rejection hurt. Her fingers curled into her palm and she bit her lip. Silent sobs threatened to choke her. She wanted him so much. She wanted things to be as they used to be. But how long would it take, she wondered, before he would be the old Mick again? The sad truth was he might never be his old self. What was it the kind doctor had said? There's always hope that the body would mend itself. But it was just that, hope.

22

It seemed to Maisie that both the world and the weather was bright with possibilities.

It had begun earlier in the week when she'd been accosted – if that was the right word – by Eddie Bridgeman. She'd been trying her best to hold Paula on her reins with one hand and carrying a shopping bag with the other.

After winding the car window down, a large cigar had appeared just before he did. 'Maisie. A word.'

He'd laughed when Paula left smudged hand marks on the gleaming black vehicle. Anyone else, he would have more than had a word with them. He wouldn't quite have cut their hands off but would have made it clear that nobody messed up his belongings. But, in a way, Paula was one of his belongings. He firmly believed she was his granddaughter.

'I've just been to Pratt and Dibble. My solicitors,' he'd added when Maisie failed to recognise the name. 'It's all settled. I'm Paula's legal guardian and am willing to let you adopt her. It's all done proper.'

Maisie had gasped and covered her mouth with one hand. 'Oh,' she'd exclaimed. 'I don't believe it.'

'If I say it is, then it is. Sorted Mavis.' He'd winked. 'As I told you, she loves money and fears me. I told her what I would do – one way and another. She never could resist me.'

He'd winked again. Maisie didn't ask whether he'd gone to see Carole's mother in person or had left it to the lawyers.

'I'll get the legal papers to you. You 'ave to sign them.'

She had been all aquiver. 'Thank you, Eddie. You cannot know how happy you've made me. I don't know how I'll ever repay you.'

His white teeth were interspersed with more gold teeth than she remembered him having. Daylight had made one of them glint like a falling star when he'd grinned and said, 'That's easy. Take care of my little girl. Bring 'er up right. That's all I ask.'

The world was moving on from war and every day seemed to bring something – even a very small thing – to confirm that. This morning, she had received the news that Sid would be docking in a week's time.

She looked from the latest telegram to where Paula was playing with a rag doll that Bridget had sent her. Her blonde curls bounced around her face just as Carole's had done. She was wearing the silver locket containing a lock of her mother's hair around her neck. Maisie allowed her to wear it, her reasoning being that the child would get used to having it with her, always connecting the locket with her mother.

What would Sid think about Paula? There was no way she could marry him if he refused to accept Paula. Ted, on the other hand, had stated unequivocally that he would.

She needed to talk things over with a close friend. Bridget was still in London prior to taking passage to the States. Phyllis was close at hand but had not visited as promised in a letter she'd sent.

Although Phyllis had not said in so many words, Maisie read between the lines and surmised the reason why. She couldn't leave Mick.

Maisie badly wanted to see her and as such the only option was for her to visit Phyllis unannounced.

'We're going for a bus ride,' she pronounced to Paula. 'Uncle Mick isn't very well, so Auntie Phyllis finds it difficult to come and see us, so we'll go and see her. Would you like that?'

Paula immediately fetched her new shoes and coat from the hallstand – more gifts from Eddie Bridgeman. Even if he couldn't find the time to call himself, he sent postal orders or even his driver with a crisp white five-pound note.

* * *

It took about an hour to reach the growing row of single-storey houses that were gradually taking over what had been fields. The city was growing and every one of these new houses was needed.

Paula pointed excitedly. The prefabs were so different to what she was used to. The streets in and around Totterdown dated from Victorian times.

'Do you think they look like dolls' houses, sweetheart?'

'Yes.'

A tired-looking Phyllis brightened on seeing the two of them standing there. 'Maisie! I can't believe it.' She placed a finger against her lips. 'Shh. Mick's having a lie-down. Come on in.'

Maisie marvelled at the interior of the little house. 'It's lovely. So light. Not like my place.' She pulled a face.

'Well. I suppose we have to be thankful for small mercies.'

Maisie guessed that deep down Phyllis really wished that things could have been as her and Mick had planned. A small prefab didn't compare favourably with a vineyard in the vast space that was Australia.

Once she'd made tea, Phyllis suggested they drank it outside.

'The garden's beginning to come together. An old man from along the road comes by with plants and advice. Both are free,' she added with a smile. 'We've got deckchairs along here at the end of the house. Mick won't be disturbed if we speak quietly.'

In order that they could talk in peace, Phyllis gave Paula a packet of seeds and a trowel. She pointed where she could dig and set the seeds in the warm earth.

'I'm so glad you came.'

Maisie sipped at her tea. 'I needed to. Sid's coming home.'

'That's marvellous!'

'He doesn't know yet about Paula. I did tell him about Carole and her baby, but he doesn't know what's happened. I need to talk it over with you.'

'Of course you do.' Phyllis regarded her friend with a concerned frown between her eyebrows.

'What do I do? Be blunt and tell him right from the start or leave it until the moment's right?'

Phyllis noted Maisie's fingers were playing with the cup, then the saucer, cradling both in her lap and eyeing the surface of the warm liquid it held. Phyllis felt for her. 'It's not an easy decision to make.'

'What would you do?'

Phyllis took a deep breath as she considered. 'If it was my own child, I would be open.' She frowned suddenly. 'I'm not sure what I would do in your situation. I suppose it all depends how attached you are to Sid.'

Maisie met her pitying gaze. A small frown fluttered between her eyebrows.

Phyllis took a deep breath. 'I think, Maisie, that only you can know the answer to that.'

Paula sang softly to herself as she scattered seeds over the earth and patted it down with a trowel. Her voice got steadily louder and more confident as she struck up 'Mary, Mary Quite Contrary'.

Maisie became suddenly aware that she had stopped singing and got to her feet. She was staring at the back door. Even before she looked round, Maisie knew that it was Mick standing there.

'Mick.' Phyllis went to him, smiling nervously. 'My friend Maisie's come to see me. And that's Paula,' she added.

Paula was standing shyly, clutching Maisie's skirt and half hidden. Her bright blue eyes were wide and her rosebud mouth hung slightly open. The tip of her pink tongue showed, hesitant like a small bird thinking of leaving the next.

There was no welcome in Mick's expression, more a questioning look. Since moving in here, he'd become something of a recluse, speaking infrequently unless he had to. The most he ever said was on hospital appointments and even then only when he had to. At home, he said little to her and never answered the door. Sometimes he stood at the kitchen or living-room window watching Mr Hargreaves tending the garden. The old man straightened to mop at his brow, spotted Mick and nodded in his direction. Mick had nodded back but still said nothing.

Now there was Maisie and a little girl with incredibly bright blonde hair. He stared at her and Paula stared back. The pink tongue retreated. A small finger pointed.

'Daddy?'

Maisie shook her head and Phyllis bit her lip. Both had tears in their eyes.

'No, darling,' said Maisie, bending her knees so that her face was level with that of Paula. 'This is Uncle Mick.'

'Mummy,' she said, pointing now at Maisie.

Maisie gasped. Never had Paula called her that. Tears filled her eyes and her heart filled with joy. 'Yes. I am now,' said Maisie, her bottom lip quivering.

Phyllis stood with her head bowed, rubbing at her arms. She didn't know what to say. The situation was not just awkward, it was extremely sad, and there was only one cause. Anger surged up from inside. 'This bloody war! All we're getting now is about rebuilding. But they're talking about buildings,' she shouted her eyes blazing. 'Not people. How do you rebuild people?'

Blind with tears, she pushed past Mick and ran into the house. Letting go of Paula's hand, Maisie ran in after her, calling her name. She found her in floods of tears, head in her hands.

'I don't think I can take much more.'

Maisie placed an arm around shoulders heaving with sobs. She buried her face in hair smelling of Palmolive. She fancied she smelt a sweeter smell she couldn't quite place.

'I'll give you the number of the phone box at the end of the street. You can phone me if you want someone to talk to. I passed your telephone box. It shouldn't be too difficult.'

Maisie felt, rather than saw, Phyllis's nod of agreement, squeezed her eyes shut and wished and wished she could turn the clock back to peacetime. Things had seemed so much simpler then.

Coming out from behind her hands, Phyllis blew her nose into a clean handkerchief Maisie gave her. 'I love Mick dearly, but I'm finding it hard. He won't even touch me. It's as if he's gone into himself and I can't seem to reach him. At times, I blame myself. I know it's stupid. But it seems that no matter what I do I can't seem to break through.' She shook her head as she gazed up into Maisie's face. 'I want this marriage to work, Maisie. But...'

'There, there.' Maisie hugged her close again, just as she might do Paula. She looked over Phyllis's head to the sideboard where she espied a used glass and a bottle of port. The bottle was almost empty. Now she knew where the sweet smell came from. Phyllis was drowning her sorrows in drink.

It wasn't the sudden realisation about Phyllis drinking that made Maisie spring to her feet. 'Oh my goodness. Paula!'

She ran out into the garden. Phyllis followed her.

Paula was gone and so too was Mick.

23

Within minutes of Phyllis and Maisie rushing inside the house, the little girl was standing immediately in front of Mick, looking up at him with those big round eyes.

Mick had found himself thinking back to home and his nephews and nieces, bouncing around, laughing and shouting, dragging him into their games. They'd made him laugh too and he'd found himself acting like a kid again himself.

Suddenly her small hand had been in his. She looked up at him appealingly.

'Walk?'

Her hand was warm in his, her expression and plaintive question irresistible.

Without really thinking, he walked with her around the side of the house and down the path to the front gate. Having barely left the house since moving in, he had no idea of where a decent walk might take him. He was quite likely to get lost. But Paula was clinging to his hand and he couldn't bring himself to let her down. Eventually, he found himself at the gate of a cottage.

'Off for a walk are ya?'

Unseen, Mr Hargreaves had limped up behind him. He was smoking a pipe and his merry eyes went from Mick to Paula.

'And who might this be?'

'Paula,' she said without a trace of shyness.

'I'm Bill. Do you like flowers?'

She nodded.

'Better show you some then, ain't we?'

Mick had not said a word and Bill didn't press him. He just led them along the pavement to where the last scarlet roses tumbled over the wall, their scent mixing with that of vegetables ready to be harvested.

An inner voice threatened to drag Mick back out of the tumultuous disarray of the cottage garden and go home. Though he was loath to admit it, the little single-storey house had become somewhere to hide away from the world and at times it felt as though his world was becoming even smaller. After all, he no longer had a place in the bigger world and perhaps, just perhaps, he wouldn't be around for much longer at all. The doctors had said...

Bill was limping badly. Mick hadn't noticed it until that moment. Neither had he noticed that the old man was missing two fingers.

He stopped torturing himself right then. Bill was saying something, pointing out his favourite plants. Paula was following his lead, pointing out the ones she liked best, and Bill was telling her their name.

'Golden rod.'

'Moon daisies.'

'Buttercups.'

He rattled them off quickly until she pointed at the profusion of scarlet poppies sticking their heads up through tall grass turned gold by the summer sun.

'Poppies.'

Paula touched their centres as their delicate petals fluttered each time they swayed in the breeze.

Bill cleared his throat. 'Do you like them the best?'

She nodded. 'Lots of poppies.'

Bill straightened. He took out a handkerchief from his waistcoat pocket and flicked at his eyes. 'Not so many as I seen.'

Mick heard the abject sorrow in his voice. He saw his injuries.

'Where did you fight?'

Bill shook his head. 'Too many places. The best thing about them battles weren't winning them. Or even surviving them. It was the poppies that began to grow the moment the army moved on.' He smiled through his tears. 'Like them scarlet poppies, life goes on.' He turned towards the house and beckoned Mick to follow. Paula picked flowers, mostly daisies and poppies.

The bench they sat on looked homemade, planks of rough wood joined onto pieces of curved iron. They looked as though they might once have circled beer barrels.

'Do you smoke?' Bill asked.

'Yes.'

He retrieved a packet of Woodbines from the pocket of his short-sleeved woolly.

Bill sat beside him puffing gently on an old-fashioned brier pipe. Together they watched Paula making her way amongst the flowers.

Mick was moved enough to remark how peaceful it was.

Bill nodded. 'You've got to 'ave known war to really appreciate peace.'

Without meaning to do so, Mick began to tell him the plans he'd had for after the war, about Australia, growing vines and bringing up a family in a country where the sun shone far more than it did in England. He told him about his injury and how he'd had to settle for a small prefab in Bristol rather than a home surrounded by space and the smell of growing vines.

When he'd finished, he waited for Bill to make comment. But the older man said nothing and when Mick looked at him, he was gazing into the distance, his eyes narrowed behind a veil of smoke.

Pipe protruding from the corner of his mouth, he finally pronounced, 'It ain't where you are, my boy. It's finding joy with who yer with and what you do. And give yerself thinking time to remember all you've been through. Our memories will be with us until the end of our days. It ain't always easy to face them. That's why I grow so many poppies. I'd grow thousands of them for the fallen if I could and even then it wouldn't be enough. So I go on living, because no matter where and what the circumstances, that's what they wanted to do.'

Mick fell to silence. Around him, the birds were singing and so was Paula. The wind disturbed the branches of trees, what remained of the wisteria hanging like bunches of faded grapes around the cottage. There was a sense of peace here but also of history, of all the years gone before when other men had gone off to be soldiers.

Whilst deep in thought, something fluttered against his cheek. It was Paula stroking his face with a bright red poppy and giggling when she found she'd disturbed him.

* * *

It hadn't taken Phyllis and Maisie too long to discover where Mick and Paula had got to. Maisie had pushed open the garden gate, fully expecting Paula to run into her arms. Instead, she saw her chatting animatedly to Mick and an elderly gentleman with grey hair and whiskers.

A bouquet of straggling, half-dead flowers was pressed into her hands and Paula looked very pleased with herself.

After Maisie had left with the tired little girl in her arms, head resting on her shoulder, Phyllis returned from the bus stop to the house.

Mick was waiting for her, standing beside the sideboard. He'd poured what remained of the port into two separate glasses.

She stood, petrified, unsure of where this was leading.

He handed her one of the glasses and took the other for himself. The empty bottle remained on the sideboard.

'I reckon us two still got a future together, no matter where we are. Here's to us.'

When they clinked glasses, it felt to Phyllis as though a window had opened deep inside and fresh air had rushed in to somewhere that had been dark and stuffy.

There was only beans on toast for supper. Mick told her he would empty the kitchen bin and lock up. She heard him lift the dustbin cover outside next to the back door. She heard the sound of breaking glass as the empty bottle of port was thrown away. Her spirit soared as she waited for him to come to bed.

For the first time in a very long time, he reached for her. His touch was gentle, his movements slow.

She wanted to remind him that there must be no jerky movements, that he had to be careful.

'I'll be careful,' he said to her, 'but we've got a lot more living to do. Nothing's over until it's over.'

24

With Paula tugging on a pair of pink leather reins, Maisie went in and out of the shops that had become familiar to her when working at W. D. &. H. O. Wills.

On spotting a horse-drawn fruit and vegetable cart, Paula pretended to be a horse and sent the bells on her harness tinkling merrily.

'Come on, horsey. I've got more shopping to do.'

By the time they got to Woolworths, Maisie's shopping bag was full.

'Maisie. I thought that was you.' Ted tipped his hat. 'Do you fancy a coffee in Carwardines?'

Maisie pulled a face in Paula's direction and suggested that an ice cream in Verecchia's might be better.

He smiled such a nice smile, one of understanding and perfect accord with her meaning. 'Better get in there then.'

The ice cream parlour had folding doors, three of which were pulled back to allow both customers and fresh air inside. Not being a smoker, Maisie chose a seat away from those who were eating ice cream at the same time as smoking a cigarette.

Paula's eyes almost popped out of her head at the ice cream sundae that appeared in front of her. Maisie had coffee in a cup and a vanilla slice sprinkled with chocolate. Ted had the same.

Ted watched as Paula scooped ice cream. A blob of it sat on her nose. Ted flicked it off with his finger and ate it. He laughed and Paula laughed too before she curved her hand around the dish and pulled it towards her.

'Looks like that's all I'm going to get,' Ted remarked and shook his head. 'I can understand you wanting to take her on. She's a lovely little kid. Anyone else would do the same.'

Maisie nodded. 'I certainly think so.'

Ted paused between a bite of vanilla slice and a sip of coffee before quietly asking if Paula knew her mother had 'passed over', as he put it.

Normally Maisie would dislike that turn of phrase, but she understood he didn't want to use the word death in front of Paula.

'She knows her mother's not coming back. I'll explain better when she's older.' Her eyes fastened on the little girl with heartfelt affection. 'She's been through enough for now. We all have.'

Being a perceptive chap, Ted latched onto the look that suddenly came to her eyes. 'Is your beau home soon?'

She dug her spoon into the vanilla slice and left it there as she answered. 'Next week.'

Ted jerked his chin at Paula who, having finished her sundae, was running her finger around the inside of the dish before tipping it onto her face so she could lick it clean. 'Does he know about her?'

'No. Not really. That is, he knew that someone with a baby was living with me. But not that I'm going to adopt her.'

'You weren't sure about that.'

'I am now.' Her eyes sparkled as she tipped her coffee cup until the last dreg was gone. 'She's been paid off by Carole's father. He wants me to bring her up. He's made me the happiest woman in the world.'

Ted winced before shaking his head in disbelief. 'Fancy that.'

'He trusts me to look after her. Besides... he is her grandfather. He's got as much right as the grandmother.' It wasn't necessarily true. Carole's mother had hinted that Eddie Bridgeman was not Carole's father. Maisie didn't so much refuse to believe that seeing as Carole's mother had put herself about a bit, it was just that she didn't want to. Anyway, Eddie had paid the awful woman enough money to have her lie to her high teeth if she had to.

Ted fiddled with his cup. Half of his vanilla slice remained on his place. 'You know where I am if you need me. I mean if you and Sid should ever decide that it won't work.'

His sheepish look caused him to look downwards, then away, then back to her, as though he might have overstepped the mark and might also be disappointed.

Maisie reached out and caressed the edge of his hand with her thumb, her brown eyes shining into his. She smiled. 'Ted, you're a sweet man and if things were different I wouldn't 'esitate. But I must see if Sid and I still 'ave something in common. You do understand that, don't you?'

His smile was hesitant and his nod of agreement was reluctant. 'I live in 'ope,' he said to her. 'I can walk you to the bus stop if you like.' He glanced at his wristwatch. 'I've got just about enough time.'

The clocking-on times at the factory were set in stone and through her years of adhering to them, Maisie knew that he would be late if he did come to the bus stop. 'I've got a bit more shopping to do, but thanks anyway.' The truth was she didn't have any more shopping but didn't want him to be late getting back and having his pay docked. 'I fancy some cockles in Bryant's,' she said and pointed in the direction she intended going.

Whether he believed it or not, he smiled as though he did. Once she'd used a handkerchief to wipe Paula's sticky features, she went out through the gap left by the open sliding doors. Outside, she paused, awkward for once and feeling guilty that yet again she'd scuppered Ted's hopes.

'I'm sorry, Ted.'

He adopted a cheery smile. 'Oh well. I live in 'ope.' The smile failed to travel to his eyes.

* * *

It had been some time since Maisie had received a letter from her brother Alf. In his last letter, he'd assured her that he was taking care of himself. She didn't doubt it but would have liked something in writing. She dreamed of him that night and when she awoke, he was still in her head. Perhaps today she would receive something from him. Just as Ted had said to her yesterday, she lived in hope.

On answering a brisk banging at the front door, she found herself facing a man with sun-darkened skin and dark dancing eyes. His smile lit up her day, especially once he mentioned having a message from Alf.

'He told me to give you this.' He pushed a wooden box towards her. 'And this.' He passed her a brown manila envelope. 'Bananas,' he said, pointing at the box. 'We just brought in the first boatload since this war began.'

Maisie spent so much time staring down at the box that she completely forgot to invite him in for a cup of tea. By the time she came to herself, he was gone. There was nothing left to do except manhandle the box along the passageway and into the kitchen. The box was made of cheap wood. The top two straps were easily broken and inside...

She wanted to toot a trumpet but instead settled for dancing around the kitchen with a bundle of bananas on her head. It had been such a long time and she couldn't stop laughing or singing.

'Look,' she said to Paula who had come to see what she was laughing and singing about. She handed her a banana. Paula held it with both chubby hands. 'It's to eat,' Maisie said to her.

Paula immediately put the unpeeled fruit into her mouth.

'No, darling,' said Maisie, took it back from her and showed her how to peel it.

Whilst Paula enjoyed the feast, Maisie read his letter.

Hi sis,

This is just to let you know that I'm not sure I will ever be home again. I'm in Jamaica. I've met somebody I'm happy with. Thing is, nobody out here cares that our relationship is a bit different. I'm a bit different, but then you already know that. Obi (short for Obidahya) has landed a job on the first banana boat to cross the Atlantic since this war began. It'll be his last trip east. Our intention is to buy a boat, do it up ourselves and sail into the Pacific. We want to be as far as possible from war. We've heard of uninhabited islands and quite fancy being alone together for a while. In the meantime, take care of yourself, sis. Think of me when the sun goes down and raise a toast – even if it's only in tea.

Enjoy your life,

Love Alf

Although inclined to run out and see if Alf's friend Obi was still around, she knew it was futile. If only she'd read the letter first, but just the smell of the bananas was irresistible. It had been so long. Such a simple thing but it said it all. Normal was something of a luxury but she couldn't help but welcome it whatever it was.

25

Eddie Bridgeman came calling with the adoption papers for Maisie to sign.

'I've already signed. Now it's your turn.' He made his way into the living room, took off his brown trilby hat and, without being invited, slumped into one of the leather armchairs placed either side of the fireplace.

Spreading the legal documents out on the dining table, Maisie's heart raced like a train as she read the details. It was all there in black and white. From now on, Paula would be her responsibility.

'I can't believe this is happening,' she said, breathless with excitement.

'The kid needs to be with someone who loves 'er. That's what I told that selfish cow Mavis.'

'So you said. She must 'ave been surprised.'

He nodded. 'Yeah. Used a load of petrol to get up there but figured it was worth it when she accepted my offer. Not that I 'ad any doubt that she would. It was always money with 'er.'

'Did she take much persuading?'

'A bit.'

A bit. What did that mean? Having known him both personally and by reputation for some years, it could be there had been violence.

'I suppose she's still with the same man?'

He shrugged. 'Don't know. Don't care. I wouldn't be surprised if she's gone off with another bloke. That one she was with looked a bit past it to me.'

Without bothering to ask for permission, he lit up a cigar and puffed it three times before smoke curled snakelike from its end.

He mistook her shocked expression. 'I didn't do anything to 'er.' A cynical expression coupled with amusement lifted one eyebrow, almost as though he was daring her to probe further. One corner of his mouth rose in a half-smile. 'Bloody tempting, though. I told 'er to write and confirm to you that Paula was yours. I should 'ave known she couldn't be bothered. And anyway I'm a man able to pay for the best legal advice.' He grinned. 'I didn't do away with 'er.'

She didn't voice her thoughts but knew he was hinting at the demise of Paula's father, the man who'd taken advantage of a young woman without realising who her father was.

'Forgive us our trespasses.' He pronounced the excerpt of the Lord's Prayer as though reading her mind and it made her smile. Eddie Bridgeman had done plenty of trespassing in his time.

A hesitant smile accompanied a slow shake of her head. 'Eddie, I don't care what you did in the past as long as whatever you've done now means Paula stays with me. For that I'll forgive you anything.'

He flicked at the brim of his hat before setting it on his head. Never had she heard him laugh so uproariously.

'You're a cheeky little madam, Maisie Miles. But you've got a 'eart of gold.' His expression turned serious. A finger stained by nicotine wagged in front of her face. 'Never doubt that I'll be there for you and the little 'un. Whatever you want, just come and see me.'

'I will. And never fear, I'll always be there for Paula.' She laughed herself suddenly. 'You know, for a while I thought you might get married and adopt her.'

He looked at her as though she'd taken leave of her senses before again breaking out with riotous laughter.

'No bloody chance of that.'

He was still laughing as he headed out of the front door and giving a last wave before he got into his car and drove away.

26

'Are you sure you'll be all right by yourself?'

Mick reached for a piece of toast and carried on reading as though he hadn't heard her.

Phyllis pulled the newspaper down to expose his face. His earlier bouts of bad temper had passed. 'I asked you if you'd be all right until I get back from the job interview.'

He gave a lopsided grin. 'I'm a big boy now, Mummy!'

'Mick Fairbrother! Stop making fun.'

She flipped a hand at the newspaper he'd brought back up to cover his face, exposing the grin he'd been hiding.

Throwing the paper to one side, he slowly got to his feet. His arms encircled her waist. 'My darling, there but for the grace of God go I.'

She pouted. 'There. You're making fun again.'

He drew her close and kissed her full on the lips. 'My darling, I can assure you that I'm not. My pension won't keep us in luxuries, that's for sure. A woman needs a bit extra. We both need a bit extra.' His look softened from humour to deep affection. 'I can't emphasise my admiration enough. You're a brave girl, that's for sure.'

He escorted her to the front door and stood there waving until the sound of her footsteps had faded away. Then he went back into the house and out to the kitchen. He'd hidden his boots beneath the kitchen sink. With an air of trepidation, like a small boy who's about to play truant, he pulled back the green gingham curtain hiding the pipes beneath the sink and pulled out his boots. For the first time in a long while, he felt excited at the day ahead.

Once he was ready, Mick locked the front door behind him and headed along the road to Mr Hargreaves, Bill as he'd been told to call him.

The old man was almost bent double pulling weeds and trimming roses. He looked up when Mick called to him and waved.

'Need a hand?'

Bill nodded. 'Pull them weeds over there. Make yer own pile. This one's big enough.'

The pile of weeds and cuttings was indeed high.

Mick set to, pulling weeds and borrowing a spare set of secateurs to trim other blowsy shrubs.

He didn't know how long he pulled and cut but was glad when Bill suggested they take a break and have a smoke and a cup of tea.

Bill produced a flask. Mick swigged back a few mouthfuls of the sweet tea.

A robin flew down and began pecking at the ground disturbed by the pulling of weeds.

'As I've already told you, it was never the plan to settle in England. The plan was to go back to Australia and plant vines. I've drank Italian and French wine but thought I could do better. As it is my injury won't allow me to travel – not yet anyway.' Mick had no idea what had led to him telling Bill all this, unloading all the angst he'd kept hidden inside. 'I keep hoping, not that I've said as such to Phyllis. I feel I've let her down, promised the earth and not been able to deliver. I want to spoil her – after all she's done and all I've put her through.'

Bill continued to smoke in silence. Once the contents of his pipe had turned to ash, he tapped the bowl on the wall of the house and got to his feet.

Mick followed him and watched as the old man picked up the secateurs and snipped at the late-blooming rose bushes. What looked to be a dozen roses were laid on the ground, red, yellow and white, their perfume strong and smelling of summer.

Bill folded them into a doubled piece of newspaper. 'Take these for your good lady to come home to. That'll surprise her.'

Mick cradled the bundle in his arm.

'Have you got a vase to put them in?' Bill asked.

Mick shrugged. 'I don't know.'

'Wait here.'

Bill went into the greenhouse and came back with a white enamel jug edged with blue.

'Take this.'

'That's very kind of you, Mr Hargreaves.'

'I told you. Call me Bill.'

'Yes. I will.'

He fancied there were tears in the old man's eyes. 'Women are like roses. Lovely to look at and smelling of heaven. Just like roses, they need looking after. Do that my boy. All that matters in this world is the two of you facing it together. I can vouch for that.'

His voice was sad. Mick didn't need Bill to tell him that he'd loved his wife and missed her.

Mick touched one of the blooms. The petal was soft, just like Phyllis's hair.

'After you've done that and 'ad a bit of lunch, come back and we can sort out some plants for your garden. What time do you expect her back?'

'About three, unless she meets up with an old friend.'

'That'll do 'er good. It did my missus good to get out. I could be a bit down in the dumps sometimes, you know, fretting about all I seen. At first, she used to think it was something she'd done, but after a good chat and a drop of water glowing under the bridge, we made allowances. That's how it must be.'

27

It occurred to Phyllis that the same butterflies that had whirled in her stomach at an earlier interview were repeating their acrobatic prowess now. The entrance to W. D. &. H. O. Wills was just as intimidating as that first time when she'd come for a job straight from school.

She was directed to the office where Miss Cayford used to hold sway. Having married and gone abroad, her place had been taken by someone else. The name on the door said Mrs Prince.

Several other women and girls sat in chairs outside waiting to be interviewed. Phyllis thought she recognised some of them but was too nervous to take much notice.

Fingers tightly interlaced, she sat staring straight ahead, hoping she wouldn't break out into a sweat. In the past, she'd often perspired when nervous, though wasn't sure of the last time it had happened. Or, for that matter, the last time she was this nervous. The island of Malta sprang to mind. *After enduring that much danger, I probably don't have any nerves left*, she thought.

A woman sat down in the spare seat next to her. A swift glance confirmed she was quite well dressed and her hair was peroxide blonde. She was also quite plump, though pleasantly so.

The blonde-topped head tilted sideways and looked up into her face. 'Didn't you used to be Phyllis Mason? One of the three Ms?'

Phyllis looked at her and tried to work out where she'd seen her before. 'Do I know you?'

Bright red lips stretched into a smile that revealed yellowish teeth. 'Yeah. Only briefly mind. You came to me mum's funeral. I'm Angela Hill. My mum was Aggie Hill. She used to be in charge of the stripping room.'

Phyllis gathered her thoughts. 'Aggie's daughter?'

'That's right. Her and me old dad used to run the Llandoger Trow down in King Street. Do you remember that?'

'I do. Of course I do. Aggie was like a mother to us girls.'

'She was a good mum all right.'

Phyllis heard the catch in Angela's voice. She recalled Aggie's daughter had worked in Eddie Bridgeman's nightclub. What had happened that a glamour girl from a nightclub was now here for a job in the tobacco factory?

Angela answered the unasked question. 'I've got two kids now. Their dad's working all the hours God sends just to pay the bills, so I said I would get a job. 'E didn't like the idea at first, but once I told 'im about the free-issue fags or tobacco, he brightened up no end.'

The door with the name Mrs Prince on the door suddenly opened. A young woman came out beaming.

'Monday,' said Mrs Prince. 'And don't be late.' Her attention turned immediately to the women waiting. 'Mrs Fairbrother?'

Phyllis raised her hand and got to her feet. 'That's me.'

'Give me a minute,' said Mrs Prince and shut the door again.

'Whoops,' said Phyllis, still stood up. 'My suspender just pinged. I need the ladies' room but I can't go. I might not be here when she pokes her nose out again.'

'Lift yer skirt,' said Angela. 'I'll fasten it for you.'

So there she was standing awkwardly with Angela doing up her suspender.

'Nice stockings,' remarked Angela. 'My old man sells stockings from a case outside Woolworths. Gets some good stockings. One shilling and sixpence. 'Ave you seen 'im there?'

'No. But if I get this job, I'll keep my eyes open for him.'

Suspender secured and skirt decently hiding her stocking tops all the way to her knees, Phyllis didn't have to wait long.

'Mrs Fairbrother?'

The name on the door might have changed but the office where Miss Cayford had held sway was basically unchanged. The lower panes of the windows were still covered in wire. A large spider plant draped its shoots over the side of the filing cabinet. A few other plants whose names she did not know took up almost the length of the windowsill. She found herself wondering whether Miss Cayford had left them behind.

Mrs Prince wore black-rimmed spectacles and her hair was tied back in a severe bun. Her high cheekbones and firm set of mouth gave her a severe look. A little lipstick and a bouncier hairstyle would have improved her looks. Phyllis cleared her mind. She wasn't here to give the woman advice. Mrs Prince was commenting on the file containing Phyllis's work record.

'I understand that your name was Mason before you married and became Mrs Harvey. You were married whilst you worked here?'

'Yes.'

A frown appeared in the clear forehead. 'You had a different married name than the one you have now.'

'Yes. Robert was my first husband. I met my present husband when I was stationed in Malta.'

Mrs Prince sat back in her chair and took off her spectacles. At first, Phyllis interpreted her look as incredulous, then decided it was more admiration.

'You served in Malta?'

'Yes.'

'They had a bit of a bashing.'

Phyllis nodded again. 'Yes.' She found herself unable to elaborate on how it had been. She looked down at her gloved hands. In her mind, the memories came flooding through the barrier she had erected to keep them at bay. At the time, she'd coped well with everything. It was only now, after the event, it hit her just how much she and her colleagues and the people of the island had endured.

Mrs Prince's next question shut it all out. 'Your first husband died?'

'Yes.'

Phyllis had the impression that Mrs Prince would have liked her to explain further, but as with the Malta episode, she wouldn't. Robert had got left behind following Dunkirk. He'd come back a changed man, his mind damaged by all that he'd seen and been through. He had taken his own life. Although their marriage had not been happy, she felt strangely protective of his memory.

Mrs Prince said nothing more but turned her attention back to Phyllis's work record. 'You've no children.'

'No.'

'Do you think you ever will?'

Phyllis tore her eyes away from her fidgeting fingers. 'I don't know. My husband was in the air force, he sustained a head injury when a bomb exploded close by on the island of Malta. The doctors aren't sure whether he'll ever be the same again. He's still an invalid. That's why I need to come back to work. With his pension and a wage, we'll manage. I need this job, Mrs Prince. I really need it.'

A smile fluttered around the thin lips, then widened. 'Of course you do. When can you start? And here. Take these.' She handed her a packet of five Woodbines. 'To celebrate,' she added. 'We are in great need of experienced people here. I'm offering you a supervisory role. Do you accept?'

'Oh yes. Yes. I do.'

* * *

Once outside in East Street and feeling both elated and relieved, Phyllis took a lungful of air. Her hands trembled as she took a cigarette out of the packet and lit it.

Shoppers loaded down with groceries staggered past, as did young women pushing prams, toddlers holding on to their skirts or fastened to the pram handle with jingling leather reins.

Her gaze followed those children and their mothers. A pang of regret tightened like wire mesh around her heart. If her daughter had lived, she too would have been their age by now – a little older, in fact.

'Well, I'm glad that's over.'

The speaker was Angela, Aggie's daughter.

'Got one to spare,' she asked, nodding at Phyllis's cigarette.

'Did she take you on?'

Angela nodded through a thick cloud of cigarette smoke. 'Yeah. I only wanted part time. Explained to 'er about the kids. She said that would be all right for now but would look at it again in six months. 'Ope they don't get rid of me when that comes round.'

'I doubt it. This country is on its knees. It's going to need all the workers it can get.'

'Hope so. Fancy going for a coffee?'

Phyllis glanced up at the big old clock hanging from a wrought-iron bracket high on the factory wall. The minute hand jerked, making her feel just a bit guilty for wanting to take Angela up on the offer when Mick would be waiting for her.

Her decision was made for her when her bus sailed past.

'Well,' she said decisively, throwing her cigarette butt into the gutter, 'there goes my bus.'

* * *

Carwardines wasn't too busy and a table was available.

A waitress came to take their order. Phyllis ordered tea and Angela ordered a teacake to go with hers and Phyllis said she would have one too.

'With loads of butter, mind you,' Angela demanded of the waitress.

Phyllis felt a little embarrassed, especially when the teacakes came and Angela ate hers in double quick time, followed by the half a teacake Phyllis couldn't manage.

They talked mostly about the war, Angela's mum and how Angela had been bombed out when living in a basement flat in Stokes Croft.

'Like that scene from *Gone with the Wind*, it was. A wall of flame. Bloody frightening, I can tell you.'

Not once did she mention her relationship with Eddie Bridgeman. Phyllis concluded that like a lot of things with this war there were going to be some things best forgotten.

The waitress brought the bill.

'Two and six,' said Phyllis.

Angela patted her coat pockets with a look of pure consternation. Phyllis guessed what was coming next.

'Bloody 'ell. Sorry about this, but I've left me purse at 'ome. Can I pay my 'alf when I sees you next?'

Phyllis said that it was all right. She also reminded Angela that it wasn't long until they began – or in her case – resumed work at the factory.

'You can settle with me then.'

* * *

Phyllis thought about Angela Hill on the bus on the way home, how glamorous she'd once been, how full of herself and downright difficult with her parents. Five years of war had marked her – just like everyone else.

As she got nearer home, she began worrying about Mick. She was late and she didn't want things to slide backwards. He'd been more like his old self of late and she wanted him to stay that way. She walked faster, so fast that she became breathless.

'Mick,' she called on entering the house.

There was no reply.

She went from room to room and peered into the bedroom with her heart in her mouth. Pray God he was only asleep and that something hadn't moved in his brain and taken him away from her. Not now. Not now they had patched things up between them.

He wasn't there, but something had changed. Perfume filled the air. A vase full of red, yellow and white roses sat in the middle of the table.

A rattly, trundling sound came from outside. When she looked out, there was Mick pushing a wheelbarrow. She gasped in amazement, her hand against her heart. A bunch of roses and a garden that was slowly filling up with plants.

Tugging the back door open, she ran into his arms. 'Oh Mick. I wondered where you were. You really must be careful.'

'My hands are dirty,' he exclaimed into the soft luxuriousness of her hair.

'And everything in the garden is lovely,' she exclaimed through a flood of tears.

'It will be,' he said, stroking her hair. 'I guarantee it will be.'

28

Bridget brought the carry cot into her old home. The moment she set it down on the sofa, her siblings were around her baby like a flock of inquisitive starlings.

Her father pronounced that her mother would have had him christened by now.

'The family have arranged it. They make a big event of it.'

There were certain things she'd never get used to with the wealthy family she'd married into. One was that she could afford almost anything she wanted – which in a way made her feel guilty. She'd been used to having little. That mindset was now a thing of the past, but still she had trouble getting used to it.

Katie and Mary insisted they be allowed to look after him.

Ethel came in with a cake.

'I thought seeing as we're all together.'

Ethel had a round pretty face and twinkling eyes. She looked every inch the motherly or even grandmotherly type. Children were what she lived for.

Bridget answered everything her siblings asked her about the baby, about her nice clothes, about whether they could visit her in America. She said that they could.

The cake was large but quickly polished off. Once it was gone, Bridget helped Ethel take the used crockery into the kitchen. Her father offered to do it, but she insisted he must keep an eye on his children and the baby.

This, she'd decided, was a convenient time to talk to Ethel about what had happened to her children.

Ethel sighed. Her hands, pink from being immersed in the dish-water, paused in the task of bringing a tea plate out of the water.

'They told me they'd have a good life, but I knew they were lying.'

Bridget frowned. 'How did you know?'

Ethel wiped her hands on a tea towel. 'I met the father of a young lad who did come back. The father had been away fighting. He had a cousin out there – a lawyer who made enquiries. He tracked the lad down. Caused a right ruckus, so I understand. Anyway, the boy got back believing 'imself an orphan. That's what they tell them.'

Bridget couldn't believe what she was hearing and yet it was exactly what she'd deduced would have happened to her if things had turned out differently. 'That's horrible.'

Ethel nodded. 'I want them back.' There was fighting spirit in her tone and on her face. 'Yer dad's already written and so's our lawyer friend. Nothing can replace yer children. Every day I think of them. Their dad's dead and gone. There's no point in grieving for him. But for my kids? I'll grieve for them until the day they come back through the front door.'

* * *

The day Maisie had long expected finally arrived. Sid was coming home.

His mother sent her a note that she was poorly so couldn't be there. *Tell 'im I'll 'ave 'is tea on the table. Bubble and squeak with bacon.*

Maisie got there half an hour before the train was expected, her heart racing and her hands sticky with perspiration.

The half-hour passed. Then another half an hour.

Nervously, she paced the platform and levered her weight from one foot to the other.

She'd wanted to get this over with, to have him home once and for all. She couldn't make any kind of decision until then.

Fifteen minutes. She'd been waiting for over an hour. Where was he?

She looked up at the stiffly moving hands and Roman numerals of the station clock, hanging there amidst a wreath of smoke and steam. The station was busy, trains coming and going on a regular basis, and the platform was packed with the families of those returning home.

Men carrying kitbags, men in uniform, men in civvies; women too.

'Isn't it marvellous,' said a woman standing close to her. 'Home. At last they're home.'

The woman's heavily made-up eyes were sparkling. They remained sparkling and her smile fixed even when she greeted her husband, though tears were rolling down her face.

'Darling!' She bent down over his wheelchair and hugged his head to her chest. 'Darling. You're home.'

Maisie watched as the woman's tears fell onto her husband's face. At first she avoided looking down at the man's legs, but the temptation was just too hard to ignore. His legs ended at his knees. Yet he looked happy and his wife looked happy. After everything he'd gone through, they still loved each other. They would have many more years together. Maisie sincerely hoped they would.

People were still thronging around those alighting from the carriages. She frowned at some of the haggard faces, clothes hanging on spare frames, eyes nervously searching the crowds for friends and relatives, parents, sweethearts, wives and children. All had once been very familiar but having been parted by a lengthy incarceration in a Japanese prisoner-of-war camp had grown older and perhaps apart.

The crowds pressed close and most of them all seemed much taller than her. She tried standing on tiptoe, but the crush was tight and steam from a train pulling out from another platform obstructed her vision.

'Where is he?'

Fear took hold and sent her heart racing. The first train to arrive was for those who didn't have life-threatening injuries. There was another train behind for those who needed stretchers and medical staff travelling with them.

Taking a deep breath of the gritty air, she mentally reread Sid's last missive. Nowhere had he mentioned being badly incapacitated. He'd sounded more reserved than usual, but that was all.

As the crowds dispersed, she found herself standing there alone. A figure at the far end of the platform emerged through the smoke and steam. For a moment she thought it was him, but as he got closer, she could see she was mistaken. Just as she realised this, a motherly figure with two children in tow ran ecstatically into his arms, her shrill voice a mix of laughter and tears.

'Rodney! Rodney!'

The two children looked up at the man. There was hesitance in their expressions – not surprising, she thought. Their father had probably been away for years. They didn't know him except as a photo on the mantelpiece or someone their mother talked to them about in an effort to remind them that he did exist.

Maisie's gaze swept up and down the platform one more time until finally accepting that Sid hadn't been on the train, that he hadn't come home. She'd left Paula with a neighbour but only until a certain time. She couldn't wait around any longer. There was nothing for it but to make her way home and wait for him to get into contact.

Disappointed but also relieved, she departed. Facing him after all this time put her nerves on edge. Would they still get on or had everything irrevocably changed? Only time would tell.

* * *

Sid swallowed and although he had lit a cigarette he hadn't inhaled a single puff of smoke.

He'd seen her from afar, had alighted from the train and taken only two steps towards her before he'd spotted his reflection in a glass window opposite and his confidence had taken a nosedive.

Sunken cheekbones accentuated angular features that he never used to have. The collar of his shirt shirked away from his scrawny neck, which in turn emphasised his Adam's apple.

He couldn't have her seeing him like this. He just couldn't.

Blending into the crowd was easy enough and panic gave wings to his feet. He hurried towards the exit and the concourse, one khaki uniform among many others. No demob suit for him until he'd put on a bit of weight. Not worth it, they'd said.

At the time, he'd felt hard done by, but now he was glad. He could head for home, where his mother would be waiting with a larder full of food. He could eat for England after the privations of the prisoner-of-war camp. Only once he looked like his old self would he seek out Maisie and perhaps, just perhaps, they could plan their future together, just the two of them walking into a happy ever after.

* * *

Maisie didn't stop worrying about what might have happened to Sid and felt at a loss to do anything about it. She told all this to Phyllis as they pulled weeds from the turned soil of the back garden at the prefab.

'Forgive me for being a misery guts,' she said after expressing the third sigh since she'd arrived. 'I was nervous about seeing him again after all this time but was getting all worked up to tell him about Paula and then he didn't turn up.'

'It could be that somebody got the muster lists wrong. Understandable, the number of men coming back, injured and otherwise.'

Maisie sighed again, then shrugged her shoulders back. 'Sorry, I can't seem to stop sighing. It's the wondering, you see. Wondering if he's injured worse than he said. Wondering if the two of us will even get on.'

'And what about Ted? It's not many girls get the choice of two men, not like you, Maisie Miles.'

Phyllis made it sound funny, but Maisie had reservations that made her unusually anxious.

Taking a tea break gave them the chance to discuss the problem further.

'I really need to speak to Sid before I make any decision about my future. And I've got Paula to think about.'

'And Sid doesn't know that you've taken her on.'

She shook her head and frowned down into what remained of her cup of tea.

'Are you going to see his mother? She might know where he is.'

'I did think of that, but, you see, Phyllis...' She paused and took a deep breath. 'I'm so nervous. I mean, me and Sid are going to be like strangers after all this time.'

'Not necessarily,' said Phyllis, her bright red lipstick leaving an imprint on the rim of her cup. 'I've known people who have known each other for years, been parted for whatever reason and struck up their old friendship as though it's only days or weeks since they've seen each other.' She was also aware that some men had come home vastly altered, strangers to both their wives and children.

'I don't know for sure if me and Sid will be like that. Still, I live in 'ope.'

The tea finished, they took the crockery into the kitchen. They paused for a moment and watched Paula digging with a small trowel at the plot her Uncle Mick said was hers.

'You and Mick are going on all right then?' Maisie asked.

'Yes,' said Phyllis, the word sounding like a sigh of relief. 'He was so disappointed when we couldn't head for Australia. We both hope that we might do some day.'

'In the meantime, he's making himself useful.' Maisie nodded at the garden where seedlings and transplanted shrubs were pushing through the earth. Beyond them, a small apple tree took centre stage amongst gooseberry, raspberry and blackcurrant bushes. 'I didn't know he was a keen gardener.'

Phyllis smiled. 'It's all thanks to Bill. They get on so well together and Bill understands how Mick feels better than I do. He's like a father to him.'

'That's good.'

'And talking of being like a father...'

There was no misunderstanding the glorious happiness making Phyllis's face shine like the sun.

'You're expecting?' Maisie gasped. 'Well, if that isn't the icing on the cake. Better than a vineyard in the sun, I should think. Does Mick think so?'

A slight strain appeared on Phyllis's face. 'He's over the moon, but it's made him even more determined to get back to Australia and fulfil his dreams.'

A shiver ran down Maisie's spine. At some point within the next few years, Phyllis would be off with Mick and her new-born to Australia.

'You'll get there. It might take a while, but I'm sure it will happen,' she said softly, and knew it would come to be.

29

BRIDGET

Since postponing her departure to America, Bridget hadn't stopped finding out more about the children who'd been sent to Australia.

To this end, she had lunch with Harry, an old friend who'd lived close to their flat but had now married his childhood sweetheart and moved out of town. He explained that he'd never really been one for city life.

'I'm a farmer's son and that's what I'm going to do. Martha is the daughter of a farmer. So how's Lyndon? I thought you would have joined him by now.'

'Oh he's fine. I just got caught up in some stuff over here.'

'Do you want to tell me about it?'

Her first inclination was to say that it would wait, but she knew it would not and neither would she. She'd lingered in this country for too long, telling herself that she couldn't leave her father all by himself. Only he wasn't by himself. He had a lady friend. Sounding a bit indignant, she'd mentioned it in a letter to Lyndon. He'd written back and told her in no uncertain terms that her father was old enough to know his own mind.

It wasn't until she was halfway through explaining about her horror on finding out about the sending of children to Australia that it came to her how much she was missing her husband. It was him she should be telling all this to. He would make the right noises in the right places, a mixture of pity and outrage, also expressing his pride in her.

In his letter, Lyndon had mentioned a new date for her departure, but the problem with letters was that there was no true nuance, tone or emotion. That only happened when people were facing each other. Everything was out in the open then. Nothing could be hidden.

'I'm going back to America shortly,' Bridget explained. 'Lyndon's booking passage for me and our baby, though I'd like to put it off until after Christmas. I'd like to spend my last Christmas here with my family and I would like to find out the truth about these children before I go. I can't help feeling angry. Shipping kids abroad from orphanages. I've managed to talk to a few people and it seems as though some of these kids were not orphans at all.' She shook her head. 'It's terrible. Just terrible.'

Harry had listened with rapt interest. Finally he said, 'Tell you what. I've got a cousin at the *Evening Standard*. What if I have a word with him. He's used to winkling out truths that people don't want winkling out.'

She burst out laughing. 'I haven't heard that word in ages. We used to go winkling on the beach at Weston-super-Mare when we were small.' A faraway look came to her eyes. 'That was when my mother was alive.' Memories melted. 'Will you do that?' she asked him.

'Yes. I will.' His eyes took on a serious look. 'As for you, Bridget O'Neill, it's time you went home. I know you're going to say that this is your home, but it's not. Not any longer.'

'Home is where the heart is,' Bridget said somewhat ruefully.

'Yes. And now I too must go. It's back to Suffolk's wide-open skies and the smell of wheat growing in the field.'

'I expect you've got a lot of work to do. I hear there's a labour shortage.'

'There is, though we've been lucky. Willem and Peter stayed on. They're German, but they don't want to go back. The town they're both from is in the Soviet zone. They've heard that the Ruskies don't trust anyone who's been in proximity with the allies – and that includes being taken a prisoner of war.'

On her way back to her flat and her baby in Chelsea, Bridget made up her mind that it was indeed time to go home. In fact she couldn't wait to get to her flat, rushing out of the taxi so quickly she almost forgot to pay him.

Once inside and with her son snuggled in her arms, she looked around the flat where she and Lyndon had been so happy together. Hardly a trace of him remained, not that masculine smell of shaving soap and cigarettes. It made her suddenly desperate to be with him. The time was now or at least very soon.

However, she wanted one more chance to see her old friends, but there was no time to write. On the off chance, she telephoned the public telephone box at the corner of the street. With a bit of luck, somebody might hear it and pick it up.

The ringing sound went on and on and finally, just when she was about to give up, somebody picked up the phone.

'Hello. I do appreciate you picking up this phone. Do you think you can take a message to Maisie Miles? I'm an old friend of hers, Bridget O'Neill. Could you tell her that I'm coming tomorrow for a fleeting visit. After that I'm off home, so goodness knows when I might see her again. Can you do that? Please?'

At first, there was no reply. She wondered if it might be children apprehensive and perhaps regretting that they'd picked up.

'Hello! Hello! Can you give her my message please?'

A male voice answered yes before the phone was put down. She could only hope that her message would get through.

* * *

Sid left the phone box, the door clanging heavily shut behind him. He thought he recognised the name, one of Maisie's old workmates. For a moment, he was undecided about what to do. Slipping his hand into his pocket, he pulled out the old photo of Maisie. During his incarceration he had directed all his hopes on that photograph. It was battered and faded now.

Taking a deep breath, he decided he'd prevaricated long enough. It had been such a long time since he'd seen her and the sudden reality check scared him. She'd written, yes, but that didn't mean she didn't have somebody else or even got married in the meantime. No matter how much he tried to reassure himself that she would have told him, the fear remained that she'd only written to keep up his spirits. God knows he'd certainly needed that!

Rumours had abounded on the ship bringing them home, in the hospital, anywhere in face where men who'd been long incarcerated away from their families shared their worst fears. He'd heard of blokes coming back to find their wives with children that couldn't possibly be theirs. Some had accepted the circumstances – the war was to blame. Others could not. In his case, he wasn't sure which way he'd swing if he found that Maisie had been unfaithful. She'd been the beacon who'd shone throughout his imprisonment. He wanted to believe that she'd been faithful. It was the only way he could see them having a future together.

He marched up and down the street, considered banging on her door, got so far, then changed his mind. It was a fairly long walk to the bus stop and all the way there he was plagued by indecision.

Back along to her street he went in a state of confusion, the indecision still with him battering like a fist against his skull.

He almost got to her door, but on seeing her step out and run after the little girl, he stalled again.

'Paula. You little minx.'

The little girl laughed back. To her, it seemed just a game. Finally, she was caught, Maisie swinging her up into the air and laughing.

'I runs faster than you, Mummy!' Paula called down at her.

He didn't hear what Maisie said in response. The child had called Maisie mummy. That one word was enough to break his heart.

Turning abruptly and blinded with tears, he tore up the photograph and marched off towards the bus stop, his world broken in two.

30

Maisie was having days of highs and lows. The high was knowing that Paula would remain with her thanks to Eddie. The low was worrying where Sid had got to. At present, she just couldn't bring herself to pay his mother a visit. What if he was there? What if he didn't want to see her?

She would have continued having a patchwork of moods if Mrs Doughty from over the street hadn't come banging on door. She looked concerned.

'Sorry to trouble you, Maisie, love, but I thought I should say that I saw some bloke watching you today. I passed 'im on the way to the bus stop and saw 'im again when I was putting the ash bin out. Looked a bit suspicious to me, so I watched 'im from behind the curtains. He took one last look before clearing off.'

'Are you sure he was watching me?'

Mrs Doughty nodded emphatically and assured her that he was.

'Nothing to do with the little girl, is 'e? Only the little 'un ran down the path whilst 'e was watching and the bloke didn't look too 'appy.'

'I shouldn't think so,' said Maisie, then rethought the possibilities. 'Can you tell me what he looked like?'

'Skinny and scrawny. That's the best way I can put it.'

'Scruffy?'

'I think 'e was wearing a uniform, but I can't recall what it was. Khaki I think. Though me eyes are not so good. But there was one thing I did notice. 'E tore something up before marching away. I don't know if it might 'elp at all, but I picked up the pieces. I would 'ave stuck them back together for you, but I ain't got any sticky tape and, besides, with my eyes I might 'ave got it all wrong.'

Once Maisie had thanked Mrs Doughty and she had gone on her way, armed with sticky tape and a pair of scissors, Maisie sat at the kitchen table. After sticking only a few pieces together, she knew what she was looking at: a photo of her, one she'd given to Sid before he'd gone marching off to war.

She leaned back in the chair and covered her face with her hands. Why had he torn up her photo? She imagined him watching her so intently that he hadn't noticed Mrs Doughty watching him. Paula had run out of the house wanting to be chased. She loved playing at being naughty. She recalled her turning round and saying that she could run faster than Maisie. She'd also called her mummy! The reconstructed scene instantly laid the truth bare.

* * *

Bridget arrived the following morning, baby in arms.

'Bridget! What are you doing here?'

'Oh blast,' said Bridget, handing her the baby. 'Let me pay the taxi a moment, then I'll tell you.'

By the time the taxi had gone and they were indoors, Bridget had explained about phoning her and leaving a message with someone who'd been passing the phone box.

'I'm afraid I had to take a chance that he would get my message to you. I must say he was a bit abrupt.'

'Oh no.' Maisie closed her eyes and shook her head. 'I can't believe this is happening.'

'What's happening?'

'And this was a man's voice?'

'Yes. He didn't say much. In fact, all he did say was yes. He didn't promise to take the message to you. I suppose I should have asked for his name or something. Who knows who it might have been.'

'I know,' said Maisie in a matter-of-fact way. 'It was Sid. It couldn't be anyone else.'

She showed Bridget the photograph.

'It's you.'

'Yes. Stuck back together.'

She went on to tell her about Mrs Doughty suggesting that this man, who she was now convinced was Sid, had been watching her.

'She said he was scrawny and that his clothes were too big for him. It had to be Sid. He's been in a Japanese prisoner-of-war camp. I've read what's been said in the papers about how they've been treated. It must be him.'

'Oh my Lord,' Bridget gasped and held a hand in front of her mouth.

Maisie looked down thoughtfully. 'I didn't see him at Temple Meads when I went in to meet the train. I thought it strange, and although I knew the best thing was to see his mother and ask if she'd seen him, I didn't.' She looked up. 'Wasn't that terrible of me?'

Bridget studied Maisie's expression and saw guilt there but also apprehension. 'You feared you'd be torn between him and Paula.' She paused. 'And we both know who you would choose.'

'I've fought so hard to keep her, even before she was born. And then Carole's mother and her selfish plans. I would have sold this house to pay her the money she wanted, but then I wouldn't have been able to provide Paula with a home. At the end of the day, it was Eddie who sorted it out.'

'Well, he would, wouldn't he,' returned Bridget. There was a hint of sarcasm in her voice and her expression.

'Hmm.'

It wasn't even a word, but Bridget picked up something about the cadence of Maisie's voice and the flickering hesitance in her eyes. There was something she wanted to say but wasn't sure that she should.

The look between them held.

'What is it?' asked Bridget.

Should she tell or not? Maisie felt she would burst if she didn't share what had been said with someone.

'Carole's mother suggested that Eddie wasn't the father. Not that she's going to admit that now. I don't know how much he paid her to leave Paula alone, but he's been making a lot of money from scrap metal. He can afford anything.'

'I can believe it with the amount of scrap metal around. A tank alone must be worth a small fortune in metal.'

Tea was poured but it went cold. There was a weightlessness to their thoughts now that the war was over, but sometimes they came back with full force and weighed heavy.

Lyndon stirred in his sleep. He lay on one end of the settee, a dozing Paula on the other.

'I need to find Sid,' Maisie finally said. 'Can you stay here and look after Paula whilst I'm out?'

'No.'

Bridget's response and the fact that she sprang to her feet took Maisie by surprise. Bridget could be adamant to the point of bloody-mindedness when she had to.

'I'll go to the phone box and call a taxi. The driver gave me the firm's number. I'm going with you. And so are the kids. They're part of our lives now. Both of our lives. Let's be honest about what we are. If Sid doesn't like it, then...'

'He'll have to lump it.'

* * *

Falling leaves blew into their faces as they alighted from the taxi. Bridget insisted on paying for him to hang around whilst they sorted the matter out.

'We won't be long,' she exclaimed.

Maisie doubted they'd be that quick, but the taxi driver seemed quite content to earn money for hanging around.

Sid's mother was scraping up leaves from the front garden. She looked both surprised and annoyed to see them walking up her garden path.

'Well,' she said, her lips setting in a tight line as her eyes alighted on Paula. 'Looks as though the mice do play when the cat's away...'

Maisie welled up with anger. 'This is Paula. Say hello, Paula.'

Paula squeaked a small hello.

'I became her mother after her real one died. A bomb blew up in the centre of Bristol. Baldwin Street, in fact. Perhaps you might remember it.'

'I do,' Sid's mother gasped. 'I didn't know that you...'

'Well I did. This mouse has not been playing around, Mrs Brewster. I can assure you of that!'

Mrs Brewster was full of apologies. 'I'm sorry. I read about it, but I didn't know...'

'Never mind.'

The apprehension Maisie had been incubating melted like ice in hot water.

'Just tell Sid, wherever he is, there's an ultimatum if he still wants to marry me. I don't come alone. I promised myself I would always take care of Paula. She's my daughter now. Tell him that...'

Tears of anger stung her eyes as she turned on her heel and made her way back to the taxi, Bridget following behind her. Bridget turned halfway down the path and said, 'Tell him I should have remembered myself to him better when we spoke on the phone the other day. Maisie's never forgotten him and from what I hear he's never forgotten her. Tell him that. Please.'

* * *

Maisie was washing the dishes whilst Bridget wiped. Paula was playing school in the patch of long grass.

Bridget made comment. 'She looks so content.'

'She is. I won't say she's forgotten her mother; I never want her to do that. But I do my best.'

They were interrupted by the sound of knocking at the front door.

Maisie left Bridget with the dishes.

On opening the front door, Maisie she saw what she first thought was the silhouette of a thin tree, a mere sapling. Her breath caught in her throat. The man standing there was a bag of bones, yet she knew him, knew that he'd been a jolly sort, one she'd at one time had fun with. His skin was greyish and his cheekbones were prominent. On reflection, she hadn't expected anything else. An iron claw seemed to squeeze at her heart.

'Sid.'

He looked awkward, gawky and with not much more weight on him than a scarecrow in a farmer's field. With stick-like hands, he pulled at his shirt collar sagging around his neck.

Had his eyes always been so deeply set above prominent cheekbones? His jacket hung from his shoulders and although his face was tanned, his skin was tight against his bones.

'Maisie. Sorry it's been so long.'

She almost laughed out loud but with flighty fingers touched the smile that played around her mouth. The urge to throw her arms around him was strong, but she held back. The years had flown and as such it was difficult to know quite how to behave.

She chose a certain amount of brevity. 'I knew it wasn't easy for you to get away, Sid, so no need to apologise.'

'Yeah. Well...' He smiled sheepishly.

'I suppose you'd better come in.' She held the door wide and turned round to find Paula close against her skirt. 'This is Paula. My daughter. Or, at least, she is now.'

'Mummy Maisie,' lisped the little girl.

'Yes, darling, but we'll never forget mummy Carole will we.'

Paula shook her head. As a special treat, she was wearing the silver locket around her neck. She'd been showing it to Bridget.

'The locket holds a piece of her mother's hair,' Maisie whispered to Sid.

Sid responded with amazement, a slight dropping of jaw, a blinking of eyes. Once he'd digested what she'd said, he smiled and said hello to Paula. Paula said a childish hello and smiled back.

Maisie felt more overwhelmed with shyness than the little girl. 'It must have been horrible out there.'

He nodded. 'It was. I was desperate for bacon sandwiches. Mind, I've put on a little bit of weight since, though I'm told it takes time for me stomach to adjust. Getting there though.' He sounded pleased and Maisie was glad for him.

The sound of Lyndon crying came from the living room at the back of the house. For a moment, Sid looked confused, until Bridget appeared with Lyndon in her arms.

'Blimey. Bridget Milligan.'

It was difficult not to be shocked at Sid's appearance, but Bridget parried her initial response with a swift retort. 'It's O'Neill now, Sid Brewster, and I've got a bone to pick with you. It was me you spoke to on the phone. Fancy not passing on my message. I could have arrived and been out on the streets.'

Maisie laughed. 'She's only joking. She wouldn't have been out on the streets at all. Now let's get the kettle on. We've a lot to catch up with. Unless you'd like a beer. I think I've got a bottle of brown ale.'

'Tea would be best. Back in the camp we used to dream of proper tea with sugar and milk. And bacon. I used to wake from a dream about bacon. Just the smell was enough to make me dribble.'

'Got any bacon, Maisie?' Bridget rocked her baby as she asked the question and Maisie answered quickly.

'I have.'

'How about making Sid a cup of tea and a bacon sandwich whilst I go upstairs and feed my hungry boy? How about you coming upstairs with me, Paula? I could do with you turning down the bedding and finding Lyndon's teddy. Shall we do that?'

Taking Paula with her was not necessary. She was giving Maisie and Sid the opportunity to be alone. They needed time to explore their emotions, to find out where they both were in their relationship. Would it be reignited or had the war turned it to ashes?

Maisie left Sid sitting in an armchair whilst she went out into the kitchen to put the kettle and the frying pan on the stove. As the bacon sizzled, tears stung her eyes and she clenched her jaw. Inside, she felt as though her bones had turned to jelly. Making a move one way or the other was incredibly difficult.

Once the bacon was cooked and the tea had mashed, she cut two slices of bread. The fat from the bacon coloured the greyish bread which was still on ration and of the same miserable quality as it had been during the war.

She was about to take the tea and bacon sandwich into him when she realised he was standing in the doorway, looking at her as though she was the most beautiful woman he'd ever seen.

'You don't look any different than I remember,' he said.

Amazement shone in his face and suddenly he was the young man she once knew.

It simply wasn't possible to say that he too had not changed because he had.

'Why did you tear my photograph into pieces?' Maisie asked him instead.

He impulsively shoved his hands into his pockets but never once took his eyes off her. 'How do you know that?'

'A neighbour was watching you. She picked up the pieces and said you were watching me. I stuck it back together.'

He looked surprised before saying, 'Looking at that photo got me through everything: 'aving mates die in front of me eyes, putting up with the beatings and being starved. Yeah, we dreamed a lot of food, but your photo...' He shook his head in a forlorn, sad manner. 'You reminded me of where I belonged.'

'You still ain't told me why you ripped it to pieces.'

In her heart, she knew the reason why, but she wanted him to say it, to admit he'd thought she'd been unfaithful and had given birth to another man's child. The truth was far from that.

'I thought that Paula was...'

'Sid, I think I should tell you right here and now that I 'ave been out on a few dates and even received a proposal of marriage. But I've never been to bed with anyone. Call me old-fashioned, but that's the way it is. I've looked after Paula even before she was born. Whether I marry or not, whoever takes me on must take Paula too. We come as a pair.'

'I shouldn't have torn it up.' Sid shook his head and smiled wryly. 'Nice to know you've stuck it back together. Like us, if you want to, that is. Stick us back together.'

For a moment, they both stood rigidly looking at each other, bacon sandwich in one of Maisie's hands, cup of tea in the other.

In an instant, she set both down on the table and threw her arms around him.

'Welcome home. Welcome home, you silly bugger.'

Her heart felt fit to burst as he wound his arms around her and buried his face and his tears in her hair. A man of bones existed beneath the sagging clothes. It would have been easy to break down and sob along with him, but deep inside she knew that what he needed most was to lean on her strength.

'Come on. The tea and your sandwich are getting cold.' She eased away. 'I'll carry it in for you. Go on. Sit down.'

Once he was settled and munching his sandwich, she went back out to the kitchen to fetch her own cup of tea. A single tear, one she could not stop from falling, trickled down her cheek. She dabbed at it with the corner of the tea towel.

On joining him, she found he'd managed only one half of the sandwich.

'I have to eat slowly,' he said without prompting. 'My stomach's shrunk. That's what the quacks said.'

She knew quacks meant doctors.

Settling in the chair opposite him, she took a sip of her tea. 'So, what next?' she asked.

His eyes were hooded as he thought about what she'd asked.

'Wills's have offered me a job. They said I could go part-time at first until I built me strength up. Course, you don't work there any more, do you?' His look was direct.

'I no longer work. I keep house and look after Paula.'

'You must miss it.'

'I do.' She lowered her eyes. Yes, she did miss the tobacco factory. Friendship had been consigned to the past because it had to be. She had responsibilities. 'I have no choice, but Paula makes up for it.'

'Well,' he said somewhat hesitantly. 'Once I get back on me feet, once I'm full time and earning a good wage...' His voice trailed away.

'Is that a proposal, Sid Brewster?'

He rummaged in his pocket, brought out a ring and placed it on her finger. 'I s'pose it is.' The look in his eyes held hers.

'As long as you accept that you'll be getting a ready-made family.'

'Only one. For now.'

He grinned cheekily, so much so that it made Maisie blush at the thought of what he was suggesting. More children. She'd never expected to have any and now here he was suggesting otherwise.

'So should I consider myself engaged?'

'And marry in spring of next year?'

Sid's face lit up like the sun. 'That should work.'

'Shall we kiss on that?'

The question took him unawares. Now it was him who blushed. Maisie got up from her chair and leaned over him.

'Sealed with a kiss,' Maisie whispered, still leaning over him.

'One more.'

His kiss was less hesitant than the first one. There was a genuine sweetness in that kiss, a fond promise, thought Maisie, of things to come.

'There's tea in the pot,' she called on hearing a set of footsteps coming down the stairs before Bridget appeared.

'Before you ask, Paula's fallen asleep on the bed. I tucked her in. Right. Now what have you two been discussing, as if I couldn't guess.'

Bridget looked at each of her friends in turn.

'You're blushing,' she said to Maisie. To Sid, 'And you need to brush those crumbs from your chops.'

Sid did as he was told, though in all honesty Maisie couldn't see any crumbs. Bridget was good at breaking the ice, getting everyone at ease.

'Sid's been offered a job back in the tobacco factory.'

'Of course he has. I didn't expect anything else. You're a valuable employee, Sid. I'm sure you'll go far.'

'And we've got engaged. We're getting married next spring. Isn't that right, Sid?' Maisie showed Bridget the engagement ring. It had a single green stone. Other women might have liked a border of diamonds, but its plainness somehow suited Maisie.

'The sooner, the better. I don't want to miss it,' said Bridget.

'We'd like you to come.' Maisie was enthused with the thought of it. Of course she'd like Bridget to come. Phyllis too. She'd like all her friends to come.

'I always thought I would one day. You two were bound to get married. I can't say I'm surprised.'

'You're not surprised. Why's that?' asked Sid. 'I might not 'ave come back.'

Bridget adopted that serene, secretive smile of hers, one that was as noticeable in her grey eyes as on her rose-pink lips. 'Come on, Sid. As long as you survived, I knew you'd be coming for her. You've written to each other more regularly than most people who didn't go through what you did. And Maisie has never had the time of day for anyone else – even though she had the offers. You two might not notice it, but you always were destined for each other. It had to be. So there, that's my sermon for today!'

Maisie looked at Sid and knew for a fact that every word Bridget had said was true. Sid was the reason she'd had plenty of one-night stands but no long-standing relationship. Sid was also the reason that she hadn't taken Ted up on his offer though he would have been a good catch and they might have been happy.

She'd gelled with Sid from the very start, and even though they'd been far apart, their love had survived.

'No going away to war ever again, Sid Brewster. I'm going to stick to you like glue.'

* * *

The next couple of hours were taken up with reminiscences about old times in the tobacco factory, old friends, those that were still around and those who were not.

'Phyllis told me about Angela, Aggie's daughter. She applied for a job on the same day that Phyllis was there.'

'Looks like I'll be in good company then when I gets back to work.' Sid smirked happily.

At mention of the tobacco factory, Bridget became uncommonly aware of the pressure of her wedding ring on the third finger of her left hand. During the past few weeks, she'd made excuses about heading for her new life with Lyndon. Seeing Sid and Maisie together had made her realise what a relationship should be. Although neither of them seemed aware, the time and distance hadn't made a jot of difference. Sid and Maisie had clung together like ivy to the garden wall. They were entwined and it made her wonder whether she was. Marrying Lyndon had been about love and attraction. The prospect of moving to another country had held her back more than she'd expected it to.

'So when do you leave?' Sid asked her.

'I'm not too sure, especially now you two are aiming to tie the knot. I'm determined to dance at your wedding. What are old friends for?'

'I would love that, but what about Lyndon?' Maisie asked.

'He knows how difficult I'm finding it to say goodbye. After all, I'm saying goodbye to my whole life. I've never lived anywhere else, except when I was serving in the nursing corps. He knows it's hard for me and that I've got to take things slowly. Anyway,' she said, 'how can he refuse me time to go to my best friend's wedding?'

Maisie wasn't fooled. Bridget was nervous about starting her new life. The Milligans' were a close-knit family and Bridget, as the eldest, had looked after the family following the death of her mother. It crossed her mind that Bridget might even be regretting having married an American. All that she'd known and loved would be left behind.

What if she were in her shoes? It was a question she found difficult to answer. From what she perceived of her life ahead, Maisie would remain in Bristol married to a fellow Bristolian. He'd already said to her that he would never go abroad ever again. 'Not even on holiday.'

There wasn't much prospect of that ever happening. 'Unless it's to Wales.'

'As long as I don't 'ave to fly there or get on a boat.'

Maisie had raised an eyebrow coupled with a smile. 'Not even the ferry across from Aust to Beachley?'

Sid's brows had folded as he considered it. 'No. That river's dangerous.'

'That's a lovely engagement ring,' Bridget said before leaving. 'That stone looks expensive.'

After she'd boarded the taxi back to the hotel, Maisie flexed her engagement finger. The green stone caught the light. The yellow metal of the ring itself certainly looked like gold. She turned it this way and that. 'Bridget's right. It does look expensive.'

'You deserve it. You waited. Some chaps ain't so lucky.'

Sid didn't tell her about that night when he'd escaped with one mate but left the third one behind. Blind and afraid, his mate had given him the ring for safekeeping.

'Just in case I don't make it.'

He hadn't said anything about who it should go to if he didn't make it. All that he knew was that the captain had a family in Norfolk and kept horses. By rights, Sid should have made the effort to find out and return the ring to them, but his heart had been so full of joy when Maisie had agreed to marry him he couldn't help himself. The ring had slid easily onto her finger. A single green emerald.

She hugged him tightly. 'Yes, I am lucky. Very lucky.'

'Glad you ain't on the other side of the Atlantic.'

'So am I, but...'

'Go on. Say it. I can't say it. Getting married in April was your idea, not mine.'

Maisie's eyes sparkled. 'If you don't want to wait...'

'I don't want to wait. The sooner, the better. I'll get a special licence if you like.'

She wound her arms around his neck, such a thin neck. He still felt so fragile, a bag of bones that had once been covered by healthy, youthful flesh. 'If that's what you want, but I don't want to rush you.'

He shook his head. 'One thing I've learned, Maisie, is to live for today.' His eyes took on a faraway and haunted look. 'That's 'ow it was out there. You fell asleep at night not sure you'd wake up the next day.' The haunted look made his eyes seem more deep-set.

She knew instinctively that he was raking through memories that were best forgotten yet sadly never would be. Thinking of marrying in April she'd thought considerate to him. She'd been wrong. The truth hit her. Deep down, he wasn't sure he'd be around in April. Living for today had been the result of that terrible prison camp.

Taking a deep breath and cupping his face in her hands, she said what had to be said.

'Okay, Sid. Give me the date and I'll be yours.'

31

At her room in the Royal Hotel, Bridget fed Lyndon and set him down for an afternoon nap.

The view out towards Park Street was busy. Remnants of buildings stood starkly against the skyline. Gaps, the result of bombing, were filled with temporary tented establishments. It was a sombre scene, yet still she felt reluctance to leave this battered city. A great many buildings in its historic heart had been destroyed. History had been what had brought her and Lyndon together. And now...

Whilst the baby slept, she immersed herself in hot water. A decent bath. No longer did she have to keep within the regulation setting. Forever after, she and many others would recall with laughter the black line drawn around the bathtub. Two inches of water. It seemed ridiculous.

She luxuriated in the soapy water as long as she could, putting off the dreadful moment of reading Lyndon's letter for the second time.

She'd not mentioned the letter to Maisie. At times, she so wanted to join Lyndon in America. At others, she felt tearful, unable to contemplate tearing herself away from home.

A towel wrapped around her wet hair and wearing a dressing gown, she poured herself a cup of tea, sat in a chair and once again read the letter from her husband.

Bridget,

I know it's hard for you to leave your family and friends in England, but it's hard for me too, living here without my wife or my son. Have you any idea how much I'm missing him? He's possibly grown a lot since I last saw him. I want him with me, Bridget. I insist in fact.

I've been patient, but there are limits. I've booked you passage on a ship leaving England in late January that's been specially commissioned to take GI brides and their families into the States. The tickets will be arriving under separate cover. I insist there are no more delays. Please be on it.

Lyndon.

She held her breath as she refolded the crisp paper. Her heart was pounding. Yet again, she was divided in two. There was no darling, no love and kisses in the curtly worded letter. Omission of such endearment suggested that Lyndon was angry with her. Quite honestly, she couldn't blame him, but at the same time she felt so sorry for herself, so reluctant to up sticks and sail away.

However, he had made quite a large concession, hadn't he? To confirm this, she reread the letter again. Lyndon hadn't seen their baby for months. A feeling of great misery came upon her at the realisation that she was being selfish. A son needed his father and a father needed his son. How could she have been so uncaring.

The time for saying last goodbyes. She would celebrate Christmas with her family for the last time. She smothered her tear-filled eyes with the towel with which she had bound her hair. How could she have been so selfish? The family was the three of them. The second reading of the letter had finally brought it home. In response, she had to explain, she had to do anything she could to keep their love and their marriage alive.

With that foremost in mind, she wiped at her wet face and wrote a letter back.

> *My darling husband,*
>
> *I've wonderful news. Sid has come home from the Far East and has proposed marriage to my dear friend Maisie.*
>
> *Forgive me for dawdling and not taking the ship you booked us passage on, but just as you've guessed I'm finding it hard to leave my father, family, friends and the city I was born in. I cannot explain how torn I feel, but my sorrow is gradually subsiding, besides which I'm missing you. I must leave everything to be with the man I love and, believe me, I do most sincerely love you. I never expected it to be easy, but it's turned out harder than I thought. But there, I've made my decision. I will be on that ship. I will be with you in the New Year.*

Once the letter was signed, folded and inside an envelope, she recalled a nice little rich girl, one from Lyndon's own social circle. His mother had pressed him to marry her but had met with his defiance and his declaration that he would marry her, a girl from a council estate who worked in the factory to which they supplied tobacco grown on their plantation. Hopefully that girl was no longer around, but if his mother had her way...

There was no doubt about it. Bridget would ensure she was on that ship.

There was time in the interim to put their affairs in order, to keep in touch with her father whilst she could. Her only regret was not being able to hang around for Maisie's wedding. Spring was a long way off.

* * *

Next morning, Bridget took a taxi to Marksbury Road.

Her two brothers were at work. So was her eldest sister. The younger girls were at school. On this visit, she wanted her father to herself so she could express her gratitude for all he'd done, for all the good things her family had taught her.

Her father was pleased to see her, asked her if she was hungry and told her he'd made faggots – big Somerset styled meatballs.

'With potatoes, cabbage and carrots.'

He sounded and looked very pleased with his newly acquired cooking skills.

She told him that she wasn't hungry. 'Not yet anyway. I wanted to speak to you, to ask your advice.'

'My advice comes at a price, which is that you allow me to hold my grandson for a while.'

He settled himself into his favourite armchair, a gurgling Lyndon cuddled close to his.

'Lovely little lad.' He smiled down into the chubby little face.

'Yes. He is.'

She couldn't help feeling anxious. In a way, it wasn't advice she wanted. It was reassurance. Her father had always reassured and soothed her nightmares away.

His attention remained fixed on his grandson. 'Yer mother would have loved him.' For a fleeting moment, his smile was sad. It was gone when a more enquiring look came to his face. 'To what do I owe this visit?'

'Do I need an excuse to see my father?'

He gave her a very direct look. 'I understood you should be in America by now. Am I right or am I right?'

She told him he was right.

There was wisdom and kindness in his eyes. Already she was

feeling calmer, decisive about what she had to say and desperate to have him guide her through the woods.

For his part, Patrick Milligan eyed his daughter with concern. She was not his biological daughter but that of an Irish aristocrat in the house where Bridget's mother had been a servant. As frequently happened back then, his dear wife Mary had fallen for the charms of a man of a different class. He'd promised to marry her, of course, and perhaps he might have done if he'd not been killed in the war of 1914 to 1918. But it had happened and his darling Mary had been living alone with her child when he'd met her. He'd fallen head over heels in love and her daughter, Bridget, had become the child of his heart.

Pity and fear fought to control his emotions.

'You don't want to go, do you.'

'Sometimes I miss him dreadfully. Sometimes I panic at the prospect of leaving Bristol, my friends – and my family. Ultimately I have to go, but it's hard to leave everything behind, far harder than I expected.'

His gaze was steady when he said, 'Do you love him?'

Bridget looked with unfettered love at her son. 'For the most part, I'm convinced that I love him. At other times, I ask myself whether it was just a wartime romance, but then it wasn't. We began seeing each other before the war began.' She frowned. 'I sometimes wonder whether we would have stayed together if the war hadn't happened. I mean, war does throw people together, doesn't it? People do adopt a live today approach. Gather ye rose-buds while you may...'

He wagged a work-gnarled finger at her. 'Don't talk like that.'

Even though he had attempted to speak quietly, the baby jolted in his grandfather's lap though not enough to wake up.

Bridget winced at the way he looked at her and guessed what he would say next.

'You must join him, Bridie. He's your husband.' His voice was soft, as he called her by her shortened name, the name he always used for her. 'Or your son will grow up without a father. That wouldn't be fair. It wouldn't be right.'

Bridget folded her arms and turned her back on him. The sight of the street beyond the window stirred her in a way she could never have imagined. She didn't just see the houses on the opposite side of the road but felt the presence of memories. They came into her mind and became visions of the past: she and her brothers and sisters playing out in the street. Her mother coming home with shopping and calling that she had two pounds of broken biscuits. 'Who wants some?' Biscuits, even if they were the cheaper ones broken into pieces, were irresistible. They'd ran in. They'd played in the snow. They'd come home soaked carrying jam jars full of tadpoles. Intruding on those memories was the remembrance of a car stopping outside. Curtains had twitched as curious neighbours watched and wondered. Lyndon, the son of a rich man, had caused a stir with both the neighbours and her workmates, though not nearly as much as he'd stirred her.

The baby's sniffles dragged her back into the present day. The scene beyond the window was much the same as it had always been. Inside her childhood home had changed. Her mother's dying had left a space that nothing could fill, though suddenly that space was filled with the biggest shock of her life.

'I'm going to get married.'

Her father's words hit her like a cricket bat.

She stopped staring out of the window and stared round-eyed at him instead. 'You're going to get married?' She couldn't help sounding surprised. 'If you're lonely I can stay... I'll tell Lyndon and—'

'No!' This time, his outburst was loud enough to wake the baby. He brushed her away when she tried to take Lyndon from him.

'Leave it. I know how to soothe a baby. I'm not helpless, Bridie. I'm not decrepit yet. Now, let's put things in perspective. You've got your own family and mine are beginning to flee the nest. Sean has a job and a girl, so I'm told.'

Bridget winced. 'Sean? He didn't tell me!'

He drew in his chin and eyed her accusingly. 'And why should he tell you? You're his big sister with a husband and baby. You'll be making your home on the other side of the world. I'll be making my home this side. Where Sean, Michael and the girls will end up is anybody's business. But it's their business. Theirs and theirs alone.'

As he lectured her, he jiggled the baby and every so often spoke soft words and pulled funny faces.

Eventually, once Lyndon had settled, he looked at his daughter in a firmer more judgemental manner. 'Your mother would want you to be with your family and that husband of yours. At the end of the day, it's all that counts. Love the one you're with every day of your life. But never stop living as well as loving. I won't. Your mother's gone, but I still feel her passing. I still love her, but it doesn't mean that I cannot love anyone else. Your mother would understand. So even if you disapprove of me remarrying, I won't listen to you. You've got your own life to live and so have I. Now go on. Get out there and live it. That's what you're meant to do.'

In that moment Bridget realised just how much she loved this man who'd taken on the responsibility of bringing her up. She also understood why her mother had fallen in love with him.

She flung her arms around his bristly neck and with tearful happiness murmured into his ear, 'You're a good and wise man, Patrick Milligan.'

'I'm no saint but I appreciate the compliment.' He chuckled and patted her arm. 'Now that's all settled what say you we have a bite to eat?'

Whilst they talked further and ate the homemade meatballs and vegetables the baby stayed asleep on the settee.

'Oh. I forgot to tell you that Sid's asked Maisie to marry him; you remember he was imprisoned by the Japanese?'

The faces of father and daughter lifted into joy.

'God bless them.'

Bridget got everything together ready to go and looked around the house as she did on every visit now. In her mind, she counted down to the end of January. Some weeks yet, enough time to say goodbye, enough time to soak in what would be her last views of the old city.

'I was reading about the Roman quay along the River Avon below St Vincent's Rocks. They reckon they've found bones there. As if we ain't got enough bones from more recent times.'

'Oh, Dad. You are only joking, I hope.'

'The human race never learns from history. In the end, it's likely to destroy us. I wonder whether people will remember anything about all this lot in one hundred years' time?'

'They'd be foolish not to learn anything from it.'

'I hope you're right, me dear. I hope you're right. For your sake and my grandson's sake.'

'Let's just put this war behind us, shall we?' She gave him a kiss on the cheek. 'I'll let you know when I'm next coming. I'll get a few more visits in before Christmas and some after, I should think.'

'That would be grand, but just remember, me darling girl, that your first duty is to that husband of yours and that bundle you've got there in yer arms.'

She promised she would, but despite the prospect of more visits before she left for good, when the taxi came it was hard to leave.

Ethel Ellard came out of her house and on seeing Bridget nodded and smiled. Vague as it was, the hesitancy, almost to the level of girlishness, in that smile said a lot. Much as she loved her father, Bridget had to say goodbye. It was time for her to leave her old family and bring up her own. It was time to travel across the Atlantic and be reunited with the man she loved, the man who loved her.

* * *

Back at reception in the Royal Hotel, a telegram awaited her. For a moment, her heart was in her mouth. Was Lyndon all right?

As it turned out, she recognised the king's head on the stamped seal.

In order to read it, she passed her baby to a hall porter who held him as if he was likely to explode.

```
Bridget. Wedding has been brought forward
to the last Saturday before Christmas. Hope
you can make it. Love, Maisie.
```

'Not bad news I hope, madam,' said the hotel manager as the porter handed back her baby.

'No. It's wonderful news. I'm going to my friend's wedding at Christmas. Can you send an acceptance on my behalf?'

'Of course, madam. A wondrous event indeed.'

'The last time I'll see my old friends. A month later, I'm off home to join my husband in New York.'

32

On the following Saturday, Eddie Bridgeman dropped in uninvited to visit his granddaughter.

Dapper as ever but still looking like a stand-in for James Cagney, he swept in like a whirlwind, beaming from ear to ear.

'So how's my little sweetheart?' he said after taking off his hat and bending his knees until he was face to face with the bright blue eyes and mass of whitish curls. 'She looks like 'er mother,' he said. 'Chip off the old block.'

There was laughter in his black eyes when he looked up at Maisie, which was quite surprising. He had the reputation of being as hard as nails. When it came to Paula, he was a marshmallow.

She explained that she was expecting a friend. 'We were going for a bus ride and a cup of tea and cakes in Dingles' teashop at the bottom of Park Street.'

There was instant understanding in his cheeky smile as he looked her up and down. She was dressed in a blue checked woollen dress Bridget had given her. She'd brushed her hair until it gleamed and her face was made up.

'A bloke, I take it.'

'None of your business, Mr Bridgeman.'

His black eyebrows, as hairy and thick as caterpillars, arched with amusement. 'Oh I think it is. My Paula lives under your roof. I wouldn't want any goings-on that a youngster shouldn't see. Get my meaning?'

He sat himself in a chair, fished around in his pockets and brought out what looked like a quarter of chocolate toffees.

Eyes bright with delight, Paula dipped her hand into the bag and brought out three.

'One at a time.' Maisie took the bag and the two extra caramels from her.

She fancied Eddie was smiling at her and knew her face had reddened. Nothing to do with the caramels but everything to do with his comment about her having a man friend.

'I got a right to know,' he said. 'That's my granddaughter.'

'So you've already pointed out,' Maisie snapped, though she couldn't really be mad with him. Neither would she ever tell him that Mavis had suggested he wasn't Carole's father. But there was no point making mountains out of molehills. After all, he had paid Mavis off. Reluctantly she had to concede that he was in charge of the situation. Everything she could do to keep Paula she would do. 'Excuse me,' she said on hearing a knocking at the door. 'It's Sid. My fiancé.'

She whispered to Sid that Eddie had dropped in. There was no need to explain who he was.

'This is Sid,' she announced on taking him into the living room. 'My fiancé.'

'Is that so?'

'Yes.' Maisie flashed her engagement ring.

Eddie's eyes widened. 'Blimey. That looks like an emerald.' He looked pointedly at Sid. 'Didn't nick it, did you?'

Sid blanched. 'I was a prisoner in the Far East. Emeralds is cheap out there.'

'Fair dos,' said Eddie in a rumbustious manner. 'You deserve a medal, let alone an emerald. So when's the happy day then?'

Sid glanced sheepishly at Maisie. 'Saturday week.'

Eddie leapt to his feet and shook Sid's hand. 'Congratulations.' Maintaining a firm grip of Sid's hand, he went on to say, 'This means you'll be my Paula's daddy.' His eyes narrowed as he assessed whether he thought Sid worthy of the task. 'You be a good dad to 'er or you'll be 'earing from me.'

Rather than being intimidated, Sid squared his shoulders and the look he gave was forthright, his tone of voice firm with resolve.

'I've dreamed of Maisie for three years. Nothing, absolutely nothing, will prevent me from making this marriage a success and this 'ouse a happy one.'

Sid's response had obviously hit the right notes as far as Eddie was concerned. 'You've got me blessing. So long as I'm invited, that is.'

Maisie and Sid exchanged looks.

'You can borrow my car and driver. And 'ow about champagne?'

'Well...'

'Anything you need, I can get it for you.'

'I don't think...' began Sid, slightly affronted by Eddie's steam-rolling attitude.

Maisie squeezed his hand in warning. 'Everything's still in short supply,' she explained. 'Even wedding dresses.'

Eddie looked surprised. 'Is that so.'

'I can't find a bridesmaid's dress for Paula.'

'Pink,' lisped Paula who was very excited about the whole thing, even though she didn't really understand the importance of it all.

'Well,' Eddie exclaimed. 'If my little darling is going to be a bridesmaid, her old grandad will foot the bill for the rest of it – if that's all right with you, son,' he said to Sid. 'Don't want to butt in where I ain't wanted.'

'I don't know about that...'

Maisie touched his arm. 'Eddie's doing this for Paula, not us.'

Eddie went on to list everything he was going to do. 'I'll provide the extras – food and booze. I've got contacts, you know, and as for the wedding car, well as I've said, my driver is at your disposal.'

'Only within reason. This is my wedding – our wedding,' Sid corrected with a nod at Maisie. 'We appreciate your 'elping, but we've waited a long time for this.'

Eddie beamed from ear to ear. 'Fine, son. I'll let you buy the wedding ring.'

33

Mick shifted nervously. He hated hospitals. He hated the bare walls, the echo of footsteps in long corridors and the bustling busyness of nurses in floaty veils and solid shoes. Most of all, he hated the smell of disinfectant, antiseptic and carbolic. They signalled serious illness. He didn't count himself as being seriously ill. He didn't feel ill or the invalid the doctors had said he was. In fact, he didn't feel any different to his old self. What was the odd headache to worry about?

'I hate this place.' Even though he only whispered it, the sound seemed to echo along the series of corridors connecting one single-storey building to another. The site had been built by the US military to accommodate wounded servicemen. Now it had been turned into a facility for head injuries. 'I don't know what I'm doing here.'

Phyllis frowned at him. 'You injured your head. They want to keep a close watch on you.'

'I'm not sure I'll bother to come again. I feel fine.'

'Don't be so stubborn. You're here because they said you needed to be here. If you want to get better.'

The more exact words should have been if you want to survive. It scared her to think her handsome Australian who had fought in the skies had been laid so low. She could only do her best to make him happy and today she had something to tell him. But not yet. Not until he'd seen the doctors.

'Better to do what? Turn into a vegetable?'

Phyllis turned away so he couldn't see the tears and anger, the fierceness with which she bit her bottom lip. 'That's not true.'

'Isn't it? I can't travel. Not even on a boat. I still want to go home, Phyllis.'

'I know and I understand it.' She felt helpless. She'd done all she could to turn their prefab into a home, though to him it was such a step down from the future he'd envisaged. A vineyard back home in Australia. She would follow him to the ends of the earth. As long as she was with him. That was all that mattered.

She told him she needed the ladies' cloakroom. 'Wait for me until I get back.'

'Yes, ma'am.' He saluted her as though she was an officer and it made her smile.

'Silly devil.'

She needed to mop at her eyes, pinch her cheeks and make herself look as though she wasn't in the least bit worried about him – even if she was.

'Excuse me. Do you happen to have an aspirin? Only I've got a terrible stomach ache.'

The woman looked to be in her late twenties and about six months pregnant.

'Yes. I think I've got some at the bottom of my bag.' Phyllis found the bottle of pills she always carried for Mick's use and unscrewed the top.' 'Will two be enough?'

'Plenty.'

Phyllis's eyes strayed to the woman's swollen stomach. 'When are you due?'

'Just after Christmas.'

'Is it your first?'

'I wish! My third. I'm in here visiting my grandad. He had a fall. Getting too old to be out and about, but he's a stubborn old sod.'

'Is there a man who isn't?'

They shared a look of agreement before Phyllis made her way back to Mick.

The sight of empty chairs in an empty corridor instantly told her that she'd taken longer than anticipated.

A uniform that looked like a senior sister was approaching her from the other end of the corridor.

'Excuse me. I was here with my husband, but he seems to have already gone in. Is it all right if I...'

There was no need to say anything further. A door opened and there was Mick.

He shouted, 'Thanks, Doc,' over his shoulder. 'That's that all over,' he said with a mighty grin.

'Oh good.'

He took hold of her arm and, looking bright and breezy, walked her along the corridor and back to the entrance.

Puzzled by his sudden cheeriness, she kept looking up at him. 'You look like the cat that got the cream.'

'We're off out of here.'

'I know that. I just hope we haven't missed the bus. These corridors go on and on forever.'

Framed by the doorway, he hugged her close and whispered in her ear: 'I'm off home. Courtesy of His Majesty's Government.'

Phyllis stared up at him. 'What do you mean?'

'I've been discharged. I can go home.'

It felt to Phyllis as though an iron hand was squeezing her heart. 'Home?'

'Australia!' People's heads turned as he shouted it out. 'I can go home.'

'Are you sure? This all seems a bit sudden. I think I need to talk to the doctor.'

He held her arm tight to stop her from doing so.

'He's a new doctor with modern ideas. He'll say the same to you as he said to me. It's my choice. If I want to go home, then I'm free to go.'

'Oh Mick.' She reached up and ran her hand down from his forehead to his chin. 'I don't know what to say.'

'Well I do. Start packing. I'll sort the documentation. It's at the Crown's expense. A final demob. Think we've waited long enough, don't you?'

Phyllis was amazed. 'I can't believe it. Are you sure?'

He stopped abruptly. 'Aren't you glad? I've got the all-clear. We're going home to make our fortune.' The laughter in his throat was accompanied by tears in his eyes.

Her jaw ached with the pressure of holding back her own news. 'We'll be taking the family with us.'

He frowned. 'What family?'

A full-blown smile lifted her face. 'Ours.'

At first he kept looking at her, trying to read her face and the happy smile she was giving him. Finally, the penny dropped.

'Jesus!' Eyes shining with amazement, he grabbed her shoulders and turned her towards him. 'Are you sure? I mean, you've just got that job at the tobacco factory...'

She took a deep breath before stating that, yes, she was sure. 'I'll write to Mrs Prince and explain why I can't take the job. I didn't think it would happen just yet and...' She didn't get chance to finish her sentence. Mick gave her the biggest hug she'd ever had. 'You're squeezing the life out of me,' she squealed as he gave her a smacker of a kiss.

Stroking her cheeks, he smiled into her face. 'It's all coming right for us.'

'You're pleased we're going to have a baby?'

'You bet I am.'

'And there's more good news.'

'There couldn't be! I'm getting everything I've ever wanted. You, a kid and the prospect of building my own business. What else could there be?'

'We've been invited to a wedding. Sid and Maisie.'

He remarked that it couldn't be better timed. 'Like a going-away party. Farewell to old friends.'

They talked excitedly on the bus home. Mick had only met Sid on one occasion and they'd got on well.

'I thought I was hard done by,' Mick said, his brow furrowing and his eyes dark with the burden of stories told him by others who'd been prisoner out there.

'Thank God it's all over.'

'Amen. But let's not dwell on the past. Let's look forward to the future. Do we have any beer at home?'

'A few,' she replied laughingly. 'I'd make an apple pie if we had some apples.'

'I'll pop along and see Bill. I'm sure he'll oblige.'

Their clasped hands tightened and both their faces were wreathed in smiles.

Phyllis so wanted this baby. She so wanted them to be happy ever after. It seemed things were going their way.

* * *

As Mick came through the gate, Bill straightened and rubbed at his back. At first, Mick's expression was full of thoughtful concern. Like a bloke that's lost a pound note and picked up a farthing, thought Bill.

It seemed Mick hadn't seen him at first. Once he did and knew he'd been noticed, his face brightened – too swiftly in Bill's opinion.

'Any chance of a few cooking apples?' Mick asked. 'And a few vegetables if you've got any to spare.'

'You sound chipper.'

'I am.' Mick was bursting to tell him right away. 'I'm going home to Australia. With Phyllis of course. I've been away a long time.'

Bill recalled Mick telling him that he wasn't allowed to travel. Perhaps not ever. All he said was, 'I'll miss you.'

Mick tilted his head back and looked up at the apple tree. Most of the apples had gone from the lower branches, but there were some good ones further up.

Bill stood with his earth-worn hands resting on the waistband of his brown corduroy trousers face turned upwards. 'You can take all you need, but it's a bit of a climb.'

'I can manage.'

'No need to manage. Make the job easier. I've got a ladder.'

Mick's long legs took the climb in his stride whilst Bill picked a few cabbages, carrots and potatoes which he tipped into a sack.

The sound of crashing branches attracted his attention. He looked back to see Mick rolling around in the dirt, surrounded by apples. His eyes were closed. His face was pale.

'Mick, lad. Are you all right?'

Mick tried to focus. He knew the voice. As the face in front of him became clearer, he realised it was Bill.

'Nothing broken?'

Hands resting on bent knees, the old man's face was full of concern.

Mick felt as though Bill's face was floating away from him. He felt sick and oddly weak.

'Come on, lad. Lean on me. I'll get you a shot of brandy.'

He set him down on one of the old wooden benches outside the front door.

Mick leaned his head back against the rough wall behind him. The floating sensation had been replaced with a dull thudding. It was as though his brain was trying to smash its way out of his skull.

Bill handed him a tin mug. 'Thought water might be best,' he said. 'Drink it slowly.'

As the water ran down Mick's throat, he could feel Bill watching him.

'I slipped,' said Mick without opening his eyes.

'You're lying.'

Mick's eyes jerked open. The old man had a way of looking right through you – *as though he was reading my mind*, thought Mick.

Mick bowed his head disconsolately. 'I want to go home, Bill. I want to live the life I want.'

'Even if it's dangerous?'

Squeezing his eyes tightly shut, Mick went over in his mind the exact words the doctor had said. He'd not said them to Phyllis, but somehow he knew that if he told Bill he would understand and keep the secret to himself.

'It doesn't matter whether I go or I stay.' He looked up and met Bill's searching look. 'The doctor said it was up to me where I die. The pressure against my cranium has increased. The only choice I have is where to draw my last breath. I want to go home, Bill,' he said in a pressing manner, determined to get there, determined to at least lay the groundwork for his dream of planting a vineyard. 'I want to put down the roots I always wanted to put down. Maybe I won't see them grow, but my wife will, so will my offspring.'

'And what does Phyllis say?'

'I haven't told her. I won't tell her, certainly not now. She's having a baby. I want him to be an Australian. I want him to carry on with whatever foundations I manage to put down.'

'Or her,' Bill added. 'It might be a girl. Sit there, son. I'll fetch a sack for your fruit and veg.'

The sack was half full by the time he'd added vegetables and fruit. In the brief time Mick had lived here, Bill had enjoyed his company. The pair of them, Mick and Phyllis, were the same age his own children would have been by now. They'd gone in the big flu epidemic just after the war, leaving him and their mother to grieve.

He understood why Mick had chosen to go home. Once there was little hope go and please yourself. That's what Mick had been told and he intended taking that advice. He was going to please himself and in the meantime he would live as he wanted to live.

By the time he got up, ready to leave, Mick wasn't looking quite so bad.

'You won't say anything,' said Mick as he took the sack.

'No.'

Bill watched him walk out of the garden gate, whistling as he marched back along the pavement to the little place he lived in. He felt envious. It wasn't everyone who got to choose their exit from this world. Under his breath, he wished him well and that he lived for as many days, weeks or years as he needed to find happiness. That was all anyone could wish for.

34

'We're not going to be wanting for bedding,' said Maisie. 'I have it on good authority that the girls at the factory have bought us bedding. Phyllis asked me what she could buy us. I told her bath and hand towels.'

'We already got enough – ain't we?'

Maisie snatched a hand towel from the pile of laundry she was folding. Holding it up with both hands, she peered through its frayed edges and poked a finger against a thin patch. 'These are pre-war. So's this one.' She held up another. 'They used to be one big bath towel. It got so thin in the middle; I made it into hand towels. Won't be long and there'll be only enough left to make face flannels or dishcloths. That's about all they're fit for.' She laughed. 'If that isn't a good reason for getting married...'

There was no response from Sid. His brow was furrowed. His gaze was fixed on the front window where her grandmother's heavy net curtains obscured the view.

'Did you hear what I said? Sid?'

He twiddled an unlit cigarette between finger and thumb but

made no attempt to light it. There had been times since his return when he was far away, feeling again the humid climate of Singapore, the daily fear of not waking up the next morning.

'Sid, if you keep twiddling that cigarette, the tobacco will 'ave fallen out of the end or it would have broken in 'alf.'

Still no response.

Worried now, she touched his arm. 'Sid.'

His eyes, dark and deep-set in his bony features, flickered before focusing on her. His was a strange look, seeing her but not seeing her, lips moving without any sound coming out.

Finally he made a big effort. 'I've got a confession to make.' He looked down at the cigarette which was now bent in half.

'Well go on. I'm all ears.' She said it glibly to hide her uneasiness at what he had done to warrant a confession.

He lit one half of the broken cigarette and blew the smoke at the window. He was half turned away from her and kept his eyes fixed on the window. 'It's about that ring.'

The uneasiness grew. 'My engagement ring?'

'Yes.'

With a start, she recalled Eddie Bridgeman noticing the ring and making comment. He'd stated the ring was valuable. 'Is it an emerald?'

Sid's curt nod and angular features were smothered in another cloud of tobacco smoke.

She was both perplexed and anguished at where the conversation was going. But now they were on this path, there seemed no point in not continuing.

'Where did you get it?'

He rubbed his hand across his eyes, index finger in one, thumb in the other.

'What is it, Sid?'

He threw the cigarette butt into the fireplace. Sucked up by the draught from the chimney, the smoke from the cigarette threaded upwards like a skein of silk. She envied its escape and almost wished she could go with it rather than listen to his confession. But she had to know.

'Tell me.'

He took a deep breath. The smell of tobacco was on his breath.

'It isn't mine. It belonged to a mate, one of them I was escaping with. 'E was blind from lack of protein. 'E asked me to look after it.' He paused. She imagined the very act of speaking about it was causing him pain. 'Poor bloke didn't make it. The Japs shot 'im.'

Maisie stared down at her flexed fingers, more particularly her ring finger. The big green stone flashed. It was like a reprimand, a reminder of where it had come from and perhaps where it should be.

'Did he 'ave a family?'

'I think so. I don't know.'

His eyes were downcast, his features dragged down with remorse, or sadness, or guilt. All three perhaps. She couldn't tell.

Maisie imagined his family receiving the dreadful news of the death of a loved one. She began tugging the ring from her finger. 'I can't keep it. I can't imagine why you should have given it me as an engagement ring. I don't want it, Sid. I can't have it.'

'I wanted to make up...' His voice faltered. 'I wanted to give you something special because you waited for me.'

Her eyes smouldered and she held her jaw so tightly that her teeth hurt. 'You have to try to contact his family, Sid. You have to.'

He flinched at first, then silently nodded.

'My mate... that was what he wished. I know what you mean though.'

He hung his head, his look downcast as he considered what she had said and how he'd taken his mate's wishes at face value. Of course he should get in touch with his parents, tell them what had transpired between them. He needed their blessing and would do his best to get that. Maisie was right.

Gradually, Maisie brought her ire under control. 'You should know me better. I've never been one for expensive jewellery or anything flash for that matter. A wedding ring is enough. More than enough.' She placed the ring in the palm of his hand and folded his fingers over it. 'It's the man I want, not a piece of rock. Your return is enough. We're going to be a little family. And here is the brightest jewel I own.'

Paula flung herself into Maisie's arms. Maisie exchanged a smile and a very profound look with Sid.

'A real jewel and all that matters.'

* * *

Everyone agreed that the post-war wedding of Maisie and Sid was also a celebration of peacetime and that the future now belonged to the young.

Paula had a wonderful day flouncing around in the pink dress that she loved so much. Bridget had paid over the odds for a white wedding dress, even though Maisie had told her to keep her money.

Sid's family, friends and neighbours filled the church.

Maisie's only regret was that her brother Alf wasn't there.

As she'd told Sid earlier, 'He's thousands of miles away and he's happy. Here's to fair winds for his boat and his friend. May the two of them find everything they want.'

Even though this should be the happiest day of her life there was also sadness. Alf wasn't here and neither was her mother to see her in the silky gown Bridget had contributed. Neither was Carole here. How proud she would have been to see Paula clutching a bunch of silk flowers. Every so often she smoothed the pink satin dress she was wearing. Maisie knew beyond doubt that it would be difficult getting her into nightclothes at bedtime. She'd want to wear it in bed.

Bridget found herself hugging her son close whilst thinking of her wartime wedding, just her and Lyndon plus a few friends, all of them still in uniform, no time to buy or change into anything else.

In a pew next to her husband, Phyllis too was thinking of her own wedding. She slid her arm through his. On feeling the increased pressure he turned and looked at her. They exchanged knowing glances. Like her he was thinking of Malta, the wedding that never happened, how happy they'd been when it had finally happened on the ship coming home.

Home. Bristol was where Maisie, Phyllis and Bridget had grown up. It was still home for Maisie and Phyllis – at least for now. For Bridget it would not be home for much longer. She would be making a new home.

'I love you,' Phyllis mouthed to her husband.

His smile was hesitant but at least it was there.

Phyllis looked towards the altar and the light flashing off the silver candlesticks and crucifix, closed her eyes and prayed.

Please God, take care of us all.

The organ wheezed then lauded out the wedding march. Bride, groom and congregation made their way happily down the aisle and out into an overcast day. Not that anyone cared about the weather that day.

Congratulations were exclaimed, hugs and kisses exchanged and dried rose petals, courtesy of Mr Hargreaves, fell soft and sweet smelling over the bride and groom.

'Right. Round the corner to the Ruskin Hall,' shouted Fred

Pinker, best man and old friend from Sid's days at the tobacco factory.

The hall was only a walk away and Mrs Brewster had overseen the spread which consisted mainly of cheese, ham, tinned salmon and corned beef sandwiches. The ingredients for the cake had been provided by Eddie Bridgeman. It was also Eddie who had provided more drink than anyone had seen since before the war.

Sid was so astounded all he could say was, 'Blimey!'

Eddie tapped the side of his nose. 'If you're wondering where it all came from, I've got contacts.'

Sid didn't press him for details.

There was joy and warmth helped in no small measure by the food and drink so generously supplied.

Full to the brim of both, Maisie made her way to the ladies' toilets. Bridget and Phyllis followed.

'Just like at Wills's,' Maisie joked. 'We always ended up chatting in here.'

'Kind of home then,' said Phyllis.

Bridget looked a bit downcast. The other two didn't probe as to what she was thinking because they were thinking the same thing too.

'It won't be long before we all go our separate ways,' said Bridget, 'though at least you and Sid will be staying here in Bristol.'

Maisie smiled sadly. 'I'll miss you.'

'So will I,' added Phyllis.

The three of them linked arms and hugged.

'Once known, never to be forgotten,' said Maisie.

All three of them held back their tears until later when finally, unable to hold them any longer, they said their goodbyes.

'Just for now,' added Maisie. 'I will be there to see you off. Promise I will.'

'My last Christmas,' said Bridget. 'And it'll be here in Bristol. For my family's sake. My dad especially.'

Maisie nodded. 'Right. Let's get back inside and have a final drink to all our yesterdays.'

Bridget sniffed. 'And another for all our tomorrows.'

'Hear, hear,' said Phyllis as they broke arms. 'And for friendship. And the rest of our lives.'

35

CHRISTMAS 1945

In the quiet of Christmas morning, Maisie sat watching Paula pulling out presents from her stocking. An old-fashioned type made of lisle and with a ladder down the back, Maisie had decorated it with sequins and a Father Christmas made from scraps of coloured felt. A pink and white rabbit, also made from felt, was proving to be Paula's favourite present. Sid had to persuade her that there was more inside.

'Look, Paula. It's an orange. It looks lovely.' He held it up for her to see better. 'And it smells lovely.' He took a big sniff. 'And it tastes lovely.'

When he made as if to eat it, she squealed and snatched it from him.

'All right then. You have that. Now what else is in there? Go on. Have a look.'

Encouraged by Sid, she dipped her hand in again and brought out a sugar mouse, closely followed by a brown paper bag full of chocolate misshapes – a present from Sid's mother who was relishing being in the company of her adopted granddaughter.

The smell of roast chicken drifted through the house and the kitchen was steaming up thanks to saucepans of vegetables which were still plentiful, especially potatoes!

Just after midday, Sid's mother arrived armed with a bottle of sherry and more chocolate misshapes given by a neighbour who worked at Carsons chocolate factory. Sid's mother had worked at Fry's so still got discount if she called in at the factory shop.

'We'll never lack for chocolates,' Maisie remarked as she took his mother's coat.

Sid's mother sniffed the air. 'That chicken smells good. Well stuffed with sage and onion, is it?'

'Plenty. I only hope it's big enough for the four of us.'

Perhaps having done without so much during the war years, the meal did indeed seem like a feast. The recipe for the Christmas pudding that came afterwards was a bit ad hoc, but tasted especially delicious once a tot of sherry was poured over it. There was custard but not cream. There was also the King's speech, the words of which they listened to with thoughtful silence, eyes brimming with tears as they remembered all they'd been through and all they'd lost.

Most poignant of all were the words that felt especially meant for them.

'*I think of the men and women of every race within the Empire returning from their long services to their own families, to their homes and to their ways of peace. I think of children freed from unnatural fears and blacked-out world celebrating this Christmas in light and happiness in a family circle once more reunited.*'

As his words fell away, the two women now united by marriage dabbed at their eyes. Sid left the table and headed into the kitchen, they presumed to go outside for a smoke.

Paula flounced out, leaving them to gather the dishes.

Outside in the still coldness of the back garden where frost still lay on the ground, Sid was leaning into the back wall, his face buried against his arm. His shoulders were heaving with sobs. There were so many others that should still be alive and looking forward to a future. Fifty million, so he'd heard. Civilians were numbered in that ghastly sum.

'What was it for?' he murmured. 'What the bloody hell was it for?'

The answer came when a small hand pushed its way into his palm.

'Daddy?'

He looked down and saw the childish concern in her eyes. Maisie had encouraged Paula to call him daddy, and having known no other father, she'd done so willingly.

'Sweetheart,' he said, blowing his nose and swiping at his eyes. 'I just needed a bit of fresh air.'

She smiled up at him. No soul-searching or other words were necessary. The reason for the war was standing right here gazing up at him. He'd fought and suffered for a safe future for her and millions like her. The future was theirs and hopefully would be a peaceful one.

* * *

There was immense joy in the Milligan household. The whole family – the boys, Sean and Michael as well as the girls – were home and so was Ethel and her youngsters.

Presents were given, food was eaten and the crackers the girls had made from newspaper were pulled, the jokes read and the half-dozen dolly mixtures inside scattered like confetti across the floor.

When it seemed they'd eaten everything, including a large cake Ethel had baked and decorated with icing sugar, Patrick got to his feet and proposed a toast. 'Ladies and gentlemen – that includes you too, Michael Milligan.'

Michael stopped chasing the scattered dolly mixtures and got to his feet.

'First,' said Patrick, raising his glass in Bridget's direction. 'This Christmas is very special to me and all my family, but it could be the last time I clap eyes on my darling Bridie for a long time. Here's to you and my grandson. May the New World be good to you. Cheers, Bridie, Lyndon Junior and Lyndon Senior.'

Those children allowed to drink raised glasses of sherry. The others made do with ginger beer.

'And next, my darlings, I have an announcement to make.' He turned to Ethel, who blushed scarlet as he invited her to come to his side. 'Me and Ethel are combining our families and getting spliced. Best of all, we've heard news that Ethel's eldest should be leaving Australia and coming home sometime in the New Year. Here's a toast to all those who applied pressure to get it done. So here's to a happy family Christmas and an even happier New Year.'

* * *

Tears of happiness at that very special Christmas, the last Bridget would spend in Bristol, were shared by everyone. There were more tears at the wedding which took place by special three-day licence just after New Year's Day, just before Bridget finally set sail.

Before she left the house for the last time, her father handed over her mother's wedding ring which he'd threaded onto a gold watch chain.

'Keep this next to your heart and me and your mother will be there too.' Not a word,' he said when she started to protest. 'Now go in peace, my girl. And may that peace last forever.'

36

One more time. That's what Maisie, Bridget and Phyllis promised themselves. One more time to be together before being scattered to the winds.

'I didn't expect this,' said Phyllis as the waiter poured champagne into her glass.

At Bridget's invitation, they were dining at the Royal Hotel. The food was a little better than in wartime, but none of them were that interested in eating. Nostalgia threw a veil of silence over them. The past was gone but the memories would hold in their minds.

Bridget proposed the toast. 'To the future.'

Three glasses clinked.

'Blimey. I never thought I'd ever drink champagne,' said Maisie once the bubbles had stopped tickling her nose. 'This is the second time.'

'I never thought I'd be going away to live in America.'

Phyllis joined in another toast. 'Or me in Australia.'

They clinked glasses and sipped some more.

Phyllis looked thoughtfully into her glass. 'Just three days until we leave.' She shook her head. Her eyes felt heavy. 'I can't believe it. It's so unreal.'

Bridget remarked, 'I bet Mick's looking forward to it.'

'He is, but...'

Both of her friends eyed her with questioning expressions.

'Are you worried?'

Phyllis sighed and sat back in her chair. 'I am, but I have to go along with what he wants to do. Must say I hate leaving my little house behind.'

Bridget frowned. 'Are you sure that's all it is? You've been a little quiet of late.'

Phyllis's fine fingers tapped the stem of her glass. 'Mick lied to me. He said he'd been signed off by the doctors.'

Maisie and Bridget exchanged looks of surprise.

'And he hasn't?'

Phyllis shook her head. 'Not exactly. I'd gone to the ladies' toilets on our last appointment.' She smiled. 'Anyway, I wasn't there when they gave him the news. I believed it when he said that he was fine to travel and was signed off.'

'And?'

'Once I'd told him we were expecting, nothing else mattered. Not to him. He wanted his boy – why is it all men believe their baby will be a boy? – to be born in Australia, the country of his own birth. "Even if I'm not around for long." That was what threw me,' she said, a more mournful expression coming to her face. 'He'd said that he was clear to travel, but then saying about not being around for long – well – that seemed like a contradiction to me.'

Her friends waited for her to collect herself and tell them what she'd found out.

'I was a bit suspicious, so I phoned the hospital and spoke to the specialist. He gave me it almost word for word. Mick had insisted on going home. The doctor talked through it with him. What was it

Mick wanted from life? He'd explained that he could give no guarantee that it would improve or get worse. Basically it was up to Mick what he wanted to do. Mick told him that if he was going to die, then he wanted to die back in his own country.' Raising her eyes, she met those of her friends. 'The same prognosis applies. Travelling is not a good idea, but ultimately...' She shrugged. 'It was up to him.'

There was a combined gasp of surprise.

'Did you tell him you found out?'

Phyllis shook her head. 'No. This war has taught me a lot – first and foremost that there is no past or future only today. We all have to live in the moment, so I understand what he means. Whatever happens, he's made his own choice and I'll be there to support him.'

Bridget ignored the alarm on Maisie's face and surveyed Phyllis. Her Titian hair and green eyes were unchanged, yet there was a new maturity about her. Phyllis had been intimidated by her first husband and had swayed alarmingly from one flawed relationship to another. She was younger then, but now...? She had the aura of a mature woman, one who could and would look after those who meant the most to her.

Bridget called for another bottle of champagne. 'I'll be there to see you off.'

'Me too,' said Maisie. 'Now drink up. We've only got three days left to finish this!'

Laughter hid the sadness of a double farewell. They would wave Phyllis and her husband off at Temple Meads Station. After that, it would be a two-week wait until Bridget too left the country.

* * *

The telegram arrived at the house in Totterdown around midday. It was addressed to Sid.

Maisie thanked the boy who'd delivered it and gave him three-pence. It was hard to resist opening it but resist she must. Sid was at work. This had to be from his friend's parents informing him about the ring and no doubt asking them to send it on.

Her wedding ring glinted. This was what really mattered.

Sid got home at around six. 'I'm starving.'

'Good. I've cooked liver and onions. With potatoes, carrots and cabbage.'

'My waistline's expanding,' he said, rubbing at his belly. 'I don't think I'll be wanting anything after.'

'I've made a jam roly-poly with custard.'

Sid groaned. 'I suppose I'd better eat it then.'

Over the weeks and months, his appetite had improved. There was more meat on his bones and his facial features were not so angular as they had been.

After he'd washed, all three of them sat at the dinner table.

He talked about how work had been, asked her about her day and allowed Paula to dip her spoon into his mashed potato.

'Paula, I don't know where you put it all. You eat more than I do. More than yer mum and she's eating for two.'

Maisie flushed at his comment and the fact that he'd referred to her as Paula's mum.

Once the little girl was safely tucked up in bed, the dishes were done and they were sitting down with a cup of tea, she brought the telegram out from behind the clock.

'This came today.'

Sid looked a bit scared when he took it from her, turned it this way and that.

'Well,' he said at last. 'Here goes.'

She sat watching him as he read it through. He looked confused rather than concerned.

After reading it a second time, he shook his head. 'I can't believe this. Looks like...' He pushed his hair back from his brow and looked at her. 'He wrote to them about the ring before he went blind. He didn't tell them where he got it but did say that he'd put it on the finger of the first girl who would have him when he got home. Listen to the rest. *'You mention having given it to your fiancée. There's no girl for our son, so perhaps it should stay on your young lady's finger.'*

'You suffered out there as much as he did. It seems right that you gained something.'

'I did,' he said, and taking her in his arms. 'I gained you.'

37

January 1946 and Operation Magic Carpet had begun. Nobody was quite sure of how many war brides were to be transported across the Atlantic. Some estimated it to be 100,000 from Britain alone.

Bridget had sent her luggage on ahead and only carried one piece of hand luggage and her baby.

Sid had to work, so Maisie had left Paula with a neighbour.

Bridget had gabbled all the way down on the train, mentioning how brave her father had been when waving her off but had declared the journey to Southampton too onerous for his aching legs. She kept fussing with young Lyndon, adjusting his clothes, trying to give him another feed from a bottle, even though he'd only just had some.

Maisie took hold of her suitcase. 'Let me take that.'

Bridget said nothing. She was looking up at the hull of the ship towering above them. It seemed overly formidable, like a giant about to gobble her up.

There was a sign up ahead saying passengers only, a gate to another world.

'Oh my,' she whispered.

'I'm with my friend. She can't carry luggage and a baby,' said Maisie when an able seaman tried to prevent her from going through the barrier onto the quay.

The quay was crowded mostly with women and their children. Relatives dabbed at their eyes, tears streaming down their cheeks. Babies cried. Toddlers and those slightly older looked bemused. There was a groundswell of noise from clanking cranes, seamen shouting orders, trollies loaded with suitcases, sea chests and other cabin luggage trundled up lower gangways to disappear into the bowels of the ship.

Finally, they came to a point where the ship's company were adamant that only passengers could go through.

The moment had come. Maisie and Bridget smiled through their tears at each other.

'You will write,' said Bridget. 'Promise me you'll write.'

Maisie just about held back a series of sobs as she nodded. 'Yes.'

'Come along now, come along!'

One voice after another rang out with the same message.

They hugged one last time.

Breaking apart was a difficult affair. Bridget consoled herself that she was at long last reuniting with her husband. Having put off this moment, fearful of leaving all that she knew, she now found herself looking forward to the great adventure that was America, Lyndon and their life together.

Maisie turned away, waved one more time, then was lost in the crowd. Bridget proceeded to board.

A seaman had taken the suitcase Maisie had carried. 'This way, ma'am.'

He spoke with an accent she thought was Spanish. Many nationalities had been based in the British Isles during the war. It amused her to think that there were still some accents she did not recognise.

SS *Argentina* was crowded. Women with babes in arms lined the guardrail eyeing Southampton docks as though it was the most beautiful place in the world, though it was far from that. Huge cranes lined the quayside against a backdrop of bland warehouses with small dirty windows. Men shouted. Engines thudded.

With Lyndon in her arms, Bridget's tear-filled eyes scanned what would be her last view of England, the land she'd grown up in, the land for which she'd served as a member of His Majesty's forces.

Like many other cities and seaports, Southampton had experienced its share of enemy raids, and although there was plenty of rubble scarring the land, progress was being made.

But you won't be here to see it, she thought with a pang of regret. *It's no longer your country.*

It seemed an age until the ship's horn sounded its intention to move.

As the ship was tugged away from the quay and the sailors prepared her to journey down Southampton Water, a host of hands from the women lining the guardrail waved down at the shore. Relatives waved back. Bridget's eyes searched for Maisie, but without success. Maisie had made her way home – just as she was doing.

'Goodbye, England,' shouted someone next to her, then burst into tears. Two toddlers clinging to her skirts, not understanding the reason but moved by her action, followed their mother's lead and wailed to high heaven.

And that was it, thought Bridget. The war brides around her weren't just waving at people, they were waving at the country, one that had been bombed and battered during the last five years. The country and its people had survived but had changed. People, women included, had taken part in battles, whether in uniform or on the home front. They now knew what they were capable of. The old ways would take time to shift, but the influx of people from all over the world had broadened people's horizons. No longer would their lives be set in stone or distinctly delineated by class or gender. In future, no place in the world would be inaccessible and foreigners would no longer be the strangers they had once been. Women had changed too. There was no way of knowing quite how that would work out.

Perhaps determining the movement of the ship, Baby Lyndon opened his eyes and began to stir. Bridget smiled down at him, then raised him up so that he too could take a last glance at the country they were leaving behind.

'Look,' she said, pointing out at the throng of people eyeing the great ship being slowly pushed out into the water. 'Wave to your grandad. Wave to Auntie Maisie. Wave to everyone we used to know.'

She waved his hand for him. He was far too young to remember this moment, but she would remember it. She would remember it for the rest of her life.

* * *

Although Bridget could not see her, Maisie was still there, waving enthusiastically with tears streaming down her face.

'It's been a long war,' said a woman next to her. 'I'll miss my daughter and her babes, but it's her future now and all I can do is pray for her happiness.'

'For all of us,' said Maisie, then shouted at the top of her voice, 'God bless, Bridget. Give my love to Lyndon. And don't forget to write.'

Even when the tugboats had successfully pushed the ship away from the quay, Maisie waved until it felt as though her arm would drop off. She waved for the years, for her first day at the tobacco factory when she'd met Bridget and Phyllis. She waved because her heart was bursting with love and her head with memories.

Back in 1939 as war had taken hold none of them could ever have imagined how their lives would change. Back then they'd called themselves the three Ms: Maisie Miles, Phyllis Mason and Bridget Milligan. They'd been through a lot both together and apart. They were now Mrs Fairbrother, Mrs O'Neill and Mrs Brewster.

No longer was the world at war but the three of them would be scattered to the four winds. In one way everything had changed. In another nothing had. They were still the three Ms, still friends and always would be.

ABOUT THE AUTHOR

Lizzie Lane is the author of over 50 books, a number of which have been bestsellers. She was born and bred in Bristol where many of her family worked in the cigarette and cigar factories. This inspired her bestselling saga series The Tobacco Girls.

Sign up to Lizzie Lane's mailing list here for news, competitions and updates on future books.

Follow Lizzie on social media:

facebook.com/jean.goodhind

x.com/baywriterallat1

instagram.com/baywriterallatsea

bookbub.com/authors/lizzie-lane

ALSO BY LIZZIE LANE

The Tobacco Girls

The Tobacco Girls

Dark Days for the Tobacco Girls

Fire and Fury for the Tobacco Girls

Heaven and Hell for the Tobacco Girls

Marriage and Mayhem for the Tobacco Girls

A Fond Farewell for the Tobacco Girls

Coronation Close

New Neighbours for Coronation Close

Shameful Secrets on Coronation Close

Dark Shadows Over Coronation Close

The Strong Trilogy

The Sugar Merchant's Wife

Secrets of the Past

Daughter of Destiny

The Sweet Sisters Trilogy

Wartime Sweethearts

War Baby

Home Sweet Home

Wives and Lovers

Wartime Brides

Coronation Wives

Mary Anne Randall

A Wartime Wife

A Wartime Family

Orchard Cottage Hospital

A New Doctor at Orchard Cottage Hospital

Standalones

War Orphans

A Wartime Friend

Secrets and Sins

A Christmas Wish

Women in War

Her Father's Daughter

Trouble for the Boat Girl

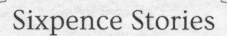

Sixpence Stories

Introducing Sixpence Stories!

Discover page-turning historical novels from your favourite authors, meet new friends and be transported back in time.

Join our book club Facebook group

https://bit.ly/SixpenceGroup

Sign up to our newsletter

https://bit.ly/SixpenceNews

Boldwood

Boldwood Books is an award-winning fiction publishing company seeking out the best stories from around the world.

Find out more at www.boldwoodbooks.com

Join our reader community for brilliant books, competitions and offers!

Follow us
@BoldwoodBooks
@TheBoldBookClub

Sign up to our weekly deals newsletter

https://bit.ly/BoldwoodBNewsletter